T0375398

DON QUIXOTE EXPLAINED

The Story of an Unconventional Hero

EMRE GURGEN

authorHOUSE®

AuthorHouse™
1663 Liberty Drive
Bloomington, IN 47403
www.authorhouse.com
Phone: 1-800-839-8640

Published by AuthorHouse 05/11/2015

ISBN: 978-1-4817-0096-2 (sc)
ISBN: 978-1-4817-0095-5 (e)

Library of Congress Control Number: 2012924001

Print information available on the last page.

Any people depicted in stock imagery provided by Thinkstock are models, and such images are being used for illustrative purposes only. Certain stock imagery © Thinkstock.

This book is printed on acid-free paper.

TABLE OF CONTENTS

INTRODUCTION

Several features motivated me to write **Don Quixote Explained**: *The Story of an Unconventional Hero*. During my undergraduate and graduate studies what fascinated me most about *Don Quixote* was its depth and sophistication in giving very significant messages to its readers, which continue to have a great deal of relevance to people's lives in today's world. For this reason I devoted considerable time, effort, and energy to *Don Quixote*, both formally and informally, in and out of academia. I studied the novel for meaning, scrutinized books of literary theory, examined journal articles of literary criticism, read detailed study guides, read doctoral dissertations and masters's theses, viewed DVDs about Cervantes's life, researched Wikipedia and Encyclopedia Britannica internet entries, and, in brief, drew on materials presented in a variety of undergraduate survey courses and graduate literary seminars. This focused study of *Don Quixote*, in turn, coupled with all of my original research on the novel, enabled me to analyze Cervantes the man, Don Quixote the book, and the philosophy behind both in relatively simple terms.

After extensive research, I found that since most criticism of *Don Quixote* focuses on how Cervantes's autobiography sheds light on the book; how Spanish literature relates to the book; how other books resemble or differ from *Don Quixote*; or a combination of these three facets, an area yet to be explored, I found, is what the book means itself exclusively. This is why I analyzed the contents of *Don Quixote* in great detail, unraveling, in layers, the complex themes and messages contained therein, absent the usual biographical discussion, comparative analyses, linguistic criticism, literary theory, or references to Spanish literature. Hence, by utilizing select library research, citing indisputable facts from the original book, and drawing logical inferences therefrom **Don Quixote Explained**: *The Story of an Unconventional Hero*, analyzes a legendary classic from a fresh and significant perspective. This, in my view, is what distinguishes, and, indeed, justifies, my study of a 415 year old book.

ESSAY 1

The Formation of True Love in Don Quixote: *How Characters Marry For Romance Not By Arrangement.*

The action of *Don Quixote* focuses on bringing together many different couples in order to ask the question: "How do we merit true-love and give it in return?" As such, the novel consists, in part, on a series of courtship and sexual tales where characters marry not by arrangement, as expected, but for romantic love, instead. Therefore, in place of marrying for usefulness or convenience, as was typical in 17th century Spain, Cervantes was intent on transitioning the domination-submission pattern of medieval marriages—where the female is a house keeper, lust satisfier, and child begetter—to the love-based pattern of modern marriages, typified by a joining of desires and a merger of personalities. Thus, he defines marriage not as a "master-servant, owner-property connection" but as a relationship of friends where each partner tries to please and advance the other.[1] As such, man's motives for selecting a wife in *Don Quixote* are not those of "a householder in search of a housekeeper, but those of a human being in need of emotional intimacy." [2] This new emotional significance of marriage, in turn, is marked by philosophic speculations about the meaning and importance of romantic love, especially in relation

---

1 Hunt, Morton, M. <u>The Natural History of Love</u>. New York: 1959. (171).

2 Hunt, Morton, M. <u>The Natural History of Love</u>. New York: 1959. (386).

to conjugal happiness and stability in marriage. Simply put, since Cervantes sees true love as the best way to choose a spouse and build a marriage, he argues that we need not be trapped by the marital customs that prevail in any given time. Rather, "by upsetting traditional patterns of [tribal] law and [established] society, [Miguel dramatizes unions that] bring new order and [breathe] new life into a stale social system."[3]

By challenging the customary view that marriage is a useful alliance defined by indissoluble law, clanship ties, and social pressures, Cervantes shows readers that any intimate partnership should be defined by a generous wish to give, benefit, and succor the beloved. This is why he diminishes the patriarchal, land-based, economic view of marriage, replacing it with the "romantic conviction that for each individual in society there is a right one out there waiting to be found."[4] This one-person-theory, in turn, is combined with Cervantes's belief in free choice: it is up to men and women alike to choose the right person based on feeling the real thing. On this view, "every unmarried person [should not only] wait, or search, until [their soul mate] is located" but also they should at last marry for romantic love; not lifelong maintenance, if they want to live a healthy mental life.[5]

Economic marriages, on the other hand, void of love, esteem, and affection, are discouraged by Cervantes when he shows readers that they are largely a manifestation of parental greed likely to create unstable unions. And unstable unions, according to Cervantes, leads to jealousy and infidelity as domestic space becomes the source of discord and anger that spreads from the bedroom to the streets. In brief, marriage for any reason other than love—such as a political alliance or a family fortune—is frowned on by Cervantes when he

---

3   Jacobson, Karin. Cliffs Complete. <u>Shakespeare's Romeo and Juliet</u>. Ed. Sidney Lamb. New York: 2000. (38).

4   Hunt, Morton, M. <u>The Natural History of Love</u>. New York: 1959. (363).

5   Hunt, Morton, M. <u>The Natural History of Love</u>. New York: 1959. (363).

shows readers that such unions are defined by mercenary tactics that often lead to marital discord.

Aside from painting a picture of married life as "a vehicle of love and emotional security," Cervantes encourages parents to not allow their daughters to select their husbands among evil and base suitors but rather to propose several good candidates and then give them free choice amongst these.[6] Short of suggesting that parents should revel in their parental authority over their children by declaring who they should and should not marry, Cervantes reasons that parents should train their sons and daughters to virtue and modesty from an early age so that they do not fall victim to unscrupulous rakes who concoct "their plans, feign their emotions, and play their parts," with convincing plausibility, so that they can "seduce and abandon without compunction."[7] Unsurprisingly, in this regard, Cervantes advises parents to guide and mold the growing characters of their children so that they learn to choose their spouses wisely.

Another aspect of romantic-love that Cervantes examines in *Don Quixote* relates to "how a person can differentiate true-love from false lust since they look the same by producing the same tears, sighs, and groans."[8] How, Cervantes wonders, if thoughts and actions are often incongruous, can we know if a lover speaks the truth about his feelings? This question, in turn, leads to broader considerations about the nature of true-love: Like the concern, for example, that the appearance of a relationship actually corresponds to its' reality: Or the idea that one can conquer lustful relationships by the avoidance and repudiation of powerful emotions that are impulsive and fickle in nature. Instead of acting on the basis of whim-driven, mercurial passions that are subject to sudden ups-and-downs—usually, without rhyme or reason—Cervantes counsels his readers to think out, in

---

6   Hunt, Morton, M. The Natural History of Love. New York: 1959. (393).

7   Hunt, Morton, M. The Natural History of Love. New York: 1959. (259).

8   Jacobson, Karin. Cliffs Complete. Shakespeare's Romeo and Juliet. Ed. Sidney Lamb. New York: 2000. (87).

full dimension, whether they feel a tender affection for someone because of who they are and what they represent or whether they feel a strong desire to have sex with someone because of their esthetic appeal. If, Cervantes reasons, the latter is true, and a relationship is purely physical, than the remedy for a young lady is to keep busy in a productive activity apart from idle infatuation, so that she thinks not of a boy-toy, or some other adolescent crush, but about finishing the job at hand instead.

Another question that Cervantes asks and answers in *Don Quixote* is whether "physical attraction is a necessary component of romantic love?"[9] If one's good looks, in terms of their body weight, physical fitness, self-grooming, dress-style, and how they carry themselves, influences their esthetic appeal to others. To answer this question Cervantes infers that "when you fall in love with a person, you don't fall in love with a disembodied spirit but with a whole person including their physical appearance."[10] To Cervantes, looks matter, since they convey a person's basic attitude towards themselves. For this reason, how his characters present themselves physically says a lot to their prospective romantic partners. Thus, posture, clothes, and grooming become a significant criterion for considering whether two people are well-suited for each other, or not. That said, however, Cervantes counsels his readers against "the belief that looks are everything. That one should spend their lives in front of a mirror trying to look [perfect.]"[11] While Cervantes emphasizes that pride in one's physical appearance is an important element of partnership formation, he also stresses that physical beauty is not everything since there are two kinds of beauty: "beauty of the soul and beauty of the body," which, to Cervantes, are both equally important (877).

---

9   Jacobson, Karin. Cliffs Complete. <u>Shakespeare's Romeo and Juliet</u>. Ed. Sidney Lamb. New York: 2000. (22).

10   Locke, Edwin. A, and Ellen Kenner. <u>The Selfish Path to Romance: How to Love with Passion and Reason.</u> Doylestown: 2011. (78).

11   Locke, Edwin. A, and Ellen Kenner. <u>The Selfish Path to Romance: How to Love with Passion and Reason.</u> Doylestown: 2011. (82).

In short, Cervantes shows us that "an interesting phenomenon often occurs regarding looks: when you ardently love your partner's soul, your partner looks more physically beautiful to you."[12]

Yet another aspect of true-love that Cervantes explores in *Don Quixote* is how good communication between partners fosters a sense of closeness, understanding, and compatibility. By talking to, listening to, and observing each other in diverse situations, characters in *Don Quixote* learn what is important to one another and why, thereby determining if a potential spouse is right for them or not. What's more, the whole process of "asking questions, and listening closely," as shown in *Don Quixote*, "establishes an atmosphere of receptiveness" in a partner's mind, which, in Sancho Panza and Teresa Panza's case, creates a "positive mindset of change".[13] Most importantly, by writing letters, crafting poems, and communicating constantly, couples in *Don Quixote* keep their love for one another alive. In sum, it is through "active listening and assertive speaking skills" that partners come to understand one another's life context, which, in turn, enables them to identify and resolve any potential sources of conflict.[14]

Also, throughout the novel, there are close friendships of habit between husband and wife, as is the case with Sancho Panza and Teresa Panza, for example. This commonality of identity, and interpenetration of life habits, in turn, shows readers that "with a romantic soul mate you get a mirror of yourself that even a close friend cannot provide."[15] In a word, Sancho Panza and Teresa Panza

---

12 Locke, Edwin. A, and Ellen Kenner. The Selfish Path to Romance: How to Love with Passion and Reason. Doylestown: 2011 (112).

13 (1) Locke, Edwin. A, and Ellen Kenner. The Selfish Path to Romance: How to Love with Passion and Reason. (Doylestown: 2011) 96. (2). Kenner, Ellen. "The Rational Basis of Romance (Part 2): Courting Success in Romance." Irvine, 2005.

14 Locke, Edwin, A. and Ellen Kenner. The Selfish Path to Romance: How to Love with Passion and Reason. Doylestown: Platform Press, 2011. (239).

15 Locke, Edwin. A, and Ellen Kenner. The Selfish Path to Romance: How to Love with Passion and Reason. Doylestown: 2011. (8).

have compatible habits of action, which, in turn, enables them to not only maintain a feeling of "mutual togetherness" with one another but "psychological closeness" to each other as well, thereby exemplifying that a hallmark of companionate love is the merger of personalities: with the cohabitation of male and female as characteristic of a romantic friendship[16]. Indeed, in this regard, conjugal love between Sancho Panza and Teresa Panza owes its existence to the cohesive power of habit, shared experience, and, above all, a similar outlook on life.

Finally, Cervantes shows his readers that in some cases, "living alone—in an unmarried state—unattended and unaccompanied by others" is the best option for a young lady. Accordingly, Miguel counsels his readers against forming hasty unions based on an arrangement where "property, inheritance, family, and a title (if there is one) are important constituents."[17] In fact, Cervantes reasons that his characters should wait until they are genuinely attracted to and care for a potential spouse: an individual with whom they find a complementary degree of companionship and a comfortable sense of fitness and with whom sensations of love derive from the recognition of these values. Thus, Cervantes shows us that sometimes "remaining single and [learning] to support oneself is better than becoming the wife of a dissipated man."[18]

Marcela's example proves that women, especially young girls, should stay single until and unless they meet the right person, otherwise they risk locking themselves into a loveless marriage. By way of background information, Marcela is the seventeen year-old daughter of a rich farmer named Guillermo who dies before his child reaches a stage in her life where the law recognizes her as an

---

16   Locke, Edwin, A. and Ellen Kenner. The Selfish Path to Romance: How to Love with Passion and Reason. Doylestown: Platform Press, 2011. (192).

17   Saccio, Peter. "The Taming of the Shrew—Getting Married in the 1590's. The Teaching Company. Virginia, 1999.

18   Hunt, Morton, M. The Natural History of Love. New York: 1959. (333).

adult. Left in the care of her guardian uncle, Marcela is beset by a variety of young men who want to marry her for her stunning looks, enormous wealth, and keen intelligence. Despite the fact that her "great beauty" vast "fortune" and moral integrity bring men from many "miles around [to] beg and pester her uncle for her hand in marriage; [he is] unwilling to marry her without first [gaining] her consent" (92). Even after her uncle "describes the qualities of each of [Marcela's] many suitors asking [his niece] to marry whoever she prefers" Marcela replies that "she doesn't want to marry yet since" she is too young (92). Since her uncle believes that "parents shouldn't provide for their children's future against their will, [he] stops asking [Marcela to marry deciding] to let her choose a [suitable] companion when she is older" (92, 93). By acknowledging that Marcela should not be forced to marry for expediencies sake but rather should marry for loves sake, her uncle gives primary consideration to her free-choice in romantic affairs, even though his niece's decision to stay single contradicts what he thinks is right for her. One reason why Marcela's uncle values her decision to stay single over his will to marry her is because if Marcela marries, she, not he, will be sharing her life with another person, therefore, she, not he, must be happy in her conjugal selection. As such, moral consideration of his niece's happiness supersedes any practical benefit Marcela's uncle may gain by forcing her into a marriage she does not want. In other words, Marcela's uncle elevates his niece's mental happiness and emotional well-being over the economic and political benefits he may gain by the allegiance his daughter makes. Therefore, with her uncle's blessing, Marcela is free to decide who she is, or is not, going to marry, and when she should wed him, or not. Thus, to avoid "rich youths, hidalgos, and farmers" Marcela dresses-up as a shepherdess and "goes into the fields" to avoid unwelcome male advances (93). Though she is accused of being "cruel [or] an ingrate [or] hardhearted," Marcela defends her right to solitude by saying that since "love must be voluntary not forced a woman who is loved for her beauty should not be obliged to love

7

[those who] love her" (93, 109). Why, asks Marcela, "do [people] think [she] should be obliged to love [them], just because [they] say [they] love [her]?" (109). It "could happen, [continues Marcela], that the lover of beauty [could be] ugly, and since that which is ugly is [undesirable], it isn't very fitting for [an ugly man] to say: "I love you because you're beautiful; you must love me [because] I'm ugly" (109). Besides highlighting physical attraction as a vital component of romantic love, Marcela also emphasizes the importance of a close mental connection between partners. This is why she says that "even if [two people] are well-matched as far as beauty goes that doesn't mean that attraction is going to be mutual because not all beauty inspires love" (109). Because Marcela thinks that she has not met anyone who can stimulate her mentally and emotionally, and because she is too young to enter into any serious relationship, she expresses a firm right "to live free [in] the solitude of the countryside [among the] company of shepherds," with nobody to stop her from living as she sees fit (109). Therefore, Marcela retreats to "the clear waters of streams [and] the [shady boughs] of trees" to escape the "arrogance [and] disdain [and] murderous intent [of disappointed suitors]" (108). This is why she dresses up as a shepherdess and enjoys a bucolic, pastoral life, roaming the countryside, with a free spirit, and a pure mind. In self-explanation Marcela insists that those "who [died for] love [of her] were killed by their own obstinacy" not her "cruelty" since she kept no man's "hopes alive" by false words or insincere actions (109, 110). Moreover, Marcela says that if she "encouraged [her lovers to continue their courtship] she [would] have been false; if [she] gratified [them with physical affection she would] have acted against her own intentions" (110). Since she "never deceived, made promises, enticed or accepted [her many suitors,] let [her] not, [Marcela says,] be called cruel or murderous by any man" (110). Thus, to defend "her good name and reputation" Marcela "warns her suitors [to] leave her alone; [to] stop courting her; [to] keep [their] distance; [to] stop following [her]" and, above all, to not commit suicide, like Grisostomo does, "because of her" (104, 110). Moreover, to rebuff men who approach her with high ethical principles Marcela says that just because a bachelor says that his "intentions [towards her] are honorable" aren't her own "honourable intentions," she wonders, significant as well—like her wish to "preserve her chastity until she is older" (110). In short, Marcela's robust moral defense of her bachelorettism "disabuses" men of the false notion that she is "disdainful, cold, and heartless." (107, 103). By depicting the moral reasoning of an ingénue who is unwilling to "bear the [responsibility] of [early] matrimony," Cervantes shows his readers that sometimes the best course of action vis-à-vis marriage is to only marry the right person at the right time in the right way (92, 93). Conversely, loveless marriages, as Sancho Panza and Teresa Panza's union almost is, constitutes immediate grounds for divorce: unless differences of opinion can be reconciled through good communication and cooperative compromise.

Sancho Panza and Teresa Panza's *potential* divorce proves that the "just ground for conjugal separation is indisposition, unfitness, and contrariety of mind, arising from a cause in nature unchangeable, hindering and ever likely to hinder the main benefits of conjugal society, which is solace, peace, and mutual [advancement]."[19] It seems that divorce *almost* applies to Sancho Panza and Teresa Panza's relationship since they dispute over Sancho Panza's career drive, their daughter's rank-elevation, Teresa Panza's social-station, and, basically, staying in their comfort zone as modest farmers versus advancing themselves in life through hard work. Teresa Panza, on the one hand, is determined to stay in her comfortable station as a peasant due to her fear of the alternative; while Sancho Panza, on the other hand, wants to enhance his career, better his life prospects, and elevate his daughter's good standing (515). This flashpoint of conflict, in turn, sours Sancho Panza and Teresa Panza's feelings for one another: until they grow to resolve their opinion-differences

---

19 Hunt, Morton, M. <u>The Natural History of Love</u>. (New York: 1959) 247. (From Milton: The Doctrine and Discipline of Divorce).

amicably. Indeed, in this regard, Sancho Panza and Teresa Panza dispute over whether to find a spouse for their daughter who is "so high-up that nobody will be able to get within sniffing distance of her without calling her your ladyship" or whether she should "marry someone who's her [social] equal [since] uneven matches never retain for long the happiness of their first days" (516, 255). Sancho Panza, it seems, favors the view that as a Governor's daughter Sanchita should marry someone high-up while Teresa Panza opines that it is "better [that she have] a poor husband [rather] than a rich lover" (516). In defense of the view that her daughter can only love her social equal, Teresa Panza says that "taking [her daughter] out of her grey-brown homespun skirt and [putting her] into a farthingale and bright silk petticoats, [thereby] turning her from 'Sanchita' and plain 'You' into 'Dona' and 'Your ladyship,' [will] render her confused [since] the poor girl won't know where she is, and she'll put her foot in it with every step she takes, and keep showing her true colours, which are humble grey and brown" (516). Concerned by his wife's unwillingness to help Sanchita grow into an affluent, respectable, young woman, Sancho Panza tells Teresa Panza that "all Sanchita needs is two or three years practice, and then grand and grave manners will fit her like a glove" (516). Unwilling to acknowledge that her daughter can retrain herself in this way, Teresa Panza says "a fine thing it would be [if] Sanchita [married] a high and mighty earl, or some other fine gentlemen, who when the fancy took him would drag her through the mud and call her peasant wench and clodhopper's daughter and tow-spinner's brat" (516). Not only does Teresa Panza assume that her daughter's future husband will abuse her if he is wealthy but she also tries to thwart Sancho Panza's career drive by urging him to "stick to [his] own station" and to not "be looking to get above [himself]" (516). In fact, Teresa Panza is insistently shrill when she says that "[she did not] raise [her] daughter" to be abused by a rich husband (516). What's more, Teresa Panza tells Sancho Panza that he shouldn't "go marrying her at those [high] courts and grand palaces of [his] where nobody will understand her and she won't know what she's doing," while Sancho Panza avers that he will not "stop [his] daughter from marrying someone who'll give [him] grandchildren who'll be called your lordship" (517). In response, Teresa Panza says that she has "always been in favour of equality [in marriage since] she can't stand people getting above themselves for no good reason" (517). In fact, Teresa Panza applies this concept to herself when she says that "Teresa [she] was christened, pure and simple, without any frills or flounces or titles stuck on the front [and she is] well content with [her] own name, without any Donnas piled on top of it" (517). Hesitant to assume the responsibilities of an aristocrat, Teresa Panza makes excuses by saying that she "doesn't want to give people seeing her dressed up as a countess or a governor's wife the excuse to say 'Look what airs the slut's giving herself now! Only yesterday she was busy spinning her tow from morning to night and there she goes today in her farthingale and her brooches and her fine airs as if we didn't know who she is'" (518). "Unwilling to expose [herself] to all that," Teresa Panza tells Sancho Panza to go ahead and be "a governor of an island, and give himself all the airs [he] likes – but [she] swears by the eternal glory of her dear mother that [she] and her daughter aren't going to budge one inch from [her] village [since] a woman's place is in the home" (518). Disappointed that Teresa Panza views a woman's role as a domestic caretaker, frustrated that his wife is unwilling to better herself and her daughter, off-put by her unwillingness to strengthen the overall prominence and cohesiveness of their family, Sancho Panza faults her for "turning [her] back on good fortune" (518). Why, Sancho Panza asks her "won't she agree [to] fall in with [his] wishes" (518)? Evidently, one of Teresa Panza's anxieties of becoming a governess is her notion that she will be slandered by "gossips [who] nit-pick," that she has found a way to go from "poor" to "rich" undeserved (518, 519). In response, Sancho Panza tells his wife to forget about her modest origins since "if [a] person that fortune has pulled out of the snow of his pond to the height of prosperity is well-mannered, generous and

11

polite to everyone, and doesn't go trying to vie with those who've been noble for ages, then [she] can be sure that nobody's going to remember what [she] used to be, but instead they'll stand in awe of what [she] is – all except envious people, and nobody's good fortune is safe from them" (519). Simply put, Sancho Panza tells his wife that she should not worry about conducting herself properly in high society since "what we can see in front of us with our own two eyes comes into our mind, is present there and stays there much better and more clearly than what's in our past" (519). Refusing, however, to agree with Sancho Panza's line-of-reasoning, Teresa Panza avers that sometimes she "doesn't understand him [therefore he should] stop making her head spin with all his highfalutin palaver" (519). Though Sancho Panza does not like his wife's defeatist attitude, he gives her time to think about what he has said to her, in hopes that either Teresa Panza comes to her good senses in time, or, alternatively, they agree to divorce. In fact, Don Quixote reinforces the rationality of divorce by telling Sancho Panza that sometimes divorce is fully justified if a man is unable to "teach [his wife], instruct her, polish all that natural coarseness of her, because everything that is gained by an intelligent [husband] is often lost and wasted by a foolish, boorish wife" (768). Moreover, Don Quixote insists that since the behavior of a leader's wife redounds on the moral characters of her followers, one in "high office" should "acquire a better wife," if needed (768). In short, discussion centered on Sancho Panza and Teresa Panza's potential divorce is based on a contrariety of mind as it relates to their social station. But since Sancho Panza and Teresa Panza develop "a healthy communication style" they come to work out their problems in an intense yet amicable way: which, in turn, serves as "good fuel for change."[20]

By "giving specific examples of their grievances, limiting their complaints to concrete issues, [and] expressing strong emotions,"

---

20 Kenner, Ellen. "The Rational Basis of Romance (Part 2): Courting Success inRomance." Irvine, 2005.

Sancho Panza and Teresa Panza talk-out issues causing anger and resentment between them thereby resolving their problems.[21] Together, they adopt the attitude that "Yes, we have problems, but we can work out these problems, if we find the strength to change together." In fact, their benevolent way of relating to each other allows Sancho Panza and Teresa Panza to: manage each other's vulnerabilities; resolve their joint problems; and formulate an action plan of change. To explain, Sancho Panza and Teresa Panza find a way to reach "an agreeable mindset for change" by: listening carefully to one another; asking questions to clarify their understanding of each other; and, most importantly, talking out their problems.[22] Instead of "leaving their problems vague, or pushing them out of their awareness," Sancho Panza and Teresa Panza "nail-down their specific grievances in words, thereby eliminating floating feelings of anger and frustration," which, if unchecked, could cause an open rift in their relationship[23]. This, in turn, fosters a healthy and happy marriage between them. What's more, when Sancho Panza and Teresa Panza communicate they do not "monopolize the conversation but share the airwaves so that both partners feel that their voices and values are important to one another."[24] Such, open, two-way dialogue between husband and wife, characterized by a series of candid conversations and defined by a set of serious actions, emphasizes that good communication is vital for sustaining any successful, romantic, relationship. Evidently, Sancho Panza and Teresa Panza's face-to-face conversations, coupled with their frank epistolary communication, proves that they have a variety of joint concerns which they talk out together to not only see

---

21   Kenner, Ellen. "The Rational Basis of Romance (Part 2): Courting Success in Romance." Irvine, 2005.

22   Kenner, Ellen. "The Rational Basis of Romance (Part 2): Courting Success in Romance." Irvine, 2005.

23   Kenner, Ellen. "The Rational Basis of Romance (Part 2): Courting Success in Romance." Irvine, 2005.

24   Kenner, Ellen. "The Rational Basis of Romance (Part 2): Courting Success in Romance." Irvine, 2005.

what is best to be done for themselves and their lives but also so that they reach joint spousal agreement on certain issues. This, in turn, fosters true-love between them. And while Sancho Panza and Teresa Panza have certain conjugal disputes that are part and parcel of any connubial relationship, ultimately, they resolve their differences by talking out their problems together. In this way, Sancho Panza and Teresa Panza reach a unity of life-energy because they speak to one another, in an assertive not in an aggressive manner to learn what is important to one another and why—thereby learning to adjust their behavior accordingly.

The dramatic action of *Don Quixote* proves that Teresa Panza reforms her basic nature, repurposes her driving energy, and reinvents her life's purpose via: a Duchess's political out-reach efforts; a page's encouraging comments; her husband's conversational guidance; and her own self-persuasion, as well. This, in turn, merits Sancho Panza's true love. First, the Aragonese Duchess eases Teresa Panza's anxiety about her husband's governorship by sending a letter to Teresa Panza in which she praises Sancho Panza's "most excellent qualities of goodness and cleverness" (825). This reassurance, in turn, relaxes Teresa Panza by showing her that Sancho Panza is capable of being a good governor. Her apprehension is further lowered by the Duchess's complimentary letters, good-will gifts, and, most of all, by her frank, down-to-earth, nature. Since the Duchess solicits a shipment of "fine fat acorns to be had in her village" Teresa Panza says that the Duchess is "a good, straightforward, down-to-earth lady [who does not] put on [any] airs or graces" but, who, instead, calls her "her friend" thus "treating her with respect" (825, 826). What's more, Teresa Panza even persuades her daughter to get used to being called "my lady" because her father is now a "governor" (830). Before Teresa Panza was adamantly opposed to her daughter becoming a lady; now she seems neutral, even excited by the prospect. Still hesitant, however, about whether such a salutation is appropriate for her daughter, Teresa Panza is unable to decide if what she "says makes any sense"

(517, 830). To comfort her again, the Duchess's page reassures her that "Senora Teresa is making more sense then she realizes" (830). Encouraged by the page's praise, Teresa Panza writes a return letter to the Duchess in which she says that it "made [her] really happy to get [her opening] letter [and that she] decided to not sit [around] waiting for opportunity to knock twice [but] to go to the capital, instead, [to buy] a loaf [of bread and] a pound [of meat]" (842). Excited by the prospect of conducting activities associated with a governor's wife, Teresa Panza asks the Duchess to "tell her husband to send her a good fair bit of money" (842). This assertion shows readers that Teresa Panza's basic attitude towards bettering herself has changed dramatically since she now wants Sancho Panza to become a Governor and her daughter to become a lady. In fact, Teresa Panza is so excited by the prospect of becoming a governor's wife that she dictates an opening letter to her husband in which she not only says that she is delighted at his being made "governor" but also that she "wants to do him credit in the capital [by] going around in a carriage" (844). Evidently, Teresa Panza starts to warm to her role as governess, for she even asks her husband to "send [her] a few strings of pearls" (844). Not only is Teresa Panza enthused about becoming governess but she is also excited by the advantages Sanchita will receive as a governor's daughter: Like not "having to work" for her marriage "trousseau," for example (844). Sancho Panza acknowledges this fact when he tells the Argonese Duchess that she "raised great hopes in [his] wife [by relaying] the news of [him] being [made] governor" (869). Here, we see that Sancho Panza is pleased by his wife's willingness to become a governess, despite her previous hesitation. In brief, Teresa Panza merits Sancho Panza's true-love by: willing herself to be a governess; assuming the responsibilities of a governess; and, lastly, by showing a willingness to prepare Sanchita for her role as a governor's daughter. It is through these remedial efforts that Sancho Panza and Teresa Panza reach a commonality of purpose, a commonality of belief, and, most importantly, a commonality of values required for any successful romantic relationship to work. Thus, they joyfully stay together, as lifelong husband and wife.

Evidently, Sancho Panza and Teresa Panza love each other very much as their repeat love declarations prove; as their separation-longings show; as their tender nicknames exemplify; as their sympathy for one another merits; as their willingness to please each other illustrates; as their good-will gifts exemplify; and finally, as their happiness at each other's good fortune represents. Clearly, Sancho Panza "loves Teresa Panza [more] than [the] lashes over his eyes" for he tries "to please [his] wife" by bringing home money (960). Obviously, Sancho Panza's attempt to satisfy Teresa Panza's financial needs shows readers that love for his wife induces Sancho Panza to create positive cash flow for her. What's more, Sancho Panza and Teresa Panza miss each other greatly since Teresa Panza declares that she is "cheered-up [to see him since her] heart [has] been so sad and out of sorts all [the] age's he has been away" while Sancho Panza declares that his "happiness at [venture questing with Don Quixote] is mixed with sadness at leaving" his wife (473). In fact, Teresa Panza declares to Sancho Panza that she "was so happy" at getting "dearest Sancho's" letter (843). Such a yearning for one another shows readers that husband-and-wife value one another's life presence. Moreover, Sancho Panza and Teresa Panza refer to each other affectionately with tender salutations like "my dear, [or] dearest, or my good Sancho," etc. (514, 829). By using terms of endearment, or special nicknames, Sancho Panza and Teresa Panza keep tenderness in their relationship alive. Moreover, the two partners foster their love for one another by giving goodwill gifts. For instance, Sancho Panza sends Teresa Panza a "green hunting outfit of [very] fine worsted" thereby showing her that even when he is away from home he thinks of her kindly (828, 843). And when Sancho Panza declares, out of frustration, that if he "wasn't expecting to be in control of an island before very long [he'd] drop down dead on the spot" Teresa Panza tells Sancho Panza that not only should he not "do that" but rather he should "live on" because "she would not want to live in this world without [him]" (844). This candid display of affection, in turn, shows Sancho Panza how important he is to his wife. What's more, Sancho Panza tries to comfort his wife when she is dejected. For instance, when Teresa Panza cries at the prospect of Sanchica Panza marrying a rich man "Sancho comforts [her] by saying that even though he [is] going to [suggest that his] girl [marry] an earl, [he'll] put it off [for] as long as he can," out of respect for his wife's feelings (520). Such consideration of his wife's sentiments shows readers how much Sancho Panza loves Teresa Panza. In fact when Teresa Panza solicits "a few strings of pearls [to wear] (on Barataria)" Sancho Panza sends her a "string of corals," instead, thereby satisfying his wife's esthetic longings (844, 828). Another concrete indication of their mutual love is proven by the fact that they are overjoyed at each other's good fortune. For example, Teresa Panza declares that she was "so happy" when she got Sancho Panza's "letter" announcing his future governorship (842). Likewise, Sancho Panza is delighted when [insert example]. In brief, all of these factual self-evidencies, when taken together, prove that Sancho Panza and Teresa Panza marriage is salvageable because it is based on true love.

Since Sancho Panza and Teresa Panza are alike in many fundamental ways—illustrated by their folksy proverbs, rustic metaphors, homely similes, and body weight—their life energy synchronizes into a personality merger, of sorts. This, in turn, connects their hearts together into a merger of co-functionality. First, as the book proves, Sancho Panza and Teresa Panza have similar speech style identities, since both individuals intersperse their oral explanations, of people and events, with agrarian metaphors. For example, when Sancho Panza tells Teresa Panza about his governorship, she says, in her typical country way, that "honey wasn't made for the mouth of [simpletons]" (473). Again, when Sancho Panza tells Teresa Panza that if he "wasn't expecting to be in control of an island before very long [he'd] drop down dead on the spot," Teresa Panza tells him to not "do that [for] the hen [should] live on though she has got the pip, and [therefore he should] live on too" (515). In reply, Sancho Panza says "that it'll be a good idea if [he] ends up in control of something worthwhile that will pull [them] out of the mire" (517). Thus, by referring to a hen's medical state, on the one hand, and rising out of a mud-bog, on the other, husband-and-wife both use natural imagery to make their points. Moreover, when Sancho Panza talks about her daughter's marriage he uses terms like "a brace of shakes," and the "twinkling of an eye," while, Teresa Panza, for her part, also refers to natural images by saying that "there are gossips everywhere in the streets like swarms of bees" (518). In a word, by using natural observations and animal imagery to make their points about lived experience, Sancho Panza and Teresa Panza's common speech-style identities bonds them together into a loving, long-term, relationship. One last example of husband-and-wife using rustic metaphors to describe natural phenomenon occurs when Sancho Panza says that "there isn't a mallet that tightens the hoops on a barrel as tight as [Teresa Panza] tightens the screws to make you do what she sets her mind on" (531). Again Sancho Panza draws analogies between manmade farm objects he uses and his wife's behavior while Teresa Panza, for her part, also analogizes Sancho Panza's behavior by referring to farm implements. This like mode of expression bonds them together. What's more, husband-and-wife both intersperse their speech with witty proverbs. Textually, this is evident when Teresa Panza not only tells her daughter that her "dear father is the father of proverbs" but also when she uses proverbs herself: like when she says that "when you're offered a heifer [its best to] make haste with the halter" (829). Even the priest, father Pero Perez, agrees that "every member of [this] breed of Panzas was born complete with a sackful of proverbs inside him [for he] hasn't met a single one who doesn't reel them off at all hours of the day and in all his conversations" (829). Hence, all of Sancho Panza and Teresa Panza's agrarian proverbs shows readers that they have similar speech style identities, which, in turn, provides a connection-point of commonality between them. But this is not the only way that husband-and-wife interpenetrate one another's characters, since Teresa Panza's "fatness [goes] well with her real name" and Sancho Panza is also "short, squat, and rotund" (941). Evidently, both conjugal spouses, as illustrated by their fleshy anatomies, like to eat heartily, to excess even, thus, they infuse one another's life-habits with an excessive yearning for food. In conclusion, since husband and wife co-operate and co-habitat in like ways, they come to love one another because they are similar to each other. Most importantly, though, all of Sancho Panza and Teresa Panza's likenesses show readers that true love, between a husband and a wife, comes, in part, from shared life-habits, common life-experiences, and a sense-of-life affinity, which, in turn, brings them closer together. In other words, the longstanding marriage between Sancho Panza and Teresa Panza renders them like one another in rather fundamental ways, thus showing readers that the joining of personalities, and the merging of life habits, is part-and-parcel of any long-term, romantic, relationship.

Another point of commonality between Sancho Panza and Teresa Panza that earns one another's true-love, is their mutual concern for and striving after money, which they talk about throughout the book, quite comprehensively. Such monetary interdependence, in turn, enables husband-and-wife to foster their romantic union through fiscal two-way support. To emphasize the importance of money to their relationship, Teresa Panza repeatedly asks "what [Sancho Panza] has got out of all of [his] squiring, how many fine skirts [he has brought back] for [her;] how many pairs of shoes for [her] children" (473). In response, Sancho Panza says that though he has brought back no money on his first sally he expects to earn money as "an earl or a governor of an island" (473). In response Teresa Panza asks "heaven [to] grant it [since] they need [money] badly enough" (473). Later, we learn that the Duke of Aragon gives Sancho Panza "two hundred gold escudos" for governing Barataria well (870). Additionally, when

Sancho Panza finds Cardenio's dead donkey lying in a stream he finds "100 gold escudos" in its "saddle bags," which he eventually brings home to his wife and children (190). Sancho Panza also provides money for his wife by providing her tangible, physical, goods, like "two donkey-mares," for example, gifted to him by Don Quixote (214). These pack-animals, in turn, enable his wife to: travel from her home to surrounding villages; transport groceries from the market place to her home; till the fields by dragging an iron plow attached to their backs, etc.. Moreover, Sancho Panza specifically asks Don Quixote for fixed wages for his squirely work so that he can "calculate pro rata what [he is] owed [in order to] be his own paymaster" (679). Don Quixote says that since Sancho Panza carries his money in a waist pouch, he can pay himself his back wages for the "twenty five days" of his second sally, which monies he shares with his wife and children when he gets home (679). Also when Senor Quixote composes his last will-and-testament he stipulates that: "it is [his wish] that in respect to certain monies in Sancho Panza's possession whatever remains after he has paid himself what [he is] owed should all be his" (978). Therefore, Sancho Panza not only receives fixed income for his job with Don Quixote but he also receives a lump, capital-sum, for his squireship, as well. In sum, since Sancho Panza acquires 300 gold escudos, 3 donkey mares, an unspecified squirely salary, and a last will bequest, he wins Teresa Panza's respect, love, and esteem for him by being a good monetary provider. Teresa Panza, in turn, also contributes money to the relationship by using the capital sum that Sancho Panza sends her to purchase seed-stock which she uses to sow the fields. In fact, we learn that what Teresa Panza and her family do not eat, she sells at market for a profit. This is why she plants corn, sows barley, and milks cows and goats and other milching-animals, which milk she churns into butter to sell at the local bazaar for a profit. Additionally, she collects and sells her hens eggs for a tidy profit. In sum, by individual monetary initiative, one in one way the other in another, Sancho Panza and Teresa Panza come to love one another because they both co-finance their relationship.

Joint nurturing of their children also gives Sancho Panza and Teresa Panza a purposive-bond that connects husband-and-wife together into a respectful, romantic, relationship, which, in turn, enables them to earn and maintain their true-love for one another. Firstly, both parents would like to see their son Sancho gainfully employed and their daughter Sanchita productively engaged. Textually, this is explicit when Teresa Panza tells Sancho Panza "that if [he is] so set on being in control of an island, [he] should take [his] son Sanchico with [him], to start teaching him to be in control too, because it is a good idea for a son to learn and inherit his father's trade" (519). In total agreement, Sancho Panza says that "as soon as [he is] put in [a governorial position he'll] send for him post haste," to train him for political leadership (519). To groom him into a future leader, Teresa Panza is concerned with educating her son, which she expresses thusly: "Sanchico's fifteen now, and it'd be a good idea if he went to school, [especially] if his uncle the priest is going to make a churchman out of him" (516). In tacit agreement, Sancho Panza discusses Sanchico's future governorship with an eye to seeing that he is well-educated. Financial self-reliance, extends to their daughter Sanchica's economic independence, as well, evidenced by Teresa Panza's statement to Sancho Panza that now that "Sanchica [is] making lace [and] earning eight clear maravedis a day that she puts in a piggy bank towards her trousseau" she is on her way to being financially self-sufficient (844). Thus, Teresa Panza and Sancho Panza's common desire to find a job for their son, their abiding concern for his developmental education, as well as some evidence regarding their daughter's economic activity, display joint concerns for their children, which, in turn, endears one to the other. Another way Teresa Panza and Sancho Panza provide for their children's material needs is by giving them clothing and food, for example. This is why Teresa Panza asks Sancho Panza "how many pairs of shoes [he] brought [back] for [his] children" upon returning from his second sally (473). Though he does not have shoes for their children at this time, later, Sancho Panza makes up for it by sending his wife "a green hunting outfit [for her to] make up into a skirt and some bodices for [their] daughter" (735). Also both parents come to love one another by suggesting an appropriate spouse for their daughter since they think that "Sanchita [would be delighted] if they searched for a fitting husband for her" (516). Obviously, Sancho Panza does not neglect his wife and children when he is away for he not only declares his intention to "stick a Dona and a ladyship on top of [his daughter's name]—thereby "fetching her out of the stubble fields and putting her under an awning onto a platform with plush pillows on it"—but also he avers that when he is away he is "sad at having to leave [her] and the children" (518, 515). In conclusion, Sancho Panza and Teresa Panza's concern for and up-keep of their children, regarding their education, occupation, material up-keep, and marital status, generates true-love between them.

To further answer the question of whether a young woman should choose a socially accepted and parentally sanctioned lover or whether she should choose a man she really loves, Cervantes juxtaposes marriage-for-love versus marriage-by-arrangement, ultimately favoring the former over the later. Take Basilio and Quiteria for example. Since Basilio and Quiteria are next door neighbors in the same village Basilio falls in love with Quiteria when he is a "boy of tender years" (610). In return, Quiteria shows her affection for Basilio with "a thousand innocent displays of affection" (610). As they grow up Basilio and Quiteria's mutual love is so pronounced that "people amuse themselves in the village by telling each other about the love affair of [these] two children" (610). Despite this fact, however, Quiteria's father is more concerned with the "material side of marriage wanting his daughter to marry a man who is able to provide for her comfort."[25] Thus, he "arranges for his daughter to marry Camacho the Rich," not Basilio the Poor, since he "does not think it wise to [let her] marry [a spouse] less well endowed by fortune" (610). Even though Basilio the Poor can: wrestle expertly; play pelota well; "run like a deer; jump further than a goat; sing like a lark"; play the guitar wonderfully; and "knock down skittles like magic"; Quiteria's father is unmoved since he thinks that these skills and talents aren't saleable (616). Since Quiteria's father is "looking for the best [economic] provider for his daughter" what impresses him most is not Basilio's athleticism but Camacho's wealth which can literally "bury Basilio in gold coins" (616).[26] This contrast, in turn, leads to discussion of whether "marriages should be arranged by parents—divorced from romantic attraction and usually for economic reasons—or based on the personal, romantic desires of a couple".[27] Sancho Panza, it seems, favors the view that people, such as Quiteria's father, should not "stop people who love each other from marrying [since love] looks through spectacles that make copper seem like gold, poverty like wealth, and water in the eyes like pearls" (611, 612). Basically, Sancho Panza helps readers to the perspective that since "true-love is an emotion in which the soul is incited to join itself willingly to objects which appear agreeable to it;" it supersedes the cash value of a romantic partner[28]. Said differently, to refute the view that marriage is largely a business transaction motivated by economic benefit and political gain, Sancho Panza believes that "romantic attraction is an adequate, and indeed the only basis for choosing one's lifelong partner." Don Quixote seconds Sancho Panza's stance by saying that

---

25 Jacobson, Karin. Cliffs Complete. <u>Shakespeare's Romeo and Juliet</u>. Ed. Sidney Lamb. New York: 2000. (50).

26 Maurer, Kate. <u>Cliff Notes The Taming of The Shrew</u>. New York: Wiley Publishing, 2001. (32).

27 Locke, Edwin, A. and Ellen Kenner. <u>The Selfish Path to Romance: How to Love with Passion and Reason</u>. Doylestown: Platform Press, 2011. (introduction xiii).

28 Hunt, Morton, M. <u>The Natural History of Love</u>. New York: 1959. (4).

"for people in love to marry [is a] most excellent end [since] love is pure joy, delight, and happiness, [especially when] the lover is in possession of the loved one" (631). Marriage, to Don Quixote, is a way of gaining the highly valued commodity of happiness, since love meets the emotional needs of the individual, gives him a sense of security, and provides him with much of the impetus and inspiration to effort. This is why he counsels "Basilio to stop devoting his time to those special skills of his, which brings him much renown but does not make him any money, and to apply himself to earning a living by honest, hard work, an option that is always available to diligent and prudent people" (631). Far from holding the view that "marriage is a phase of feudal business-management consisting of the joining of lands, the cementing of loyalties, and the production of heirs and future defenders," Don Quixote reasons that true love should be fostered by a strong work ethic, especially since "need and poverty are absolute enemies" of romantic love (631).[29]

Cervantes inevitably leads women and men into "marriage-for-love [not] marriage-by-arrangement" by having them marry their childhood sweethearts, even if they are relatively poor.[30] One way he does this is by having Basilio the Poor stop Quiteria the Fair from marrying Camacho the Rich by: ramming the steel spike of his walking stick into the ground; pulling its scabbard off to reveal a medium length rapier hidden inside; and, most astonishingly, throwing himself onto its jutting blade with such firm resolve that it seems to pass through his body. Then Basilio lies wallowing on the ground, stretched in a pool of his own fake blood, sighing pitiful moans and groans from time-to-time, pretending to come in-and-out of consciousness all to convince Quiteria that she should follow her heart by marrying him instantly. One argument Basilio uses to convince Quiteria to marry him is to "not turn [her] back on his own pure love for another man's riches" because wealth alone will

---

29   Hunt, Morton, M. <u>The Natural History of Love</u>. New York: 1959. (137).

30   Hunt, Morton, M. <u>The Natural History of Love</u>. New York: 1959. (217).

not bring her happiness (626). Moreover, Basilio declares that since "his own efforts [will eventually] increase [his] fortunes" she should not be off-put by his temporary lack of money (625). After waiting for Quiteria to gather her thoughts Basilio tells her that if she is "willing to give [him her] hand as [his] bride it [will] enable [him] to attain the bliss of being [hers]" (626). It seems that Basilio believes that his "identity is now entwined with" Quiteria's, since, only with her, will he be whole, because "the portion of his self that belongs to her" will only be complete if he is with her.[31] More largely, the action of this scene raises the question: "Does love depend on parent's arranging suitable matches among their children or should marriage be governed by personal affection instead?" Evidently, Quiteria thinks that husbands and wives should freely find and freely choose each other; and that true love should be the principal bond that holds romantic partners together. For this reason she "kneels by [Basilio's] side, asks him for his hand, and says that since 'no force would be sufficient to bend [her] will, it is with total freedom that she gives [him her] hand as [his] lawful wedded wife'" (628). In return, Quiteria will "accept [Basilio's] hand, [only if he], too, gives it [to her] of [his] own free will, unimpaired and underanged by the calamity that [he] has brought upon [himself] by [his] wild ideas" (628). Such emphasis on love and mutual attraction between bride and groom shows readers that husbands and wives should be as two sweet friends in the golden book of love. Just the fact that Quiteria and Basilio "choose their own lovers rather than marrying for convenience indicates their strength."[32]

In Cervantes's world, true-love, on the one hand, is shown to be powerful enough to mend social rifts, while arranged marriages, on the other hand, catalyze hostility, conflict, opposition, and antagonism between rival suitors, especially when parents try to force a match that

---

31   Jacobson, Karin. Cliffs Complete. Shakespeare's Romeo and Juliet. Ed. Sidney Lamb. New York: 2000. (131).

32   Jacobson, Karin. Cliffs Complete. Shakespeare's Romeo and Juliet. Ed. Sidney Lamb. New York: 2000. (132).

their children do not want. Take Basilio's, Quiteria's, and Camacho's love triangle, for example. Since "Camacho feels humiliated" that Quiteria loves a poor county shepherd better then himself he "entrusts [his] vengeance to [his] own hands [by] unsheathing [his] sword [and] falling upon Basilio" (629). Immediately, "many more swords are drawn," both by Camacho's supporters and by Basilio's friends, and, in an instant, an armed conflict *almost* ensues (629). Had not Father Pero Perez and Don Quixote intervened—one by speaking many "wise and well-meaning words" the other by brandishing his sword—these antagonists would have certainly injured each other, perhaps fatally (629). But since the creative passion of true-love conquers the destructive rage of a spurned lover, calmer heads prevail. In fact, as Camacho sees it, "more thanks are due to heaven for having taken Quiteria from him than for having given her to him" since she would "have continued to love Basilio [even] after he married her" (629). With these words, both groups of men "return their swords to their proper places," and once again the streets are safe and quiet (629). The larger point here is that "rather than presenting a carefree image of marriage [between Quiteria and Camacho, Cervantes] intertwines images of love and death; vignettes of joy and sorrow," to emphasize the point that if parents insist on forcing their children into matches they don't like, what can, and often does, result, are intense pre-marital disagreements that can spill-over as violence erupts in the streets.[33] And, this, in turn, can lead to nasty blood feuds: like the clash between the Caplets and the Montagues in *Romeo and Juliet*, for example. Another illustration of this concept in action occurs when Luscinda's parents force her to marry Don Fernando against her will. Due to their "persuasion that Don Fernando will be a better match" for their daughter they inadvertently create a dangerous situation where her rival suitors almost battle (237). But Don Fernando's true-love for Dorotea stops him from unsheathing his sword, since she

---

33 Jacobson, Karin. Cliffs Complete. <u>Shakespeare's Romeo and Juliet</u>. Ed. Sidney Lamb. New York: 2000. (103).

"clasps his legs, kisses them, and holds onto him," all the while saying, with "tears flowing down her cheeks," that since he has, at his "feet," his true and lawful "wife," he should be content with that and not jeopardize his life out of a mistaken sense of honor (351, 343). Due to the wisdom of this plea "Don Fernando brings himself to tranquility, thereby showing all the world that reason has more power over [him] than passion" (343). As these examples prove, a repeating theme in *Don Quixote* is the idea that true love restores tranquility between and among lovers so that peace, law, and order prevails.

Another point that Cervantes explores in *Don Quixote* is the idea that when two-human beings enjoy a very special, loving, relationship, they should not try one another's love by administering unnecessary love tests.

As Camila, Anselmo, and Lotario's love triangle proves in the *"Tale of the Inappropriate Curiosity,"* when true-love exists between partners, unnecessary "love tests" should not be administered, otherwise death, destruction, and seclusion, can result for all persons involved. To explain, Anselmo feels that he is "the angriest and bitterest man in the world because he is assailed and tormented by the urge to find out whether his wife, Camila, is as virtuous and perfect as he thinks she is" (297, 298). Hence, to convince himself of the truth of his wife's virtue, Anselmo tests her purity by asking his friend, Lotario, to tempt and entice Camila. Thus, he asks his best friend: to stay alone with her in his house for three days; to eat dinner with her repeatedly so he can praise her fine mind; and admirable looks; to write her complimentary poetry and other romantic love letters winning over her mind through eloquent, loving words; and give her money and jewels in token of his affection. Since Lotario is a good friend he tries to convince Anselmo not to test Camila's virtue and to just be happy that he has a fine lady. Reasons he gives Anselmo not to test her are: **1)** Camila's virtue will not be improved by testing it; **2)** If Anselmo doubts Camila's virtue he should confront her directly, not, play, childish, psychological mind-games that are

27

meant to entrap, weaken, and destroy, her love for him; **3)** If his best friend keeps his project a secret just knowing about it himself will be enough to torment and destroy him; **4)** Anselmo's honor will be undermined if he is successful, since, his wife will shame him by no longer loving him; **5)** He will be as wretched as a man can be if he is successful in undermining Camila's love for him, because his sole, romantic, value, will leave him; **6)** If he is successful in undoing Camila's virtue by romantic love-testing, ultimately, he will cause his own undoing by decoupling her from him. Despite Lotario's good advice, though, Anselmo refuses his moral guidance. Instead, he insists that his best friend test Camila's love for him by subjecting her to a pretend romantic trial. Thus, in an attempt to placate his friend, Lotario reluctantly agrees and starts to fall in love with Camilla. So, he professes his love to Camilla through sweet words, and, even gives her "four thousand escudos [of Anselmo's] cash and jewels," which causes the narrator to ask: "What [Anselmo] is doing? What is he plotting? What is he trying to bring about? Why is he trying to [generate his] own destruction" (310). Essentially, the narrator opines on Anselmo's motivations, as well as their disastrous effects, to show readers that a positive conjugal relationship should not be undone by unnecessary love tests, especially when a "wife, [such as] Camila is a good woman [that should be cherished] in peace and security" (310). Due to his inappropriate curiosity, however, Anselmo rushes headlong down the path of his own self-destruction: proven by the fact that his wife elopes with his best friend; they take his treasure trove of valuables; his servants run away—like Leonela, for example, who makes a "rope" out of "sheets" and climbs out of her "window,"— and, in short, he is left in a dejected and confused mind-state (335). In this instance, we, as readers, understand – through the events of the plot – that, though Camila remains resolute for a while, ultimately her resolve breaks down, in the face of this love testing. Sadly, Camilla buckles under Lotario's advances, and, as a result: Anselmo's honor is undermined because his wife cheats on him with Lotario; her virtue is diminished by this rigorous love undoing; and, because he is successful in breaking his wife's resolve to be loyal to him, Anslemo causes his own death. In his last will and testament, then, Anselmo writes that: **A)** a "stupid and inappropriate desire had taken his life; **B)** That he "manufactured his own dishonor;" and; **C)** that he "forgives his wife Camila" since her elopement with Lotario is his own fault (337). Evidently, Anselmo's inappropriate curiosity leads the narrator to call him "unfortunate and ill-advised for plotting his own dishonor and bringing about his own destruction" (337). And, as Lotario presciently warns Anselmo at the outset of his little experiment with Camila, he should "consider how he would feel without her and how justly he'd reproach himself for being the cause of her downfall and his own too [since] if she falters, and can't withstand the trial," he'll be "the cause of a triple tragedy" (303). But, Anselmo does not listen. Instead, his stupid curiosity, causes: him to die in bed agonizingly due to a broken heart; Lotario to die in the "battle of Crepinolga" against the Ottomans; and Camila's death at the unforgiving hands of sadness and melancholy" wallowing alone in a convent. (endnotes, 337). In conclusion, the moral of this unfortunate tragedy is that when one has true-love with another person they should not spoil that love with unnecessary love-trials, otherwise they risk jeopardizing their own long-term happiness by unraveling a very special, intimate, romantic relationship that they already have, or can grow.

Despite the fact that Cervantes favors romantic young lovers over the authority of the family, he satirizes the grand seduction techniques used in *Don Quixote* to make the point that parents should, at times, take an active role in their children's love lives, otherwise their children can be tempted into wrong acts and beliefs based on a false (or mercenary) promise of marriage. Case in point is a sixteen-year-old girl named Leandra whose father fails to internalize good conduct in his daughter during childhood. Though "fame of her exquisite beauty, rare intelligence, elegance, and virtue [causes] countless men to ask for her hand in marriage," her father fails to

teach Leandra how to distinguish right from wrong when it comes
to the emotional dealings between men and women (462). Instead of
teaching her that substance is more important than ornament when
evaluating the character of a potential spouse, he fails to prepare
his daughter for sly sexual predators who target and exploit naïve
young girls just like her for mercenary gains. In lieu of proposing
that Leandra marry a legitimate suitor named Eugenio—a young
man of "good family, in the prime of his life, rich in worldly goods,"
and fairly "intelligent," too—or, alternatively, instead of "proposing
several good candidates and giving her free choice among these,"
Leandra's father "off-puts [her suitors] with talk of how young she
is" (463). Unwilling "to refer the matter to Leandra herself,"—which,
Eugenio tells us, is "an example that could well be followed by all
parents in search of spouses for their children—" Leandra's father
dissuades young bachelors with an assortment of "generalities" meant
to release him from his fatherly "obligations" (463). Though "sixteen"
may be too young for a teenage girl to marry, Leandra's father, as we
have seen, is remiss in not telling his daughter that legitimate suitors
are courting her (462). Thus, when a fashionable young rake named
Vicente de la Rosa shows up at Leandra's home village she is ready to
believe his declarations.

Dressed as all "soldiers like to dress" Vicente de la Rosa: wears a
"thousand different colored" suits and plumes; "covers [himself] in
glass trinkets and little steel chains" of all kinds; and combines all his
"baubles, geegaws, garters, and hoses" in clever variations (463). "One
day he wears one flimsy, artificial, tawdry, worthless" outfit, the next
day he wears another, "ringing in the changes of his finery" in such
a way that he gives people the impression that he owns "more than
ten suits and more than twenty plumes," when, in fact, he owns only
"three" outfits (463). Not only does Vicente de la Rosa seek to impress
Leandra through his vulgar ostentation, he also tries to evoke a false
sense of hero worship in her by saying that there isn't "a land in the
world he [hasn't] been to, not a battle he [hasn't] fought in" (463, 464).

According to him "he [has] slaughtered more Moors than there are in Morocco and has taken part in more single combats [than] Gante y Luna" (464). Feigning invincibility, Vicente de la Rosa claims to have won all of his prearranged duels "without ever having been made to shed a single drop of blood" (464). In testimony he shows people imaginary "scars he says he has but that [they] cannot see, [claiming, all the while] that they are from gunshot wounds received in various [battles] and raids" (464). "In addition to all of [his] bravado," Vicente de la Rosa "strums" his guitar, sings doleful songs, and recites original poetry about "every trifling incident in the life of the village, [ensuring to] distribute at least twenty copies" of his endless "ballads" (464). "Often seen and gazed upon by Leandra from a window in her house this hero, this man of fashion, this musician, this poet," captivates her young heart with his flashy clothes, heroic braggadocio, mediocre guitar playing, and poetic doggerel (464). Bamboozled by his persuasive picture-painting, Leandra: "falls in love with his gaudy clothes; is captivated by his [mile-long] ballads; [marvels] at the feats he claims to have performed; [and, in the end,] falls in love with the man himself" (464). Evidently, Leandra is infatuated by the heroic fantasy that Vicente de la Rosa creates for himself rather than his true nature. So much so, in fact, that "before he has the presumption to try his luck with her, Leandra [strikes up a conversation with Vicente de la Rosa]" thereby providing him with the opportunity he needs to "persuade her to [elope to] Naples [with him]" (464, 465). "Ill-advised and beguiled enough to believe him, [Leandra] robs her father's [household] money and valuable jewels," and disappears with Vicente de la Rosa in the still of the night, only to be found, "three days" later, in a "mountain cave wearing only a chemise" (464, 465). Evidently, Vicente de la Rosa's artificial love posturing shows readers that he is a dedicated seducer; a sly predator who "plays his part with the skill of an actor and the dedication of a soldier—all without the slightest hint of emotional involvement."[34] Primarily "he views other

---

34   Hunt, Morton, M. <u>The Natural History of Love</u>. New York: 1959. (279).

human beings as [sacrificial] objects that either fit, or fail to fit, his needs, using them at his pleasure without suffering guilty feelings."[35] Accordingly, Vicente de la Rosa tries to master women's minds and control their flesh as well to extract what he wants from them. Despite Vicente de La Rosa's culpability, however, Leandra, too, is at fault, since she did not get to know Vicente De La Rosa's true nature before running away with him.

Conspicuously absent from Leandra's rush-off alone—or total flight from her family—is a thorough investigation of Vicente de la Rosa's inner character comprised of: asking him upfront questions; extracting direct answers; and "drawing him out" to find out if he is good for her or not. In other words, instead of learning "who [Leandra] has in front of her" by asking pointed questions, receiving direct answers, and scrutinizing subtle evidence, Leandra falls in love with the verbal fantasy that Vicente de la Rosa creates for himself, without directly learning something about his "character, opinions, and plans for living."[36] Since she does not talk about money, children, where to live, his life philosophy, and Vicente's occupation, Leandra does not extract the information that she needs to form an accurate picture of his goals, dreams, practices, and beliefs. Totally missing from Leandra and Vicente de La Rosa's relationship is an educational process that gradually leads from playful heterosexual behavior to companionship and love capable of initiating and sustaining a successful marriage. Instead of asking him questions first, and looking for love later, Leandra simply believes the appealing fantasy Vicente de la Rosa creates for himself, without verifying if what he says is true or not. Without observing Vicente de la Rosa in action to see how he handles different situations, Leandra simply believes the truth of his statements, even though he lies often. Perhaps, if

---

35   Hunt, Morton, M. The Natural History of Love. New York: 1959. (50).

36   Kenner, Ellen. "The Rational Basis of Romance (Part 2): Courting Success in Romance." Irvine, 2005. And Hunt, Morton, M. The Natural History of Love. New York: 1959. (359).

Leandra's father took a more active role in his daughter's love life she would not have been beguiled and abandoned by a man whose false bravado is a masquerade—a tough exterior designed to hide his inner evil.

Short of suggesting that parents should force their children into matches they don't like, Cervantes warns readers that

> if everybody married the person they [think] they love, parents would lose their power to marry their children when and to whom they should; and if it were left to daughters to choose their husbands as they pleased, one would pick her father's servant, and another a man she has seen walking down the street and who she thinks looks jaunty and dashing—even though he is in reality some wild swashbuckler—because [infatuation] and fancy easily blind the eyes of the understanding, which are so necessary when making decisions about settling down in life"
>
> (611). Here, Cervantes emphasizes selectivity when choosing a lifelong partner by acknowledging that a young adult, and her parents, can find a fitting spouse together. In this regard, Cervantes emphasizes that trust, or the confident dependence on the character, ability, strength, and truth-telling of a spouse, is absolutely vital in forming a beneficial union. Hence, Don Quixote says that "before a prudent man sets out on a long journey, he [should] look for someone trustworthy and agreeable to keep him company" (611). He continues that just as a journeyman looks for a companion who is likely to live up to his word, "someone setting out on the journey of life" should also select an appropriate partner "since the person he chooses will keep him company in bed, at table, and everywhere else, just as a wife does her husband
>
> (611).

From the opposite viewpoint, Cervantes, as author and narrator, presents compelling evidence that caring too much, as opposed to not caring enough, can lead to idle infatuation, which is itself a form of madness that thwarts true love by off-putting a true-lover. Evidently, Altisidora's actions prove that she is too fond of Don Quixote for she repeatedly laments that she burns, pines, and perishes out of aching love for him. "Demonstratively sentimental, melancholic, tempestuous, and tearful, according to the occasion," sometimes Altisidora weeps. At other times she cultivates a pallor and adopts a look of suffering.[37] Due to her wounded feminine pride at Don Quixote's rejection, Altisidora recites a long list of wrongs that seem false. For example, she accuses Don Quixote of "sinful callousness and obstinacy" of "deception" of "stealing [her] love" of "bad faith" of "cruelty," because she "adores him," not because these charges are true (795, 870, 953). In fact Don Quixote responds to her "deliberate outrageousness" by saying that "when love is dawning to be undeceived is the best cure" (792).[38] Hence, he not only sings her a ballad, on page 793 (suggesting that he does not love her) but he also reiterates, seventy nine pages later, that "the maiden speaks as one in love, something for which [he is] not to blame" (872). We must now ask ourselves, is such upfront candor a sign of hardheartedness? Did Don Quixote ever encourage Altisidora's idle lust for him? Did he ever lie to Altisidora, deceive her, cheat on her? Obviously, the answer to these questions is an emphatic no! A better explanation, one that I believe, is that she behaves with the green-judgement typical of a wild, foolish, and fickle fourteen-year-old adolescent. Basically, Altisidora is a prime example of the clinging-vine character of a thoughtless ingénue who suffocates Don Quixote by always gushing about her love for him. This, in turn, displeases him, ultimately creating a desire for him to push her away. Yet, Don Quixote rejects

---

37   Hunt, Morton, M. <u>The Natural History of Love</u>. New York: 1959. (309).

38   Saccio, Peter. "The Taming of the Shrew—Getting Married in the 1590's. <u>The Teaching Company</u>. Virginia, 1999.

Altisidora tactfully, by giving her sound advice on how she can turn her thoughts away from idle-lust by keeping busy.

In order to differentiate true love from idle infatuation, Cervantes suggests—through his mouthpiece characters—that a prudent woman can turn her thoughts away from an inordinate desire to have sex with someone by decent and continuous occupation away from the lust object. Thus, to undercut Altisidora's sudden and capricious carnal lust for Don Quixote, he tells her that since lust "counts on careless sloth to aid and abet, much sewing and embroidery and ceaseless occupation are the antidotes to the virulence of amorous inclination" (793). Sancho Panza seconds this sentiment by saying that "all of [Altisidora's] problems are born out of idleness, the remedy of which is honest and constant occupation" (960). Furthermore, during the catafalque scene, where Altisidora pretends to wake from the dead, Don Quixote tells the Duchess that Altisidora can truly resurrect herself "by applying herself to [the] activity [of lace making]; because so long as she is busy with her bobbins, the image or images of her desires will not be busy in her mind" (960). Sancho Panza validates Don Quixote's opinion by swearing that "never [has he] in all [his] life seen a lacemaker who died of love, [since] busy girls think more about finishing the job in hand than about their boyfriends" (960). Sancho Panza applies this assertion to his own life experience by saying that "while [he is] digging [a ditch he] hasn't got a thought for Teresa Panza" (960). Evidently, the Duchess agrees with this assessment by saying that "from now on [she'll] see to it that Altisidora [is] kept busy with some needlework, [especially] since she [is] incredibly good at it" (960). Most importantly, by saying that "errant knights who err at court will dally with flighty [maidens] but [will] marry the chaste sort," Don Quixote emphasizes that while idle infatuation invites unremorseful seduction and abandonment, true-love tends to generate lasting, successful, romantic relationships (794).

Theoretically speaking, by disparaging Altisidora's wild, reckless, fickle behavior induced from excessive passion, Cervantes highlights, by opposite contrast, the idea that reasonable, careful, stable thinking in romantic relationships can only be created by a form of moderate passion motivated by true-love. Indeed, comments made by the Duchess, Don Quixote, and Sancho Panza, in this regard, suggest that Altisidora would do well to learn that the tempered, realistic, moderate love of a mature adult is agreeable, while excessive "love is a heavy burden, a cause of toil, trouble and frustration, a type of madness, an overpowering force that robs a woman of her self-control and wise judgement, a destructive passion that makes the rational woman act wildly."[39] Put positively, Cervantes suggests that Altisidora would benefit herself enormously by realizing that moderate love is an enlightening saneness, a healing force that cures and uplifts an individual while lovesickness is a tragic madness, a ruinous disease that is "habit forming, causes frenzied and irrational actions that consumes the lover's strength and wastes his substance." [40]

One more reason that true-love does not develop between Don Quixote and Altisidora is because of their vast age difference and different maturity levels, which makes it difficult for them to have interesting conversations about topics they both enjoy. Since Altisidora is a "fourteen year old teenager" and Don Quixote is a "forty-nine year old" adult, a thirty-five year time gap marks unequal intellectual outlooks thus signaling, to Don Quixote at least, the impossibility of any romantic relationship growing between them (784, 25). "Fond of life, literature, and learned woman," Don Quixote is unattracted to Altisidora since she is not: well "read; highly skilled in [creative] writing and [philosophic] conversation; and capable of handling worldly and political matters."[41] Hence, as Altisidora's words and actions prove she is an unlearned child, without "glamour, sophistication, intellectuality, or experience in the ways of attracting

---

39 Hunt, Morton, M. <u>The Natural History of Love</u>. New York: 1959. (41).

40 Hunt, Morton, M. <u>The Natural History of Love</u>. New York: 1959. (61).

41 Hunt, Morton, M. <u>The Natural History of Love</u>. New York: 1959. (200, 181).

men."[42] Most crucially, their mental discrepancy shows readers that romantic partners should share some common interests otherwise they will spend less time together and may drift apart emotionally.

By way of proving, textually, that physical chemistry is a necessary component of romantic love, characters in *Don Quixote* are not only attracted to one another for their: anatomies; dress-style; hair-color; skin-tone; countenance; body postures; and physical gestures, but, more importantly, they view their partners as the most beautiful and attractive people in the world—at least to them personally. This physical attraction, in turn, facilitates one another's true love. Take, Captain Viedma and Lela Zoraida, for example. His "fine, robust, muscular physique" attracts Lela Zoraida's to him while her good looks inspires admiration in him (351). Therefore, when she comes before him with "pearls hanging from her neck, ears and tresses, [wearing] ankle rings of the purest gold [inset] with many diamonds, [he] can't begin to describe [to readers the] beauty and grace [of] her rich and elegant attire" (380). Indeed, "at that moment she [is] so magnificently attired and so very beautiful that she seems to [him] the loveliest woman that [he'd] ever seen: a goddess who had come down to earth for [his] delight and deliverance" (380). In a later conversation, when Lela Zoraida suggests that the reason why Captain Viedma is so "keen to go back [to Spain is] to be with [his] wife again," he replies that not only is he "not married" but, more importantly, he has "given his word to marry [her] as soon as he reaches Spain" (381). Encouraged by this response, Lela Zoraida asks Captain Viedma if she is "very beautiful" (381). In response, Captain Viedma assures her that "she [is] so very beautiful" (381). Evidently, Captain Viedma's great love for Lela Zoraida, and Lela Zoraida's great love for Captain Viedma, is motivated, at least in part, by one another's physical beauty, which, in turn, leads them into marriage.

But they are not the only couple in *Don Quixote* who are attracted to one another's good looks. Take Cardenio and Luscinda, for

---

42   Hunt, Morton, M. <u>The Natural History of Love</u>. New York: 1959. (21).

example. Cardenio is attracted to Luscinda for her: "lovely blond hair; [delicate] white hands; [and her] incomparable beauty" (239, 235, 340, 235). Luscinda, on the other hand, is "amazed" by "Cardenio's good looks" (289). Together, they present a view of love that emphasizes its physical aspects. In fact, Cardenio accentuates the importance of beauty to a romantic relationship when he describes Luscinda as "richly dressed and adorned as her beauty deserves" since the "crimson and white [colors of her dress, along with] the glinting of the jewels in her hair and on her clothes" marks her "singular beauty" (239). So great is Cardenio's admiration for Luscinda's good looks, indeed, that "he extols her beauty" often (233).

Besides these two examples, there are a variety of women in Don Quixote, like Marcela, for example, or Leandra, for instance, who "readily inspire admiration through their beauty."[43] So much so, in fact, that men flock around them. But since the physical yearnings of their admirers are mostly attributed to animal heat—not spiritual love—they are summarily rejected, ignored, or spurned by their lady loves. As for the notion that a person should view their romantic companion as the most beautiful person in the world, at least to them personally, Don Quixote's great love for Dulcinea proves this. Evidently, since Dulcinea is "the most beautiful woman in the world" to Don Quixote she is superlative (699). This is why he describes her as the "most beauteous and eminent lady" on earth (126). Basically, Don Quixote sees Dulcinea as "a beautiful woman, a delightful [individual,] loving her for her body as well as her inspirational value."[44] In short, Cervantes presents the view that beauty as seen in bodies, but especially in faces, creates a strong desire for the joining of souls and the merger of lives. What's more, Cervantes shows readers that physical beauty is such a draw to men and women that romantic

---

43   Maurer, Kate. <u>Cliff Notes The Taming of The Shrew</u>. New York: Wiley Publishing, 2001. (23).

44   Hunt, Morton, M. <u>The Natural History of Love</u>. New York: 1959. (50).

love depends, at least in part, on the appreciation of a lover's body as well as the desire for the sensation of bodily pleasure.

Contrary to the view that sexual love is a foul connection practiced by sinful creatures, Cervantes presents the view that sex is a normal, healthful means of affirming a very special relationship between two human beings. For this reason Miguel imbues love and sex with emotional meaning by showing readers that sexual expression is legitimate where love exists. For example, Leonela, a maid in a Florentine household, tells her mistress that she is seeing a "well-born young man" from an unnamed city in Tuscany and that her relationship has already gone beyond words (318). Very much in a way to be in love, one night Leonela copulates with her lover saying that "there is no force [in this world] that can resist [true love]" (318). Basically, Leonela emphasizes that love and sex are intertwined and she obviously enjoys both. But she is not the only one. Don Fernando's love for Dorotea directly results in his desire to "penetrate and be absorbed by her."[45] Evidently, since Don Fernando "loves this [very] beautiful farmer's daughter [he] decides to conquer her virginity [by] giving her his word of marriage" (200). For her part Dorotea is attracted to Don Fernando since he is a "charming, attractive, young man, of generous and amorous disposition" (199). Therefore, one night, when Don Fernando gains entrance to Dorotea's room, her "maid leaves and [she] stops being one" (255). Even though Don Fernando's lovemaking is imputed, at least at first, to his overwhelming sexual appetite for Dorotea, eventually, he proves that he really loves her when he not only tells her that "it isn't right for the woman [he] holds in [his] heart to be kneeling at his feet" but also when he says that he now "holds [her] in the esteem [that she] deserves" (345). In summary, "Don Fernando takes with his lips a part of the prize gained by his love" thereby illustrating that his love longs to have complete union with Dorotea

---

45   Hunt, Morton, M. <u>The Natural History of Love</u>. New York: 1959. (62). (From *De Rerum Natura* by Catullus).

(428). Here we see that Cervantes does not portray sex as so sinful and disgusting after all, since men and women in his novel begin to associate it with true-love. Moreover, Cervantes suggests that, on the one hand, the "stifling of biologically inevitable emotions results in human sickness" and destructive conduct while, on the other hand, all the pure-minded sexual episodes in the book mark lovemaking as natural and beneficial.[46] Accordingly, Cervantes refutes the twin misconceptions that: true love should be unsullied by sex; and that sex is simply a physically pleasing bodily function, with no deep bond with the person you are with. On the contrary, Cervantes presents romantic love as a strong, emotionally intimate relationship between consenting adults that combines an intense valuing of a partner on the deepest level and the enjoyment of sexual pleasure with that partner. Lovemaking, though, which is based on an affinity of values, should not be confused with lechery, since one is based on a strong mental and physical connection, while the other is based on sensual gratification only.

Sex, when not motivated by love, is penalized by Cervantes to show readers that a carnal "relationship that does not combine the intense valuing of a partner on the deepest level and the enjoyment of sexual pleasure with that partner is not a romantic relationship."[47] Take Maritornes's prostitution with a Muleteer, for example. She treats sex as a business transaction divorced from any deeper meaning. As such, Maritornes promises this muleteer "that as soon as the [inn] guests settle down and her master and mistress are asleep she will go to him and give him all the pleasure he can wish for" (125, 124). Making good on her promise, Maritornes "creeps forward with her arms held out in front of her" in search of her client (126). But when she "bumps into Don Quixote's arms, he seizes her by the wrist and pulls her towards him and makes her sit on his bed" (126). Dismayed

---

46 Hunt, Morton, M. <u>The Natural History of Love</u>. New York: 1959. (280).

47 Locke, Edwin. A, and Ellen Kenner. <u>The Selfish Path to Romance: How to Love with Passion and Reason.</u> Doylestown: 2011. (5).

at seeing herself in Don Quixote's clutches, Maritornes "struggles [to] break loose" of his iron grip (126). This imbroglio causes the muleteer to creep up to Don Quixote's bed and "deliver such a punch [to his] lantern jaw that his mouth [begins to stream] blood" (127). Since Don Quixote's rickety bed cannot bear the weight of Don Quixote, the Muleteer, and Maritornes, they come crashing to the ground. During all this commotion Maritornes "takes refuge" in Sancho Panza's bed waking him from a dream in which he is battling some insolent knight" (127). Thinking that he is under attack, Sancho Panza "begins to flail about with his fists" punching Maritornes several times in the process (127). Seeing herself so rudely treated, Maritornes throws all "modesty" aside and begins to grapple and wrestle with Sancho Panza in the "fiercest and funniest skirmish imaginable" (127). This rowdy brawl continues until a member of the holy brotherhood of Toledo enters the fray ordering the combats to stop fighting in the name of the law. This amusing episode, then, shows readers that if sex becomes a commodity divorced from any deeper meaning what can, and often results, is the moral decline of the participants, which, in some cases, results in violence, ridicule, and shame. In brief, while sexual love is often linked with the essentially good and beautiful of human existence, concupiscence is a degrading experience which jeopardizes the good standing of those involved.

More largely, all of this talk of love and sex essentializes the point that when looking for your soul mate you want a partner you are attracted to both mentally and physically. By alternating between serious conversations and sexual love in *Don Quixote*, Cervantes emphasizes that love balances the mental and the physical. Take Don Fernando and Dorotea's relationship, for example. When Don Fernando sees Dorotea in church he looks upon her with "loving eyes" since her: "peerless beauty;" gorgeous face; and freely flowing "[long] blond hair" is attractive to him (251, 248). In fact, "the moment [his] eyes catch sight of [her] he [is in a way] to fall deeply in love [with her] as his later demonstrations indicate" (252). Ways

Don Fernando communicates his love for Dorotea include writing her romantic "love-letters full of words of passion; giving [her] presents and offering her relations favors; [and vouchsafing] more offers and vows than signs of the alphabet" (252). Though Dorotea is pleased "to read Don Fernando's praises in his letters," and though Don Fernando's rational "gallantry gives her a very special thrill of happiness to be loved and esteemed by such an eminent gentlemen" her sense of virtue [causes her to take] defenses and precautions," lest he is untrue (252, 253). Thus, when he "produces tears to support his words and sighs to vouch for his passions" she is moved to "honest compassion:" nothing less, nothing more (253). Hence, she tells Don Fernando that though she is his "tenant [she] is not [his] slave [since] the nobility of his blood does not give [him] the authority to [denigrate] the humility of [hers since she] holds [herself], a lowly farmer's daughter, in quite as much esteem as [he,] a lord and gentlemen does" (253). Hence, Dorotea avers that "all [his] words will not deceive her, all his wealth will be powerless [to move her], all his sighs and tears will [not] effect [her since] it is unthinkable that any man who is not legitimately married to [her] can gain anything from [her]" (253). After: promising her his "hand in marriage; [in front of] a holy image [for verification]; repeating and confirming his oath" in front of her witness-maid; and finally, "calling down a thousand curses on himself if he [fails] to carry out his promises," Dorotea consummates their union by making love to him (254, 255). Before leave-taking, Don Fernando "takes a fine ring from his finger and puts it on her [finger]" swearing that she should "feel certain of his faithfulness [since] his oaths [are] firm and true" (256). Notice, here, how physical love is combined with proper and contractual love, which shows readers that true-love has a mental two-way component, which distinguishes it from pure physical gratification. Despite all of Don Fernando's promises, however, he almost marries another young woman named Luscinda "a month later" (256). In the end, however, Don Fernando marries Dorotea when she reminds him that "his own words are [testament to his love of her] and they cannot and must not be false ones" (342). Moved by this, and other cogent arguments, Don Fernando admits that Dorotea has "won [since] nobody could have the heart to deny such an assemblage of truths" (342). Throughout the rest of the book, Don Fernando and Dorotea partake in a series of chivalric and physical adventures together— using their minds and their bodies in union. Due to all this textual evidence, it is reasonable to say that Don Fernando and Dorotea "create their own world of love: one that combines spiritual and physical pleasures."[48] The larger, theoretical, point here is that since real love is based on mental attraction and physical pair bonding, husband and wife should not only enjoy companionate sex together but also loving, mind-to-mind, conversations, as well. And, contrary to the view that husband and wife are mere bodily pleasure givers, couples in the book look for people who can "spar wits with them, challenge them, and excite them, intellectually, emotionally, and physically".[49] Besides emphasizing the point that "love[50] based sex is a glorious union of mind and body—since a person's capacity for sexual pleasure comes from the mind and the body"—Cervantes also shows readers that one must win over their soul mates to generate true love between them.

Not only does Don Luis and Clara Viedma's relationship emphasize that persistence, dedication, and tenacity is required to win one's mate permanently, but, above all, Dorotea's great courage, in the face of very challenging circumstances, shows readers that one must court their mates, intellectually, emotionally, and physically, to earn their true love. To illustrate this fact, consider the intricate courtship between Don Luis and Clara Viedma. In the story, Donna Clara is

48 Jacobson, Karin. Cliffs Complete. Shakespeare's Romeo and Juliet. Ed. Sidney Lamb. New York: 2000. (63).

49 Maurer, Kate. Cliff Notes The Taming of The Shrew. New York: Wiley Publishing, 2001. (68).

50 Locke, Edwin. A, and Ellen Kenner. The Selfish Path to Romance: How to Love with Passion and Reason. Doylestown: 2011. (184).

a young woman who travels with her father to Mexico City—where he will take up a post as a "Supreme Court judge." Her childhood sweetheart, Don Luis, loves Donna Clara so much that he follows the pair, on Spanish highways and byways, disguised as a modest footman, walking, and hitch-hiking, hundreds of miles, to convince her to marry him (397). So intent is Don Luis to win over Donna Clara that he hides from her father—when they meet on lanes and at inns—so that he does not frustrate their love. But, once in Granada, when her father is not with her, Don Luis serenades Donna Clara from the street below her window, comparing her beauty to "a distant lodestar that guides a mariner to safety in the darkest nights" (401). In another verse-stanza, Don Luis avows that despite her coyness towards him, he intends "to keep [a] firm, straight line [since] no sluggard ever gained the triumphs and laurels of love to adorn his brow" (403). Finally, Don Luis concludes his sonnet by saying that "love will persevere" since joy that is hard-won is appreciated more and will last longer (403). After Don Luis concludes his poem, Donna Clara declares to her girlfriend, Dorotea, that she appreciates his poetry, love-gestures, and persistence, because she "cannot live without him" (404). This is why she says that "so long as Don Luis does not give-up the manner of her heart, he'll never be ejected from it" (402). Thus, Camila not only wants, but also expects, Don Luis to be persistent in his suit to win her over. And he is. Don Luis's serenading, then, along with Donna Clara's favorable reaction to it, begins to ease her maidenly bashfulness, thus, fostering their incipient love affair. Thus, when Don Luis's father's servants try to take him back home, saying that his father would be at a loss without his son and sole heir, Don Luis replies that "on no account can he [go home] until he settles a matter that involves his life, honour, and soul" (413). This statement show's readers that to win Camila's mind and heart Don Luis has to be persistently assertive. This is why Don Luis tells his father's servants that since he is "free to do as he pleases, he will return home if he feels like it, and if he doesn't feel like it none of them are going to force him

[to]" (413). Judge Viedma, seconds Don Luis's control over his own love life by telling Don Luis's "four [servants] to calm down and be patient, since a satisfactory solution will [soon] be found" (414). This statement deescalates tensions for a while. Don then shows his future father in law that he really loves his daughter by saying that "from the very moment [he] set eyes on Dona Clara, he made her the mistress of his heart" (416). This is why, according to him, he leaves "home, puts on [his] footman's clothes, [and] follows Donna Clara where she goes" so that he seizes the opportunity to convince her to marry him (416). This shows judge Viedma that Don Luis truly loves his daughter because he endures many trials, tribulations, and hardships for her. Moreover, to convince Judge Viedma to "make [him] a perfectly happy man" he asks him not to "prevent" their "marriage" since he not only ardently loves his daughter, and will therefore do his utmost to make her happy, but also because his "sole heir [status to all his] parents wealth and nobility [may be] motives enough for [him] to make him [his] son" (416). Moved by this appeal, Judge Viedma tells Don Luis to "calm down and to procrastinate with his [father's] servants so that they do not take him back that day, leaving time to consider what [is] best for all parties" (416). Eventually, due to Don Luis's persistence, and judge Viedma's persuasion, Don Luis's father's "servant's agree to everything he wants, which [makes] Dona Clara so happy that nobody can see her face and not know the joy in her soul" (426). In sum, Don Luis's consistent persistence—in the face of great hardship—merits Donna Clara's true-love, which makes the point that when you really love someone, and she loves you back, one must be tenacious, persistent, and indefatigable, in their suit until they marry the woman they love.

An opposite example of a woman winning a man's true-love applies to Dorotea's relationship with Don Fernando, which shows readers that sometimes it is moral and right for a woman to pursue and court a man to secure her future happiness. This is why Dorotea dresses as a farm boy, and, in the silence of the night, travels to a nearby city in search of Don Fernando to convince him that he should honor his vow to marry her, not Luscinda. Upon discovering, then, that Don Fernando has already left Luscinda's parents house, Dorotea forms an action-plan to win him back. With her mind focused on finding Don Fernando, Dorotea travels up hill and down valley, with nimble, bipedal alacrity, since "a town crier's announcement declaring a large reward for anyone who finds her" hastens her departure (258). To avoid apprehension, then, Dorotea leaves the city, with her man servant, and hides in a densely wooded part of a nearby forest. But when her man-servant tries to take advantage of "the seclusion he thinks the forest offers him" by forcing himself upon her, Dorotea defends her body by "pushing him off a nearby precipice," thereby leaving him contorted on the valley floor below (259). Even in the face of rape and molestation Dorotea is so determined to find Don Fernando, she makes her way deep into the mountain chain to avoid her father's prying eyes. During her wanderings in the Sierra Morena, Dorotea meets a country herdsmen named Guillermo, who hires her as a herdboy. After he discovers that she is a beautiful woman dressed as a man, his sexual appetite is aroused by her great beauty. So much so, in fact, that Dorotea thinks he will rape her. To avoid this gross bodily violation, she runs away and hides in the wilds of the countryside, rather than "trying her strength against him, or inventing excuses to get away from him" (259). Thus, to secure Don Fernando's love, she overcomes two very dangerous assaults from men who either try, or are set, to rape her. Such warding off of two potentially dangerous bodily assaults, coupled with cunning wit deployed to ward off her father's searchers, shows readers Dorotea's determination is to find and declare her love for Don Fernando. And, when, Dorotea encounters Don Fernando, she marshals a series of reasonable arguments about why he should marry her. Among these are that she is virtuous, honorable, and comes from a family of affluent tenant farmers "who have always served his parents well" (342). In addition to these arguments Dorotea says that "it is easier to make a woman who adores him the object of his love, as opposed to forcing a woman, like Luscinda, who despises him to love him." To this Don Fernando listens with a will. And, thus, Dorotea's well-reasoned speech, distressed sighs, and doleful sobs, ultimately convinces him that she is right. Moved to tender compassion by Dorotea's eloquent speech, Don Fernando gives-in because "nobody can have the heart to deny such an assemblage of truths" (341, 342). Don Fernando even apologizes for his former neglect of her, vowing that he has found in her all that he desires. Basically, this romantic union shows readers that, in some cases it is a woman who does take, and should take, bold initiative, to secure her husband, especially if she knows what he needs to know to be happy in the long run. Thus, Dorotea takes concrete actions to foster her long-term joyousness. Said differently, all of this determined love-action between Don Luis and Donna Clara, on the one hand, and Dorotea and Don Fernando, on the other, shows readers that when a man loves a woman, or a woman loves a man, they must reason, and/or, act to gain, and/or, keep, that mate, especially if true-love exists between them.

In conclusion, questions Cervantes asks and answers in *Don Quixote* are: what is true love? Why do you need and want true love for yourself? How can true love be created between two individuals? When should true love be realized in an intimate relationship? And, most importantly, how can one avoid emotional traps that are not based on true love? One answer that Cervantes presents readers is that true love is a close trust relationship between "self-respecting equals which involves friendship, mutual interests, tenderness, moments of intensity, waves of compassion, and joyous sexual play."[51] Another answer he provides is that true-love is a mental union based on compatible ethics, involving respect and admiration, which achieves value by fulfilling a loved one's needs as well as one's own. Yet another answer Cervantes provides readers is that true-love is unique, not to be found twice in life, each person having one ideal soul mate.

---

51   Hunt, Morton, M. <u>The Natural History of Love</u>. New York: 1959. (371).

Contrary to the view that marriage is a business transaction used to elevate one's social standing as much as possible, Cervantes argues that love does not depend merely on material wealth for creation and sustenance but psychological and emotional closeness, as well. Therefore, drawing up a marriage contract simply on a monetary basis—where a family fortune is at the heart of a marriage—is shown, by Cervantes, to be an inadequate basis for romance. Thus, through the events of the plotline, the author argues against marrying purely for money, with no underlying mental-and-physical attraction between partners. In other words, Cervantes, as author and narrator, presents compelling evidence that marrying solely for financial reasons to make the best fiscal alliance one can for oneself—especially when such a union is empty of two-way love—is shown capable of bringing only fleeting material satisfaction, not long-term happiness. This is why Cervantes shows readers, by the characters in his story, that love is not a genetic device, with household and welfare functions among the lower classes, and economic and political value for the propertied classes. Rather, he sees true-love as a mental, emotional, and physical affinity between husband-and-wife—a relationship, not based merely on the cash value of a significant other, but deep personality traits instead. This is why none of Cervantes characters marry, solely, for money. And, thus, the effect of money value on the emotional aspects of courtship is shown to be negligible, at best, since a person's character, sense-of-life, and mental-and-emotional traits should be the basis of formulating a long-term, romantic relationship. And, as such, many scenes, and romantic relationships in the novel, are motivated by the desire to love and be loved, not by a desire to forge a fiscal union, empty of all values. This, then, is how Cervantes tries to discover a new meaning of marriage and [romantic love] within an old framework of traditional customs.

As we have seen through the book's romantic relationships, any healthy and growing erotic liaison between two human beings should be a relationship of self-respecting equals, since your loved one is an irreplaceable personal treasure, someone to be nurtured and protected, with whom you want to grow and thrive as an equal life-long partner. Thus, interdependent love, as we have seen, should exist between companions, where both are connected with and reliant on each other to the advantage of both. Point of fact, Teresa and Sancho Panza's symbiosis proves to readers that marriage should be one of equals, because, their marriage is one of equality. Because of this, they find a harmonizing balance in their relationship fostered by jointly raising their children, jointly earning money, like habits—which fosters a sense of intimacy—and similar, speech style identities. Simply put, as Sancho Panza and Teresa Panza's relationship proves, equal love is a romantic connection that makes both parties happy because they both get what they want. Observe the goal, as Cervantes infers, of any loving relationship "is to ensure that each partner gets what he or she wants." 72 In other words, love that achieves value by considering the loved one's desires as well as one's own, is typified by a genuinely mutual relationship, involving two-way respect and admiration. Hence, love is a reciprocity of the soul: where, husbands and wives should be pleased with one another's company and in their general enjoyment of each other.

For this reason, a romantic relationship, as shown in the novel, is ideally a partnership of equals with joint decision making shown as a sign of mutual love and respect. Thus, one way satisfaction, or mental and bodily pleasure for one partner, without the other also enjoying, as illustrated in the book, does not work. True-love, as instantiated through the events of the story, must be two-sided, with mutual joy as its primary tenet. Formulated another way, by critiquing the many symbiotic partnerships in the novel, we can conclude that equalitarian marriage is a union where women are not submissive, pleasing, housewives, but equals capable of friendship with their husbands. For this reason, "some sociologists see modern love as having its basis in equalitarian marriage in harmony with modern democracy." Said differently, Cervantes expresses the idea that the genesis of modern romantic pair-bonding, which, he shows in the book, represents a huge forward stride in human relationships, grants to love a life-preserving value since it meets two creatures' emotional needs and in the process continues the species and society. Observe, that the goal in any loving relationship is that each partner gets what he or she wants. Thus, a romantic relationship is ideally a partnership of equals, with joint decision making as a sign of love and respect. Hence, one way satisfaction or pleasure between partners doesn't work, since, true love, as shown through the events of the story, must be two sided, with mutual joy as its primary tenet. And contemporary marriage, based on the values of modern romance, upholds the ideal of sexual equality between husband and wife, where both partners derive mental and physical gratification, from an intimate, mind-body, connection. In this regard, husbands and wives should be pleased with one another's company, and in their general enjoyment of one another, expressed through the medium of loving conversations, as well as through the act of sexual copulation. Therefore, as we have seen throughout the novel, love and mutual attraction between bride and groom is an integral unity point of a marriage, since normally, "people tend to fall in love with other people whose emotional needs complement their own."

As we have seen, then, characters in Don Quixote, like Luscinda and Dorotea are "good daughters, but they are not blindly obedient to their parent's wishes."77 And, though "not willfully disobedient [these two young women] do what they think is the right thing to do, instead of giving into their parents [wishes],"essentially because they want to "create their own ideas of love rather than accepting the views of others." 78. Thus, throughout the novel, questions arise asking us to contemplate if we trust so and so's parents. If they seem genuinely concerned with their daughter's welfare, in terms of her true-love-passion, or, alternatively, if they strive to match their daughters with wealthy, or connected people, against their wills. And though wealth and power in the novel is not necessarily seen as a bad thing to have or be aligned with, if a convenient arrangement is based only on this—especially if it goes against a son or daughter's free will—it is shown capable of achieving only a fleeting type of happiness as partners learn and confront the truth about one another, ultimately finding that they are locked in a loveless marriage. This, in essence, is why Cervantes encourages his characters to live and love as they see fit.

In conclusion, as illustrated in Don Quixote, the goal of any intimate, romantic, relationship is to bring compatible human beings together as lifelong friends and lovers, which, in essence, is what true love and marriage is all about. Obviously, a subject that receives so much of Cervantes's attention involves an important human need. As such, it is the job, indeed the moral obligation, for every unmarried person to wait and search for their soul mate to be located, for true-love is unique, not to be found twice in life, each person having one ideal partner. And, by showing that romantic love is responsible for a variety of different unions, Cervantes argues that all love involves the balancing of one's interests "as they move into a deep relationship with someone."76 In brief, by showing readers in Don Quixote that many different couples attain happiness after great difficulty – even though they are beset by a wide variety of challenges – Cervantes presents the view that while the "course of true-love might not run smoothly, it should run. It should triumph eventually." 75. And, in Don Quixote, because true love is the basis of many different relationships, romantic love wins in the end.

Select Bibliography

Bernstein, Andrew. "Objectivist Values and Virtues." University of North Carolina Chapel Hill. North Carolina. October 10 2010.

Hunt, Morton, M. <u>The Natural History of Love</u>. New York: Alfred A. Knopf, 1959.

Jacobson, Karin. Cliffs Complete. <u>Shakespeare's Romeo and Juliet</u>. Ed. Sidney Lamb. New York: 2000.

Kenner, Ellen. "The Rational Basis of Romance (Part 2): Courting Success in Romance." Irvine, 2005.

Locke, Edwin, A. and Ellen Kenner. <u>The Selfish Path to Romance: How to Love with Passion and Reason</u>. Doylestown: Platform Press, 2011.

Maurer, Kate. <u>Cliff Notes The Taming of The Shrew</u>. New York: Wiley Publishing, 2001.

Saccio, Peter. "The Taming of the Shrew—Getting Married in the 1590's. <u>The Teaching Company</u>. Virginia, 1999.

ESSAY 2

Cervantes's Treatment of Religious Extremism in Don Quixote: *The Opening of a Free Society.*

The institutionalized religious practice of rigid "conservative conformity" is satirized by Cervantes to show readers that people should be free to think and act for themselves in a more open, libertarian society that permits some degree of unorthodoxy[1]. Since a person's ability to self-determine constitutes personal control over his life, Cervantes shows readers that human beings should be free to worship (or not worship) in their own way. For this reason, mandatory self-flagellation, or the ascetic practice of purifying one's body by lash strokes, is mocked by Cervantes to undercut the idea that "people living on earth are somehow cosmically unworthy" to enjoy their lives and must therefore prepare their wicked souls for the afterlife by mortifying their flesh.[2] Similarly, forcing people out of their homes, stripping them of their livelihoods, and compelling them to leave their native country for having unorthodox beliefs is impugned by Cervantes when he shows that ostracism: severs families, strains romantic relationships, causes risk of life, undermines people's consciences, and inflicts hardship on innocents. Likewise, the arbitrary seizure of a person's wealth and property based on false

---

1   Herzman, Ronald, B. "Miguel de Cervantes." The Teaching Company. Lafayette, Virginia. 2004.

2   Ghate, Onkar. "Seminar on Ayn Rand's Philosophy of Objectivism." The Ayn Rand Institute. Irvine, California. October 2008-March 2009.

charges to extort their monetary assets or because of their unpopular association with an alienated minority group is undercut when Cervantes has Ricote bury his riches in a secret location. Clerical interference in people's everyday lives is also mocked by Cervantes when he blasts a conservative clergyman for his: strict narrow-mindedness; harsh public criticism; flawed argumentation; quick temper; suppression of free choice and, lastly, intolerance of a moral code not based on Christian ethics, like meekness, but based on chivalric bravery instead. Moreover the religious symbols of heaven-and-hell, angels-and-demons, and condemnation-and-death, are ridiculed by Cervantes when he stages a series of mock ecclesiastical episodes where everything becomes a sham. By presenting paganism as a viable alternative to Godly Christianity, Cervantes diminishes the significance of faith and sacrifice in one's life while emphasizing the importance of pride, courage, prowess and honor as the best within men. Cervantes also criticizes the religious policy of stigmatizing controversial books for their content by not only having several of his characters convey their respect for creativity, imagination and works of the mind but also by having a priest and a barber refuse to burn a score of well-conceived books, which they justify on firm intellectual grounds. In addition, the Church's disparagement of pre-marital sex is undercut when Cervantes couples several of his characters out-of-wedlock. Not only does Cervantes challenge the Church's influence in the bedroom he also challenges the Church's authority in the courtroom by having his characters elude the Holy Brotherhood. Similarly, Cervantes challenges divine miracles by undercutting Church myths, like virgin births, for example. In all these ways, and more, Cervantes opposes religious control of Spanish society so that people are free to think and say what they like throughout their lives without fear of punishment.

Cervantes satirizes original sin—or the notion that a person is flawed from birth and must therefore harm their bodies to erase their inborn blemishes—by mocking the belief that a person can purify their inner soul by punishing their outer body. By having Sancho Panza refuse to whip himself to disenchant Dulcinea, Cervantes rejects the idea that a person can enter heaven through a self-imposed process of physical pain. This is why Sancho Panza rejects Merlin's request to thrash himself 3, 300 times: "I'm not talking about three thousand strokes of the lash, I won't give myself so much as three of them" (729). To avoid this scenario Sancho Panza makes a series of rhetorical statements like: "I don't see what my bum has got to do with magic spells!" (729). Because he cannot connect lashing his posterior to Dulcinea's well-being Sancho Panza refuses to tear his skin to shreds for the sake of lifting a dubious magic spell cast on a quasi-imaginary person. It is on these grounds that Sancho Panza asserts: "if Senor Merlin hasn't found a better way to disenchant the lady Dulcinea del Toboso, she'll have to go enchanted to her grave!" (729). Evidently, Sancho Panza rejects whipping his body to save another person's soul because he is a simple country farmer, "not some monk to get up in the middle of his sleep [to] start scourging [himself methodically]" (944). When asked to whip himself Sancho Panza dismisses self-flogging altogether: "they come asking me to lash myself of my own free will, when I'd as soon do that as turn into an Indian chief!" (731). But Merlin persists. This time, however, he offers a positive incentive: "if [Sancho Panza] wishes to abate his atonement by one half of the thrashing, [he can] have it administered by another hand" (729). And again Sancho Panza refuses lash-strokes when he says: "No hand's going to touch me not someone else's nor my own, not heavy nor light." (729). "He is not, indeed, a symbol of the claims of the body over the life of an ascetic [monk]."[3] Rather, he does what he must to spare himself pain. So he resorts to trickery to avoid taking lashes. When Don Quixote, for instance, listens from a distance to make sure that Sancho Panza whips himself he does not "hit his back [but] hit the trees instead heaving [loud] sighs from

---

3   Grierson, Sir Herbert Jon Clifford. <u>Don Quixote: Some War-Time Reflections On Its Character and Influence (1921)</u>. New York: Cornell University Press. (12).

time to time [that sounded like he] was tearing his soul from his body." (963). So effective is Sancho Panza at faking his flogging that Don Quixote grows concerned and asks him to stop: "Upon my soul, friend, do let the matter rest now; this medicine seems a very drastic one" (964). It is in this way that Sancho Panza escapes ripping his skin open for Dulcinea.

When Sancho Panza refuses to whip himself for Dulcinea the idea arises that each person has an individual soul that he should administer with freewill and a good conscience not by mental compulsion or physical force. This concept becomes clear when Don Quixote threatens to tie Sancho Panza to a tree to flog him yet Merlin objects by saying: "the worthy Sancho must take his lashing of his own free will, not by force" (729). Since Christianity teaches each man that he should save his own soul and never give up hope of his own salvation, Sancho Panza is told to choose for himself when deciding what to do. So when Don Quixote "tries to scourge [Sancho Panza his squire] pins him to the ground [with] his wrists held down [to remind him that] lashes have got to be voluntary, not forced, and right now [he] doesn't feel like lashing himself." (892). Chastened by Sancho Panza's physical self-defense, "Don Quixote swear[s] [on] his life [to] not lay a finger on Sancho Panza and to leave it to him to choose with absolute freedom" what to do (893). This statement suggests Cervantes's primary thesis that each person has a sovereign soul that they can choose to prepare for the afterlife, or not. It is up to them. Belief in God, infers the author, has to come from within not from without. Thus, Sancho's reluctance to whip himself for God coupled with Merlin's defense of religious freedom suggests that faith-based self-devotion must not be compelled but chosen, if it must, by one's own mind.

If Cervantes is so adamant against self-flagellation, why, then, does Sancho Panza whip himself at all? Does not lashing his backside justify self-torture as a means of denying the self in preparation for the afterlife? Objectively speaking, no, it does not, because Sancho

Panza whips himself not as a method of helping another person who is of no value to him or as a means of suppressing his needs to prepare his body for the afterlife, rather he self-flagellates for his own selfish reasons. Consider this. When Sancho Panza whips himself he does so not out of a sense of self-sacrifice but out of a sense of egotistical gain (i.e. financial gain). When Don Quixote, for example, realizes that Sancho Panza will not self-flagellate for nothing, he says: "you decide, Sancho, how much money you want, and then lash yourself, and pay yourself in ready cash, since you are carrying my money" (962). At the promise of ready money Sancho Panza's "eyes and ears gape open, and he inwardly agrees to lash himself with a will: Very well, sir, I'm agreeable to go along with your will as long as there is something in it for me" (962). Afterwards Sancho Panza "puts" the highest reasonable "price" he can on each lash stroke, deciding that "eight hundred and twenty-five reals" total is a fair price (962). In fact he "won't take any less even if the whole world tells [him] to" (962). In this case, Sancho Panza exercises his business acumen to calculate a proper price for his troubles because the money he is to gain from self-imposed lash strokes is of greater value to him then a bit of physical pain. Because Sancho Panza wants to enhance his living standards he agrees to endure an unpleasant experience, essentially out of "love for [his] dear wife and children" (962). But first he sets all sorts of moderating preconditions like the twin-provisos that he is "not to make [himself] bleed, and if some of [his] lash strokes turn out to be more like [fly swats] they're still valid" (733). True to his word he eases the force of his self-whipping by stroking his backside gently with the palm of his "hand," only (734). And when Sancho Panza thinks that he must whip himself to earn his pay he strokes himself with his donkey's halter a few times mildly. The rest of the time either he strips the bark of trees with a knotted rope; or does not whip himself at all. In sum, without causing himself great physical harm Sancho Panza earns material riches, betters his life prospects, makes his wife-and-children happy, and calms Don Quixote down,

59

too. Above all, Sancho Panza's reluctance to whip himself for another person moves readers away from a faith-based sense of life where warped impulses of self-flagellation tend to surface in human affairs to a view of existence where natural thoughts of self-preservation become the goal of one's actions.

In an attempt to move rational clergymen to a pro-life view of reality not a pro-death view of existence, Cervantes logic chops a self-destructive philosophy of death by showing readers that self-abnegation is not the right way to view a human being's temporal existence on earth because such an ideology has nothing positive to offer forth. He adopts this policy to persuade logical penitents that they should take good care of themselves, while alive, in the here-and-now, so that they pursue not a death hastening mode of suppression but a life-enhancing way of being. In other words, Cervantes seeks to persuade open-minded prelates to embrace the light of self-concern by highlighting selfish incentives to do, or not to do, something. So he tempers his criticisms of organized religion so that clergymen will at least listen to his ideas and perhaps agree with some of them as opposed to dismissing his reasoning outright as a polemic attack against their view of firm principle. Put another way, Cervantes wants his ideas on religion to be viewed not as a negative attack against all values associated with religion but rather as a positive alternative to a faith based moral code. So he shows us that religion is a package deal that mixes elements of value-centric moral-ethical guidance with concepts that are irrational and mystical and untrue in that they do not correspond to the logical proofs of scientific reality—no not at all.

In an attempt to eliminate religion's unsubstantiated, unprovable tenets, Cervantes discredits mystical supposition, magical omens, divine miracles, and numinous prognostications, so that these unrealities do not corrupt the minds-and-emotions of naïve people who are willing to believe almost anything associated with religion just because its moral code happens to offer some positive ethical guidance presented in a systematic, comprehensive way. For this reason, natural omens, which purport to transmit Godly mysticism, are discounted by Cervantes. For example, Sancho Panza does not take "the sight of a hare dashing through the fields chased by greyhounds [as] a bad sign [as Don Quixote does]" but rather as a phenomena irrelevant to their venture-quest (971). After challenging the concept that the rabbit represents Dulcinea and that the greyhounds pursuing her are "knavish enchanters that turned her into a peasant girl" Sancho Panza tells Don Quixote "that [his] omens have come to naught [because] to [his] mind they haven't got any more to do with [their] affairs then last year's [vapor] clouds" (971, 972). In fact Sancho Panza tells Don Quixote "that sensible Christian persons shouldn't pay any attention to [the] nonsense of omens" to remind him "that all Christians who heed omens [need a reality check]" (972). This speech suggests to readers that many religious zealots simply go along with what their clergymen tells them is true instead of verifying or rejecting with their own minds what they are told is, or is not, the case. This happens for two reasons: either because they fail to form first-hand value-judgments for themselves or because they shy away from asserting a contrary viewpoint because they want to be embraced by their belief group, even though they know that something is, or is not, true. To counter this mentality, Cervantes undercuts the notion that spiritual forces can inhabit physical objects and can transmit heavenly or hellish voices through them. This, he does, by discrediting the "magical mystery" of an enchanted plaster bust by explaining its ingenious contrivance, which, though:

> resembling the effigy of a Roman emperor was [actually a] hollow [tube that] fitted into a hole in [a rock slab] so perfectly that the join was invisible. There was also a hollow in the pedestal, exactly under the hollow of a bust, and all this opened into a room underneath. Through [a] system of holes in the bust, slab, and pedestal, a tin tube was neatly fitted so nobody could see it. In the room below the man who

was to reply was stationed, with his mouth to the tin tube, and the voice downstairs went up to it, as clearly articulated as through an ear trumpet, and so it was impossible to discover the trick

(913).

By revealing a clever mechanical ploy for what it is, Cervantes shows us that it is impossible for simple material objects to speak as if possessed. In fact Cervantes argues that the omniscience of the bust speaker stems not from an all knowing intuitive insight generated by a profound connection to God but rather from the intellect of a: "Sharp witted [young] student who is coached by his uncle to provide a quick and precise answer to [his] first question; and then to improvise [replies] to other [inquires]" (913). In fact Cervantes questions divine miracles further when he exposes the power behind a fortune telling ape:

> Before going into a village with his puppet show and his ape [Master Pedro] would find out from a previous village, or from the best source he came across, what notable events had happened there, and to whom, and he'd carefully memorize them [then according to] the questioner's ability to pay he charged two reals [per question and] whenever he walked by where there were people living about whom he'd receive information he'd make the sign of the ape, and then say it had told him this and that and the other, all of it tallying with exactly what had happened [and] this would earn [him] an incredible reputation [and so with this technique he convinced simple minded people that his] monkey could divine miracles [hence] making monkeys of them all [to] fill his money bags

> (672).

Here Cervantes shows us that a human wit lies behind the secret of a prognosticating ape not some mystical supernatural power. This exposure shows readers that animals cannot predict the future through divine communication. Likewise religious drama depicting divine miracles is also scorned by Cervantes. For example, he criticizes dramaturgy that features heavenly miracles by asking: "what about plays on religious subjects? How many false miracles they invent, how many apocryphal and misunderstood events [they depict]" (445). Besides undermining devotional plays that give rise to mysticism-and-magic, Cervantes discredits the notion that a dead person can be resurrected by an act of divine revival. This, he does, by explaining the ingenuity behind Basilio's revival:

> the stick that Basilio thrust into the ground and threw himself on [was] nothing more than a hollow iron tube full of blood which he fashion[ed] in such a way so that it did not pass through him

(628).

Flabbergasted at Basilio's supposed resurrection a group of onlookers cry: "A miracle, a miracle, [but Basilio replies]: 'No miracle, no miracle: ingenuity, ingenuity' (628). Examples of this sort abound in *Don Quixote*, the main point here is that human beings should be free to use their minds, to the best of their ability, to sort truth from falsehood, actuality from unreality, to figure out what is or is not the case.

Besides logic-chopping irrational elements of religion, Cervantes challenges the notion that one should live for the sake of another and not for themselves, that one should sacrifice what is of greater value to them for what is of lesser (or no) value to them, and, ultimately, that one should abandon their selfish-interests in this world to enter an alleged heaven. By not whipping himself to remove Dulcinea's magic spell, by not pin-pricking himself to awaken Altisidora, and by not pinching himself to resurrect a swooning damsel, Sancho Panza challenges the religionist idea that one should sacrifice themselves to save another person's soul. In fact he opposes the concept of divine altruism altogether when he says that Dulcinea's life is not his concern because he did not "give birth to her," therefore he "[should not] have to pay for her sins [by lash stroke]" (952). Because Sancho Panza did not conceive Dulcinea; or raise her; or put effort and energy into her development, her well-being, or lack thereof, is none of his business. If Don Quixote loves Dulcinea so much, says Sancho Panza, then he should whip himself for her sake because "[his] master's the one who every five minutes [calls] her his life and his soul and his support and his stay, so he can and should do everything that's needed to disenchant her." (729). Why, Sancho Panza asks, does he have "to be the general scapegoat to sort out other people's problems [when it is not] a good idea for [him] to do [himself] harm for someone else's benefit." (734). Again Sancho Panza is asked to sacrifice himself—this time by three judges of Hell who ask him to pinch, pinprick, and slap himself to revive Altisidora—and again he declines on the grounds that it would not be wise for him to do himself mischief for the sake of another. Astounded by a renewed request to re-injury himself, especially when he rejected the original overture to do so, Sancho Panza says: "it would be a fine thing if [I subjected myself to a shellacking for other people's sake]" (953). Evidently, he is very reluctant to hurt himself for others – to such a degree, in fact, that he accuses his tormentors of wanting to get rid of him: "All you lot need to do is get a nice big stone, tie it around my neck and chuck me down a well." (953). This quote suggests that if Sancho Panza yields to Altisidora's demand that he pinch, pinprick, and slap himself, or if he yields to a vigorous back-lashing he would sacrifice himself to death. Since sacrificing himself to death is not a part of Sancho Panza's plan he refuses to whip himself to save Dulcinea, or pinprick himself to rouse Altisidora, because he not only fails to see how such a self-sacrificial action will disenchant or awaken them but also because he thinks that he should be the primary beneficiary of his actions not someone else. In fact Sancho Panza embraces the earth in sensual, self-gratifying, worldly terms not in ascetic, self-sacrificial, altruistic ones. In short, by rejecting the notion that life finds its ultimate meaning in suffering and death, Cervantes shows readers that it is futile to visit harm on oneself as a means of spiritual salvation.

Another aspect of religious extremism that Cervantes undercuts is the practice of expelling people from a nation because of their cultural beliefs or because they look or speak or think atypically. Case in point is the 1609 expulsion of the Moriscos from Spain by King Phillip the III who decreed that "all Moriscos must depart Spain, under pain of death and confiscation, without trial or sentence, [and] to take with them no money, bullion, jewels or bills of exchange, just what they could carry."[4] In the space of months King Phillip emptied Spain of its Moriscos in this way. Cervantes portrays this historical dislocation in *Don Quixote* when he depicts the expulsion of a Morisco family from Iberia.

The Ricote family, like all Morisco family's, are Moorish descendents who were forced to convert to Christianity to live in Spain. Despite changing their faith from Islam to Christianity the Holy Inquisition still expels them for their cultural affiliation. Upon deportation by the crown a Morisco girl named Anna Felix emigrates with her aunt and uncle to Algiers while her father travels to Germany, disguised as a pilgrim, to search for better accommodations for his family. But before Ricote leaves home he makes "arrangements to go look for somewhere [he] can take his family in comfort without the haste of other Moriscos" (854). So he decides on Germany because in "most of Germany there is freedom of conscience [and] Moriscos live in greater liberty there [because] people don't bother much about niceties and everyone lives as he pleases" (854, 855). But his daughter, Anna Felix, goes to Algiers because it is the only place that will readily accept her. In this way not only are father and daughter forcibly

---

4   http://en.wikipedia.org/wiki/Spanish_Inquisition/Repression. (6).

parted for a time but Anna Felix is also torn from her neighbors as well. In fact "when [Anna Felix goes] away everyone in the village [comes] out to see [her]" (857). In return she "cries and hugs all her friends and acquaintances" wishing them well without her (857). Evidently, the expulsion of the Moriscos from Spain severs whole sets of social relationships—like friendships between fellow villagers, for example, or intimate father/daughter relationships, for instance. We are told, for example, that "Moriscos who can speak Spanish well [typically] abandon their wives and their children, such is their love for Spain" (854). By leaving their families to return home many Morisco women, like Anna Felix, live alone in foreign places, under hardship conditions, struggling to survive.

Besides disjointing many Morisco families, the banishment of the Moriscos also diminishes the cohesion of many Christian families as well. Take, the Gregario family, for example. The Gregorio family, though Christian, breaks apart when the family's youngest member, a sixteen-year-old boy named Don Gasper Gregorio leaves Spain and goes to Algiers to find Anna Felix—a runaway Morisco. Don Gregario's flight to Africa separates parents and siblings from their son and brother for quite a long time. Away from each other for months, years even, the Gregarios eventually reunite in Spain thanks to a Moorish Renegade who frees Don Gregario from captivity. By depicting their heartfelt reunion in this way, Cervantes highlights the consequences over the lives of ordinary Spanish citizens of the expulsion of the Moriscos.

This theme is expanded when Cervantes examines how close friendships between Moriscos and Spaniards are put at risk by their expulsion. Take, for instance, the relationship between Ricote and Sancho Panza. The former is a village shop keeper while the latter is a village farmer yet they are parted when Ricote is forced to leave Spain. Fortune has it, however, that Ricote and Sancho Panza meet each other near Barcelona on a dusty country road. When Ricote recognizes Sancho Panza he hugs him tight and says: "Lord

Almighty! What's this I see? Is it possible that I'm holding my dear friend and good neighbor Sancho Panza in my arms?" (852). Sancho Panza responds by throwing "his arms around [Ricote's] neck" and by asking who "turned [him] into a bloody foreigner, and what made [him] do such a silly thing as return to Spain?" (852). Ricote rejoins that he "left his village [to] obey the edict of His Majesty's with all those terrible threats [issued] against the unfortunate people of [his] race" (852). Afterwards they sit down and have a picnic together where they "eat with intense pleasure savoring every morsel" (853). Their fellowship continues when they "lift their arms and bottles into the air, and with their mouths pressed up against the mouths of their bottles [they] empty the entrails of [their] vessels into their own stomachs" (853). Despite celebrating their sudden reunion in this way everything is not 100% fine between Sancho Panza and Ricote because their friendship is not the same as it used to be for a degree of separation now exists between them. On the one hand, Sancho Panza swears he will not turn Ricote in for defying Holy exile. On the other hand, he does not want to "betray his king by helping his enemies" (856). Here Sancho Panza is conflicted between loyalty to a friend on personal grounds and loyalty to the state on political grounds. Since the Holy "Inquisition stimulated distrust among neighbors and denunciations amongst close friends were not uncommon" Sancho Panza does not know how to treat Ricote[5]. In this sense, the Holy Inquisition erects a wall of separation between Morisco's and their Spanish countrymen who question whether they should be loyal to their *friends*, for personal reasons, or loyal to their *King*, for state fidelity. This, in turn, sows conflict in the minds and hearts of many Moriscos who, like Ricote, are hurt and dejected that they are exiled from Spain for no good reason yet they still "weep for Spain" because Spain is their homeland and "love for one's country is sweet" (854). Though patriotic, many Spanish Moriscos feel that marching away from their motherland is their best bet, especially when faced with

---

5   http://en.wikipedia.org/wiki/Spanish_Inquisition/Accusation (13).

the grim alternative between leaving their home country to fend for themselves abroad or risking their lives by remaining in Spain. Despite the difficulty of this choice some Spanish Moriscos are lucky enough to meet high ranking Spanish officials who secure their freedom out of a deep sense of sympathy and mercy and compassion.

Moral guilt is a feeling that not only cements a Spanish Admiral, a Spanish Viceroy, and a Spanish noblemen together in a bond of sympathy for innocent Moriscoes but it also compels them to take firm steps on behalf of two endangered citizens. Take, for example, the mistreatment of Anna Felix. Though born of Morisco parents, Anna Felix is Christian and Catholic but she is banished from Spain anyway. So strong is her desire to live in Spain, however, she risks her life to return home. At great self-peril Anna Felix dresses as an Ottoman sea captain and sets sail for Spain. During her voyage she risks drowning in the waters of the Mediterranean; she risks being sold into slavery at the hands of pirates; and, above all, she risks being executed as a foreign hostile by a Spanish navy quick to punish transgressors. In fact this is almost what happens when two drunken Ottoman soldiers under Anna Felix's seeming command kill two Spanish soldiers who try to board her brigantine. Since Anna Felix is dressed as an Ottoman sea captain the blame for the murders falls to her. Found responsible for the Spaniards deaths, she is ordered to be hanged by the neck until she is dead. But she pleads for her life by swearing that she is a true-and-firm Christian woman who had nothing to do with the fatalities of the two Spanish soldiers. Since she claims that she was forced to dress up as an Ottoman sea captain to escape Algiers—but really she is a Spaniard of pure Christian stock— the Admiral waits a moment before he hangs her from a nearby yardarm. After hearing her back-story, a Spanish Viceroy, moved "by tender compassion, stops the execution [by] remov[ing] the rope that [binds Anna Felix's] hands together" (924). The Viceroy's sympathy for Anna Felix extends further when he asks Don Antonio Moreno "to treat her with the utmost kindness and consideration so great [is] the benevolence and sympathy that [her] plight inspires in his breast." (925). In this scene a deep feeling of mercy and compassion prompts the Viceroy to not only see "how it might be arranged for Ana Felix and her father to stay in Spain" but his sympathy also spurs him to provide material aid and support for their comfort (933). So he is "happy for Ricote to stay with him until" Don Antonio negotiates a satisfactory solution in the capital. (933, 934). Clearly, the Viceroys moral sense of what is right and wrong, fair or unfair, reasonable or unreasonable, governs his thoughts, actions, and sentiments. Hence he acts swiftly on behalf of two innocent Moriscos. Compassion for Anna Felix and her father extends further when Don Antonio – a Spanish aristocrat – lets them stay in his house. Besides "offering [them] everything his house contained for their pleasure" he travels to Madrid to negotiate a lasting solution that will enable them to stay in Spain because he can't see "any harm in allowing such a Christian daughter and such an apparently well-meaning father to remain [there]." (933). By means of giving the "right gifts" and dispensing the "right favors" to the "right people" Don Antonio overcomes many difficulties "in Madrid" to win the Ricote's a safe home in Spain. In sum, because an Admiral frees Anna Felix, because a Viceroy negotiates on her behalf, and because a Spanish aristocrat shelters her in his house, many high-ranking Spanish citizens seek to contain, even reverse, the harms visited on the Moriscos. In this sense, Cervantes criticizes religious intolerance for unorthodoxy and difference through a series of stand-in characters, who find fault with, criticize, and even seek to reverse official Spanish policy.

The Crown's decision to expel the entire Morisco population from Spain not only breaks-up families, sunders friendships, and splits neighbors apart it also strains romantic relationships as well. Take the courtship between Anna Felix, a 16 year old Morisco girl, and Don Gasper Gregario, a hot-blooded young Spanish lad. He is the eldest son of a lord from a Spanish village who falls deeply in-love with Anna Felix, a catholic girl of Morisco lineage. When she is exiled to Algiers he follows her there hoping to win her over. But when Anna Felix realizes that Don Gregario is in Algiers, she dresses him up as a Moorish woman because she thinks that "handsome boys are much more valued by Ottoman men over any woman, however beautiful she may be" (922). She does this so they can be together. But when Anna Felix takes Don Gregario before the Barbary King to plead that they be permitted to return to Spain together, the King is thunderstruck by Don Gregario's feminine beauty. So he decides to keep Don Gregario as a present for Sultan Selim. But the Barbary King allows Anna Felix to return to Spain, under the watch of two Ottoman soldiers, on the promise of a rich reward in return for her liberty. Despite being parted twice, once by the Holy Inquisition, and once by a covetous Algerian King, Anna Felix and Don Gregario find a way to be together. True love triumphs, here, despite the Holy Inquisition's attempt to drive a wedge-of-intolerance between two young people.

Not only does a Christian and a Morisco consummate their love for each other despite formidable external opposition, but Cervantes also tries to repair the damage done to many Moriscos by giving them credit-and-recognition for developing Spanish society. He does this by crediting them for originating several Spanish terms like "all the words that begin with al, such as: almohaza, almorzar, and alfombra and other [Morisco words like] borcegui, zaquizami, and marvedi" (942). By identifying several words coined by Spanish Moriscos, Cervantes tries to build a degree of goodwill for them within his country. To extend this goodwill among Spaniards, Cervantes highlights their Spanish value presence by giving the translator of his book the lineage of a Christian Morisco. Since acceptance, tolerance, and kindness is what Cervantes tries to inspire in the minds-and-hearts of his readers, he accentuates the positive qualities of the Moriscos so they are embraced by their fellow countrymen. Therefore, he criticizes countrywide expulsions of select groups of people for having a different ethical belief system, for having a different physical appearance, or for practicing a different moral code. He does this so a more libertarian, tolerant, and accepting society could emerge; one that encourages Spaniard's to choose their own belief system without fear of discrimination, persecution, ridicule, or force. For this reason, Cervantes, speaking through his mouthpiece characters, objects to the Holy Inquisition's extortion of other people's wealth by dramatizing how an intelligent Moriscoe avoids this prospect by secreting his money in a hidden location.

Some clever Moriscos, like Ricote, hid their money from the Holy Inquisition so that when they were denounced and deported for being heretics the Spanish Crown could not "seize" and dispense their financial assets.[6] This is why Ricote has the foresight to bury "pearls and gems of great value, as well as money in the form of gold cruzados and gold doubloons, in a [secret] hiding place outside [his] village" before his expulsion (855, 922). With this money Ricote: secures Don Gregario's freedom; matches Don Gregario with his daughter; and bribes Spanish officials to let him stay in Spain. Thus, he gains favor with the Spanish authorities by allocating his riches wisely. By payment he gains permanent legal residence in Spain; by purchasing Don Gregario's freedom he gains favor with a Spanish Lord; by giving his daughter a handsome dowry he hopes to ally his family with powerful relations of old Christian stock. In short, Ricote uses his wealth to gain advantage in whatever way he can. Besides his pre-expulsion treasure trove, Ricote gathers and stores a moderate amount of wealth for himself when he "wanders [about] the Spanish countryside" dressed as a pilgrim gathering alms being "wined and dined" along the way for free (855). In this way some lucky Morisco pilgrims, like Ricote, accumulated great wealth by "the end of their travels, which they [quickly] converted to gold and smuggled out of Spain; [often] hidden in hollows in their staffs or sewn into the patches of their cloaks or in whatever way they [could] devise, despite all the precautions that were taken in the customs-houses where

---

6   http://en.wikipedia.org/wiki/Spanish_Inquisition/Confiscations (18).

money had to be declared." (855). This, then, is how Ricote manages to stay relatively wealthy despite official attempts to seize his money.

Besides dramatizing the oppression of the Morisco's in *Don Quixote*, Cervantes undermines unwelcome religious interference in aristocratic court society by mocking a meddling churchman who intrudes into the lives of a Duke and Duchess. This grave Churchman is introduced in a rather negative light:

> with the Duke and Duchess came one of those grave churchmen who rule noblemen's houses: one of those who, not having been born noble themselves, never manage to teach those who are noble how to live up to their rank; one of those who want the greatness of the great to be measured by their own narrowness of mind; one of those who, in their attempts to teach people they rule to avoid extravagance, turn them into misers, he must have been one of those grave churchmen who came with the Duke and the Duchess to receive Don Quixote

(696).

Immediately, the grave Churchman is established as a nosy interloper who is unqualified to give advice to the Duke and Duchess: A person who butts-in where he is not wanted. For instance, when Sancho Panza "tells a story about who should sit where [at dinner]" the Grave Churchman calls him "a chatter" tells him to "get a move on with his story without delay" and "reacts with displeasure to the leisurely pace of Sancho's [words]" (698). Then he tells "Don Idiot [to] go back home and see to the upbringing of [his] children and [to] look after [his] property, and [to] stop wandering about the world frittering [his] time away [by] turning himself into a laughing-stock of all who know [him] and all who do not know [him]." (700). Later, he challenges Don Quixote's chivalric beliefs when he asks him "where [he] unearthed the notion that knights errant have ever existed or do exist or any of the rest of the nonsense written about [them]?" (700). The grave Churchman also censors reading materials when he berates the Duke for reading Don Quixote's book: "it [is] an absurdity to read such absurdities" (699). In fact he calls the Duke "a fool" for joking with Don Quixote in the first place (702). Then he forbids the Duke from "encourage[ing] Don Quixote to perform [more of] his preposterous and ludicrous antics" by warning him that he "will have to answer to [God] for this fellows [sayings and] doings" (699). After watching the Duke anoint Sancho Panza governor of Barataria the grave Churchman "is on the verge of calling his grace as much a fool as this [here] pair of sinners [for] how can they fail to be mad when sane men sanction their madness?" (702). Evidently the grave Churchman shows: intolerance for the opinions of others; narrow-mindedness by rigidly defining what is right and proper; public harshness by openly criticizing the faults of others; inaccurate information, which he marshals to support his arguments; a short-temper, as his unjustified outbursts show; and authoritarianism, when he tells people what to do and how to do it. Despite his truculence, however, the grave Churchman gets his comeuppance when Don Quixote rebuts his criticisms with a few of his own.

Don Quixote faults the grave Churchman for issuing "infamous insults" instead of giving "good advice," for "reproving [him] so harshly in public," for calling sinners fools and idiots "without any knowledge of the sin," for telling him to "go back home to take charge of his wife and his children without knowing whether he has any," for "bursting into other men's houses to rule their lives," and, above all, for passing moral judgement on knights errant and chivalry when he has "seen no more of the world [then] the narrow confines of [his] residence hall." (700,701). Don Quixote even defends chivalry on the grounds that it is not "empty nonsense and a waste of time to wander about the world in search of the rough and rutted footpath up which the virtuous climb" (701). Since Don Quixote is criticized not by "a grandee" or a "highborn" person or a "noblemen" but "by

[a] scholar who [has] never ventured along the path of chivalry [the grave churchman's insults] do not concern [Don Quixote] one iota." (701). A "knight [he] is and a knight [he] shall die" and his "intentions are always directed towards worthy ends to do good to all and harm to none" (701). Later, he asks the Duke and Duchess "whether [a] man who believes [in chivalry] deserves to be called a fool?" (701). Pleased by Don Quixote's robust self-defense, the Duke expresses his pleasure as follows: "You have answered so absolutely splendidly for yourself" (702). In short, Don Quixote rebuts the grave Churchman's arguments, especially in regard to chivalry, which line of reasoning Sancho Panza soon picks-up on.

Sancho Panza criticizes the grave churchman further when he faults him for claiming that knights errant do not exist and have never existed: "if this here gentlemen denies as he does deny that knights errant exist or have existed, it isn't surprising that he doesn't know what he's talking about, is it now?" (701). He even says that if "Amadis or any of his infinite progeny had heard him say such a thing they'd have taken their swords and split him open from top to toe like a pomegranate" (703). It seems that members of aristocratic court society also mock the grave churchman by laughing at his unprovoked anger.

The Duke and the Duchess of Aragon are twice delighted that Don Quixote and Sancho Panza have the moxy to stand up to the grave Churchman's intrusions. For example, when the prelate is "displeased with the leisurely pace of Sancho's story" the Duke and Duchess are "extremely pleased" at his irritation (698). Later, when the grave Churchman objects to Sancho Panza's Governorship "the Duke [does not say] very much, hindered as he [is] by the laughter that the priest's untimely anger stirs in him" (702). Since the Duke and the Duchess are fed-up with the grave churchman's intrusion into their lives they are glad to entertain two funny guests who are not afraid to tell this reverend gentlemen exactly what they think. In fact the Duchess is "ready to die with laughter" when Sancho

Panza threatens to give the grave Churchman " a smack on the chops that would keep him quiet for the next three years" (703, 704). This laughter comes not out of a sense of mean spiritedness, or ill-will, rather it comes out of a sense of contentment upon seeing the serious cleric finally put in his place. In conclusion, the grave Churchman is painted as a meddlesome, pesky interloper whose presence in the Duke and Duchess's castle is unwelcome.

Besides mocking the Church's presence in royal life, Cervantes also ridicules the Holy Inquisition's symbols of life-and-death, heaven-and-hell, and condemnation-and-suffering, when he stages a series of joke-scenarios where everything becomes a sham. Take, for example, Altisidora's revival ceremony where two hellish judges tell Sancho Panza what he must do to restore her life. At this time one of the Duke's servants places a cardboard cone over Sancho Panza's head with devils painted on it only to have Sancho Panza remove the cardboard cone and place it on his donkey's head instead. Here, a dunce cap, instead of marking-out a heretic for holy punishment is used as a mock object to drape an ass in ridicule. We, as readers, learn just how laughable the Church becomes when a priest dresses-up as a woman and Don Quixote fashions a grotesque shirt-tail rosary out of a dirty piece of cloth. The abuse of religious symbols continues further. This time in Montesinos's cave when Don Quixote envisions "a ridiculous rosary" made of "a string on which beads larger than fair-sized walnuts [abound] with every tenth one being as big as an ordinary ostrich egg" (639).[7] This confabulated distortion of Don Quixote's mind suggests to readers that God will not be found among Montesinos or his companions. Cervantes also mocks religious symbols of the afterlife when Don Quixote runs into a group of play actors personifying Death, an Angel, and the Devil, respectively. As personifications of the hereafter these characters are supposed to be taken seriously. Instead they are mocked with derision when a

---

7   Duran, Manuel, <u>Cervantes</u>. Eds. Gerald E. Wade and Janet Winecoff Diaz on Spain. (Boston: Twayne Publishers, 1974. (136).

bell-jingling, bladder-thumping clown jumps on Dapple's back and begins thumping him with his inflated cow stomachs. By making fun of figures associated with life, death, and the afterlife, Cervantes challenges the institutional dogma of religious extremism, which, in severe cases, seeks to instill the fear of God in a person's soul as a means of subjugating that person's judgement and will to the whimsical dictates of a theological tyrant. In this sense, he purposely disrespects religious symbols to show a salient opposition between religious faith, on the one hand, with altruistic self-sacrifice as its ultimate value, and chivalric bravery, on the other hand, which is more egocentric in nature.

In his presentation of two different moral codes with respect to the human condition, Cervantes dramatizes the contrast between a self-centered, earthly, code of morality achieved through honor and bravery, and a self–sacrificial, divine, code of morality achieved through altruism and faith. This stark contrast between two contrary sets of values becomes most apparent when Don Quixote says: "the difference between [religious] knights and me is that they [are] saints, and fight in the manner of Angels, [whereas] I am a mortal [who] fight[s] in the manner of men" (874). Don Quixote desire is, to a large extent, worldly and self-gratifying, not divine or self-sacrificial, therefore his belief system is meant to revive a moral code where one's virtue, one's prowess, and one's lady, is most significant, not God. So he ushers in Quixoticism, a new belief-system, whose founder and prophet Don Quixote is. In this new value hierarchy, a distinction is made between fighting for God and faith, on the one hand, and fighting for honor and glory, on the other. This principle is exemplified when Don Quixote commends himself to Dulcinea before going into battle. This is significant because "during moments of danger, when death is a real possibility" chivalric knights did not turn to God to save their souls rather they appealed to their ladies to give them the strength to succeed (98). Besides undermining what "a Christian is [supposed] to do" before dying, Don Quixote's chivalric dream-quest functions to identify one's value-quest as the ultimate meaning of their lives not subordinating themselves to a faith-based sense of service. The Duchess echoes this viewpoint when she says that what motivates the Duke of Aragon to act is not divine altruism, or self-sacrifice, or irrational mysticism, but chivalric bravery instead—for though her "husband mightn't be all that errant that doesn't stop him from being a knight" (716). As such, the Duke makes Sancho Panza a governor because "once a knight makes a promise he strives to keep it" (716). On this view, strength-and-honor trump faith-and-sacrifice as primary virtues hence we are told that "knight errantry has a smack of Pagan about it" for it challenges a whole host of normative religious values (98).

Cervantes does indeed revive polytheistic paganism, as opposed to monotheistic Christianity, in a number of ways. First, he mentions a variety of Roman Gods as sources of inspiration like: "Apollo" the god of the sun and light; "Vulcan" the god of fire and forges; "Silenus" the god of merriment and laughter; "Jupiter" the god of sky and thunder; "Mars" the god of war and virility; "Cupid" the god of love and affection; "Aurora" the Goddess of dusk and dawn; "Diana" the Goddess of hunting and tracking; "Venus" the Goddess of love and beauty; and "Hercules" the demigod of strength and leadership (20, 31, 57, 941, 963, 168, 120, 494, 154, 477, 553, 619, 620, 622, 574, 616, 316, 870, 944, 569). By presenting compelling depictions of many Pagan Gods, Cervantes introduces a system of ideas that rivals Christianity as a source of inspiration. Second, Cervantes purposely creates the Knight of the Forest: a character that identifies with and compares himself to a pagan demigod, not a Christian knight. When the Knight of the Forest describes his relationship with his lady Casildea de Vandalia, for example, he says that she tests his "honest affection by imposing on [him] many different perilous labours like Hercules stepmother did onto him" (569). In hopes of attaining the goal of his "chaste desires" he must complete a "chain of toils" to prove that he is worthy of her love (569). It seems that the Knight of the Forest refers to pagan mythology, not Christian mysticism, when speaking about love. This, in turn, signals a subtle paradigm shift—a turn away from Christian altruism to pagan egoism instead. Third, Cervantes describes sacred places of Pagan worship in vivid detail, like the "temple of all the Gods [in] Pagan Rome," or "the tombs of Pagan [heroes like] Julius Caesar [who lies in honor at] Saint Peters needle" (535, 537). Fourth, Cervantes relates historic knights to pagan adventurers like the Knight Malumbrino "a Pagan [who was] prudent indeed;" or "Pagan Doria, a [legendary] knight of Malta and a generous man [too] (167, 365). Fifth, Cervantes describes pagan emperors in admiring terms like the Caesars of Rome, for example, or Alexander of Macedonia, for instance. Sixth, Cervantes exults ancient pagan poets by reminding us that "the poet Homer stayed awake to give us the light of his work" and "Virgil showed us in the person of Aeneas the courage of a dutiful son and the sagacity of a brave and able captain" (508, 207). In this sense Cervantes juxtaposes his creation of *Don Quixote* to Homer's creation of the *Adventures of Odysseus* to draw a comparative connection between the two. This is how Miguel implies that like Homer's *Odysseus*, his *Don Quixote* is an epic tale about a brave hero motivated by a Pagan moral code. By focusing on popular pagan Greek heroes in this way, Cervantes moves his readers away from the values of Christianity, which depends on mysticism and sacrifice for realization, to the values of paganism instead, which holds that the primary virtue in life is heroism in action complemented by the glory one gains by surpassing all mortal men in creating a world safe for humans to reside in. This is why Don Quixote, like Hercules, tries to bring peace and prosperity to humanity by battling giants and monsters and juggernauts of all sorts. Seventh, Cervantes has Don Quixote attribute his metaphysical actions to a pagan code of astronomy. For example, when Don Quixote ponders the nature of his exploits he says that: "from this inclination of

[his], [he] must have been born under the influence of the planet Mars" (524). Here, Don Quixote relates his violent deeds to the marshal prowess of Mars, the God of War. Eighth, Cervantes has his Castilian translator draw inspiration from the Gods when narrating events. For example, when telling the story of Sancho Panza's governorship the translator begins his tale thusly:

> O perpetual discoverer of the antipodes, torch of the world, eye of heaven, sweet sawyer of wine coolers, Thymbrius here, Phoebus there, now archer, now physician, father of poetry, inventor of music; O you who always rise and never set, despite all appearances! On you I call, O sun, with whose help man begets man; on you I call to help me and lighten the darkness of my wits so that I can proceed step by step through the narration of the great Sancho Panza's governorship

> (785).

Like Achilles called upon the Gods to give him the strength to sack Troy, or Hector appealed to Zeus to defend him during his time of need, *Don Quixote's* translator sings a prayer to the Pagan Gods to inspire him to write. In sum, by presenting heroic Pagan ideals particular to classical Greek antiquity, Cervantes weakens faith and the hereafter as sources of moral guidance, directing people to classical figures represented in good books instead.

The Holy Inquisition's "indexes of prohibited books," as well as their burning of blasphemous materials, are undermined by Cervantes when he depicts several of his characters admiring books for their ideas.[8] Therefore, when father Perez, the curate, and master Nicholas, the barber, examine Alonso Quixano's library together they preserve many of Don Quixote's books because they find intellectual value in them. Right away the priest shows some tolerance for Don

---

8   http://en.wikipedia.org/wiki/Spanish_Inquisition/Censorship (8).

Quixote's book collection by refusing "to throw [all of Don Quixote's books] out the window" (52). Only after "read[ing] the title[s]" of the books will he know what to do (52). So the "priest [tells] the barber to hand him books one by one so that he [can] see what [is] in them, since he might find some that [don't] deserve to be committed to the flames." (52). So begins a rigorous process of literary scrutiny that starts with the Priest defending "The Four Books of Amadis of Gaul" claiming that they are "the very best of all the books of this kind [and therefore] ought to be pardoned" (52). The Priest shows further restraint when he says that *Palmerin of England*:

> deserves respect for three reasons: because it is excellent in its own right; because it is said to have been written by a wise king of Portugal; [and because] all the adventures in Princess Miraguarda's castle are superb and splendidly contrived; and the speeches are courtly and clear; and have due regard for the character of the speakers, with precision and sensitivity

> (55).

On these grounds he orders that it "be saved from the flames." (55). Again he is lenient when the "History of the Famous Knight Tirante the White" falls at the priest's feet and he cries:

> Good heavens fancy Tirante the White being here! As far as its style is concerned this is the best book in the world. In it knights eat and sleep and die in their beds and make wills before they die; and other such things that are usually not expected from books of this sort. Take it home and read it, and you'll see that what I say is true

> (56).

This time he saves a good book from the bonfire because of its' realism.

It is not just *some* chivalry books that are spared from the flames but *all* poetry books as well. Poetry books are "saved" because they "don't deserve to be burned with the others, because these are books of the intellect, [that cause] no harm" (56). Respect for learning and the imagination is also illustrated when the priest shows tolerance for three unique books written in Spanish heroic verse. Since these "three books are the best written in heroic verse in the Castilian language [the priests asks that they be] preserved as the finest pieces of poetry Spain possesses" (58). And when Don Quixote's "remaining books" are burned by his housekeeper we are told that "if the Priest had examined them they wouldn't have received such a severe sentence" (59). Here we see a fictional easing of literary activity in Spain enacted by a Spanish priest and a local barber, who, together, begin lifting a long-imposed silence on the learned, so that a slow-and-gradual intellectual awakening can grow in the minds of Cervantes's readers. It is no coincidence that a member of the church and a commoner examine Don Quixote's library together to determine what books are worthy to be read and why. The priest represents scholarly learning associated with the cloister. While the barber represents practical shrewdness associated with *La Mancha*. Although they have different social stations, different economic backgrounds, and a different way of sensing life, they can both identify a good book when they read it. In short, the priest and the Barber's common identification of great books of the western literary cannon conveys the idea that there is something universal about quality creative prose which can be seen and appreciated and praised by all people despite their superficial differences.

Even though a priest shows enthusiasm for the human imagination, the Holy Brotherhood is not so understanding in its' day-to-day dealings with Holy law breakers.

The "Holy Brotherhood was a kind of lodge whose members were sworn to keep the highways safe from bandits."[9] They would offer protection against highwaymen, rural criminals, and lawless nobles, because local kings could not afford to do so. In this sense they were "a centrally organized police force" operating under the authority of the crown, with "large powers of summary jurisdiction."[10] Though they were instituted on a temporary basis they soon became a fixed characteristic of municipal life in Spain. Cervantes undermines the authority of this rural police squad when Don Quixote frees a coffle of prisoners marching to the King's galleys. Thinking that physical torture, lash strokes, and years of rowing is too great a punishment for pilfering linen, stealing horses, and selling sex, Don Quixote frees the King's slaves. By releasing these outlaws in the countryside Don Quixote undermines the Holy Brotherhood's power to judge, punish, and arrests outliers. But the real deathblow to the Holy Brotherhood's ability to enforce divine justice comes when Don Quixote thrashes a peace-officer for trying to arrest him. When a warrant-officer detains Don Quixote for "setting [a group of] convicts free" Don Quixote "grabs the officer by the throat with both hands" and would have squeezed the life out of him "had his companions not intervened" (424). Despite trying, the Holy Brotherhood's use of force as a means of compulsion does not work on Don Quixote for try as they do they cannot take him prisoner. He is too combative. Fighting between Don Quixote and the Holy Brotherhood is finally stopped when Don Fernando "prises the peace-officer and Don Quixote apart [by] unhooking their hands, one from a tabard collar and the other from a throat." (424). Instead of assisting the Holy Brotherhood by "tying" Don Quixote up to "deliver him to their charge" as expected, Don Fernando saves Don Quixote from a lengthy prison term (424). Not only does he hamper the Holy Brotherhood's arrest attempt by word, when provoked, Don Fernando even "tramples away at a

---

9   Milton, Joyce. <u>Barron's Book Notes: Miguel De Cervantes Don Quixote</u>. New York: Barron's Educational Series, 1985. (105).

10   http://en.wikipedia.org/wiki/Holy_Brotherhood (1).

peace officer under his feet to his heart's content" (422). Beaten-up and cast aside the Holy Brotherhood has "little success in their tussle with Don Fernando" so they "withdraw from the conflict" to avoid fighting a man of high rank. This is when a priest intervenes on Don Quixote's behalf by "explain[ing] to the peace officers that the knight was out of his senses" when he freed the King's prisoners therefore "if they arrest him and take him away, he'd be released immediately as a madman" (425, 426). On these grounds the Priest appeals to the Holy Brotherhood to "let him off just this once" for he "knows not what he does" (426). Such high-level effort to secure Don Quixote's freedom greatly undermines the Holy Brotherhood's ability to enforce a corrupt form of divine law because it sends the message that warped Holy Law may be transgressed without any major harm redounding to the offender. Greater still is Don Quixote's taunt that members of the Holy Brotherhood "are not officers of the law but officers of lawlessness" (425). He even insults their rank-and-file members with pejorative epithets like "blockhead," for example (131). Because Don Quixote chokes a warrant officer, because he breaks the Holy Brotherhood's laws, and because he gets away with it, his actions set a counter example of noncompliance which results in a metaphorical loosening of the Holy Brotherhood's iron-clad grip over the lives of Spanish nationals. No longer are they seen as the "agents of self-discipline" they once were. Rather they are presented as a feckless, waning police force whose representatives can be eluded, defeated, even overturned by a set of determined individuals who stop at nothing to see justice done. Besides depicting the weakening of the Holy Brotherhood's authority over social affairs Cervantes also challenges Church mythos like virgin births for example.

Cervantes not only questions the "superstitious excesses of the cult of the Virgin Mary" but also undermines the notion that a person can conjure rain by praying to a wooden statue or that he can restore his health by imbibing a quack religious miracle potion.[11] By depicting a procession of penitents who hope to summon rain with Mary's wooden statue, Cervantes says with irony: "Here is your Church. Here is a group of educated men—priests and other luminaries of the town. What are these presumed intelligent men doing? They are prancing around in the woods with a lot of hocus-pocus and a wooden statue, mumbling and prating a lot of mumbo jumbo and expecting thereby to cause clouds to appear in the sky or to cause precipitation in the upper air."[12] Utterly disgusted with this scene Don Quixote "advances on the penitents and delivers such a blow to the shoulder of his enemy's sword arm [that he] tumbles to the ground in dire straits" (469, 471). After Don Quixote knocks Mary's statue down "the other processionists swarm around the Holy image brandishing their scourges awaiting [Don Quixote's] assault determined to defend themselves and even attack their assailants if they can" (471). Don Quixote's attack on these penitents is Cervantes's "indirect attack on members of the clergy" who parade divine miracles, superstition, and hypocrisy to persuade simple-minded people to believe in myths associated with religion.[13] For a similar reason, Cervantes takes direct aim at quack religious cures, like the Balsam of Fierbras, for example, which, "in Carolingian legend is purported to have miraculous properties because it was used to embalm Christ."(chapter 10, endnote 3). But such nostrums are shown to have no healing properties whatsoever. Quite the reverse, they make one violently ill. Don Quixote, "vomits, retches, writhes, and sweats" after he drinks the Balsam of Fierbras and Sancho Panza begins "to gush at both ends, with such seizures and spasms that [he] thought that his life had come

---

11   Milton, Joyce. Barron's Book Notes: Miguel De Cervantes Don Quixote. New York: Barron's Educational Series, 1985. (63).

12   Johnson, Caesar. The Great Quixote Hoax; or, Why Wasn't Cervantes Burned at the Stake. New York: Exposition Press, 1972. (60, 61).

13   Suarez, Manuel F., and Bartolomeo Pinelli. The Revelations of Don Quixote. New York: Harbinger House, 1947. (92).

to an end" (131, 133). In conclusion, by mocking divine mythos like virgin births, for example, Cervantes pours scorn on a moral code that claims that objects have divine powers, that liquids have miraculous properties, and that a woman can give birth to a demi-god without making love.

Though he makes no direct mention of the Church's sexual doctrines, Cervantes, in his "artful and hidden" way, wants to "spell out" that the Church has no authority to prohibit premarital sex[14]. Therefore, despite the ever-present threat of being denounced for sexual immorality, several of Cervantes's characters become intimately involved before marriage. Take Dorotea and Don Fernando, for example. She is the daughter of a rich farmer and he is the son of a Grandee of Spain. Don Fernando sneaks into Dorotea's room "presses [her] tight in his arms [and] satisfies [his physical needs]" (255). Then he is gone for "over a month" (256). Only on the strength of an "oath [that is] firm and true" along with a "promise to marry" does Don Fernando and Dorotea become prenuptial lovers. Contrary to inquisitional decree, they do not wed first. The same is true of other characters as well. Take, for instance, Maritornes, the inn's scullery maid, who "agrees to have some fun and games together" with a muleteer (124). Evidently they do not have a problem with pre-marital sex either. Likewise, a hog driver pays a local woman to sleep with him during Sancho Panza's governorship. They, too, break inquisitional bans by having premarital sex. In conclusion, by dramatizing popular ignorance of, or disregard for, the Inquisition's ban on pre-marital sex, Cervantes, in a veil of laughter, levels criticism at the Church's stringent sex policies.

Cervantes was interested in creating a novel where "freedom of belief could have full range" of expression, especially in a restrictive

---

14   Johnson, Caesar. <u>The Great Quixote Hoax; or, Why Wasn't Cervantes Burned at the Stake?</u> New York: Exposition Press, 1972. (61).

society dominated by religious dogma[15]. "Aware of the wrongs and the injustices [of] his times, Cervantes pointed them out in an attempt to correct them."[16] At a period when the Inquisition was the sole power and law in Spain, the Church is shown to be a stifling force of conservative conformity that visits suffering, punishment, harm, and even death on freethinkers. By listing a number of wrongs committed by the Church, Cervantes criticizes abuses practiced in the name of God, religion, faith, and the afterlife, in an attempt to generate positive social change. Since "Church reform" is Cervantes's primary aim he is critical of some of its more ascetic practices, like punishing one's body to prepare one's soul for heaven.[17] By having one of his main characters refuse to methodically beat and punish his body Cervantes questions the prevailing attitudes toward physical penance. This is why he highlights a belief in the integrity of the individual soul, especially within the context of self-flagellation, which view conflicts with religion's ceaseless call on blind faith. By showing readers that a human being can grasp profound truths about life and morality on their own, unassisted, Cervantes questions the deterministic nature of organized religion. At heart *Don Quixote* is a book that criticizes religious intolerance for people because of their cultural background. This is why Cervantes condemns, in fairly straightforward terms, the expulsion of the Moriscos from a country dominated by concepts of racial purity. In fact the Inquisition's "surveillance of faith and punishment of transgressors" is sidestepped when a crafty Morisco named Ricote avoids the capture of his wealth.[18] His example symbolizes the steps that many Moriscos took to hide their money from Holy extortion. Likewise, Cervantes criticizes the church by

---

15   Duran, Manuel, <u>Cervantes</u>. eds. Gerald E. Wade and Janet Winecoff Diaz on Spain. (Boston: Twayne Publishers, 1974. (132).

16   Suarez, Manuel F., and Bartolomeo Pinelli. <u>The Revelations of Don Quixote</u>. New York: Harbinger House, 1947. (17).

17   Herzman, Ronald, B. "Miguel de Cervantes." The Teaching Company. Lafayette, Virginia. 2004.

18   http://en.wikipedia.org/wiki/Spanish_Inquisition/Precedents (2).

ridiculing its members like a nosy priest, for example, who butts into the lives of others, criticizes them harshly, offers unasked for advice, and leaves in anger. Although Cervantes's anticlerical message is, at times, hidden carefully, it is nevertheless there to show how the clergy can misbehave. Symbols associated with convicted heretics and blasphemers, like hellish frocks and restrictive cones, for example, are also ridiculed by Cervantes to show readers how laughable the Holy Inquisition paraphernalia is. In order to restore freedom of thought and expression to humanity the Holy Inquisition's campaign to burn and censor books is undercut when Cervantes argues for the diffusion of learning and culture in Spain by passing positive judgement on a wide variety of writings. Since "true religion does not seek to destroy knowledge" but rather seeks to educate people, Cervantes reminds us that the Inquisition was only imposed in the name of religion to still men's minds and silence their tongues by dictating their thoughts and proscribing their life practices—even their sexual ones.[19] For this reason the Holy prohibition of sex before marriage is logic-chopped when Cervantes shows us that "simple fornication" between consenting adults was commonplace in 17th century Spain.[20] By portraying a wide-variety of characters who are unafraid to have sex outside of marriage, Cervantes shows readers that one can enjoy earthly pleasures without sinning. Finally, divine miracles, like virgin births, for example, are challenged when Don Quixote attacks a group of penitents carrying Mary's statue. The protagonist's assault on the sacred image of the Virgin Mary is not an attack on religion's values per say but it does call into question Roman Catholic adulation of her.

While many of Cervantes's criticisms of the church of his times are humorous and entertaining, his jokes are nevertheless made at the expense of the established religious order—so he had to find a

---

19   Suarez, Manuel F., and Bartolomeo Pinelli. <u>The Revelations of Don Quixote</u>. New York: Harbinger House, 1947. (87).

20   http://en.wikipedia.org/wiki/Spanish_Inquisition/Blasphemy (10).

way to get around the censors of his times to avoid suffering the consequences of direct criticism. Therefore, to avoid being denounced as a heretic and tortured for his confession, Cervantes deployed the use of satire and irony and humor in his book so that he could criticize the clergy without appearing to do so. If his criticisms were taken directly, without the smokescreen of humor, the Church would have punished him severely. So comic irony is deployed, in the form of religious satire, to convey a sense of frustration in Spain for the clergy's growing intolerance of unorthodox thought. In short, in an age of religious conformity characterized by the twin-dangers of theologic dogma and religious authoritarianism, Cervantes wrote *Don Quixote* as a creative response to the harsh limitation imposed by the Holy office. So he focuses on the liberation of the common man from the shackles of religious power in a fictive world where the free use of one's mind becomes respectable again.

Select Bibliography

Duran, Manuel, Cervantes. eds. Gerald E. Wade and Janet Winecoff Diaz on Spain. Boston: Twayne Publishers, 1974.

Herzman, Ronald, B. "Miguel de Cervantes." The Teaching Company. Lafayette, Virginia, 2004.

Ghate, Onkar. Seminar on the Philosophy of Objectivism (Internet Course). Irvine, California, 2008.

Grierson, Sir Herbert Jon Clifford. Don Quixote: Some War-Time Reflections on Its Character and Influence (1921). New York: Corne II University Press.

Johnson, Caesar. The Great Quixote Hoax; or, Why Wasn't Cervantes Burned at the Stake? New York: Exposition Press, 1972.

Milton, Joyce. Barron's Book Notes: Miguel De Cervantes Don Quixote. New York: Barron's Educational Series, 1985.

Suarez, Manuel F., and Bartolomeo Pinelli. <u>The Revelations of Don Quixote</u>. New York: Harbinger House, 1947.

http://en.wikipedia.org/wiki/Battle of Lepanto

http://en.wikipedia.org/wiki/Cat_0%27_nine_tails

http://en.wikipedia.org/wiki/Holy_Brotherhood

http://en.wikipedia.org/wiki/Moriscos

http://en.wikipedia.org/wiki/Ricote_(Don Quixote)

http://en.wikipedia.org/wiki/self-flagellation

http://en.wikipedia.org/wiki/Spanish_Inquisition

ESSAY 3

Don Quixote and Sancho Panza's Relationship:
Foils that Evoke the Best in Each Other.

Don Quixote and Sancho Panza check-and-balance each other through a set of opposite characteristics since one is delusional, the other is realistic, one is succinct, the other is chatty, one is brave, the other is timid, one is sad, the other is cheerful, one is a knight, the other is a squire, one is book-lorish, the other is folk-lorish, one is literate, the other is illiterate, one is theoretical, the other is practical, one is urbane, the other is rustic, one is idealistic, the other is pragmatic, one is noble, the other is simple, and finally, one is a gentlemen, the other is a farmer. It this though these opposite characteristics that Don Quixote and Sancho Panza stabilize one another because: when one talks too much the other quiets him down; when one fails to listen the other encourages him to attend to the conversation; when one is rash and foolhardy the other is brave and careful; when one turns frightened the other inspires bravery; when one stands alone the other shows him that friends are sometimes needed; when one is stuck leading a dead-end life the other creates a scenario where he can advance; when one is ignorant of book knowledge the other teaches him the value of letters; when one is unlearned in Spanish folklore the other recites Iberian maxims; when one is so abstract and theoretical that he lacks common sense the other shows him what it takes to live in hard reality; and lastly, when one's thinking is short-term and concrete bound the other teaches him to project long-term moral values. It is through an inter-penetrative process of give-and-take, push-and-shove, live-and-let-live, that Don Quixote and Sancho Panza realize a constructive synergy where both partners connect with and rely on each other to the advantage of both.

The first instance of one partner enhancing the other partner's external awareness comes when Sancho Panza corrects Don Quixote's visual, auditory, olfactory, and tactile hallucinations by identifying people, places, objects, smells, spaces, and sounds by their actual physical properties rather than what Don Quixote takes them to be. For example, when Don Quixote thinks that "forty windmills standing on [a] plain" are forty "monstrous giants" obstructing his path with "arms almost six miles long" Sancho Panza says that they are "not giants [at all but] windmills [not with] arms [but with] sails [so that] when the wind [blows they can] turn and make the millstones [inside them] go round" (63, 64). Similarly when Don Quixote spots "large water-mills standing in the middle of [a] river" and cries "there stands [a] fortress hold[ing] some knight or distressed queen under duress" Sancho Panza claims that what he really sees is a milling station used to crush, pound, and churn vegetable matter into fine particles and powder. Similarly, when Don Quixote thinks that inns are splendid castles replete with "moats, and towers, portcullises and drawbridges," Sancho Panza says that they are not fortresses at all but simple road-side taverns (964). Likewise, when Don Quixote claims that Sancho Panza is blanket-tossed by a group of enchanted ghosts, Sancho Panza says that the pranksters he sees are the same muleteers that Don Quixote stoned earlier. Not only does Sancho Panza evaluate people for who they really are he also sees man-made objects for what they really are. Take Mambrino's helmet, for example. When Don Quixote thinks that a man wearing a shiny yellow object on his head is a golden-helmeted knight named Mambrino, Sancho Panza points out that the alleged warrior is a simple country barber, with an overturned copper-basin on his head, which he uses to avoid staining his hat during a rain storm. Again, when Don Quixote mistakes a stationary wooden mare for a flying horse, Sancho Panza suggests that the pegasus is not a unicorn at all but an elaborate fabrication designed to make fun of them. Likewise, when Don Quixote claims that a chopped-off head gushing blood belongs to a headless ogre he has slain in battle, Sancho Panza says that what he has defeated is not a monster at all but a liquid filled pig skin containing twenty gallons of red-wine. Sancho Panza also corrects Don Quixote's auditory hallucinations. For example, when he mistakes the bleating of two flocks of sheep for the sounds of two clashing armies, Sancho Panza says that sounds created by grazing animals differ from noises produced by warrior knights in battle. Sancho Panza also uses his eyes to identify spatial relationships by their relative distances. For instance, when Don Quixote claims that they are on a transoceanic ship, traversing the Atlantic Ocean, bisecting the equator, Sancho Panza looks around and says that they are on a dingy floating on the river Ebro, five yards from its' bank, and two yards downstream from where their horse and donkey are tied. Similarly, when Don Quixote hears far-off voices that indicate their elevated altitude, Sancho Panza says that the sounds he hears are near-by thus they cannot be that high up. Sancho Panza also uses his vision to identify agricultural crops for what they are; not what Don Quixote wants them to be. For instance, when Don Quixote thinks that a peasant girl sifts pearls of the orient, Sancho Panza identifies the sun-specked objects as grains of buckwheat—nothing less, nothing more. Not only does he identify wheat by its visual appearance he also detects smells by their actual physical odor. For example, when Don Quixote smells perfumed fragrances coming from the body of a damsel, Sancho Panza smells work-sweat coming from the body of a farmgirl. In addition, Sancho Panza uses his sense of touch to detect feelings on his skin. For instance, when they ride a supposed flying horse, instead of thinking that the earth's wind is blowing them about as Don Quixote does, Sancho Panza claims that the breeze he feels is similar to the air-currents produced by a thousand large bellows.

Examples of this sort abound in Don Quixote. The main point here is that Sancho Panza uses his eyes to identify man-made objects by their physical properties – he uses his vision to identify people by their physical characteristics – he uses his sight to identify agricultural crops by their appearance – he uses his mind to identify where he is in time-and-space – he uses his ears to identify animals by sound – he uses his consciousness to measure geographical distances – he uses his nose to identify aromas by smell – and, lastly, he uses his sense of touch to identify tactile sensations by feel.

This, then, is how Sancho Panza dismisses Don Quixote's external misperceptions to identify concrete reality when he sees it, hears it, feels it, smells it, and tastes it, with his own five senses. Because Sancho Panza points out a number of perceptual-sensuous-facts that cannot be rationally disputed, Don Quixote creates a complex explanation for his misperceptions by claiming that he is hounded by a set of wicked enchanters who have the ability to transform persons, places, and things into whatever appearance they like just to spite him. But Sancho Panza does not fall for this line of reasoning either – for he points out, many times that the people they meet are not enchanted at all. For example, Sancho Panza uses his mind's eye to refute Don Quixote's claim that a group of malicious enchanters can shapeshift at will to impede his progress. Specifically, when Don Quixote claims that the "men who [blanket tossed his squire] are ghosts and creatures from another world" Sancho Panza claims that the people who "had fun with him weren't ghosts or enchanted men [at all] but men of flesh and blood" (137). When Don Quixote says that an evil spell immobilized him when he tried to help Sancho Panza, his squire says that the reason why Don Quixote was "not able to get over the [garden] wall or even off [his] horse was not [due to] enchantments [but because of] something else [altogether]" (137). When Don Quixote believes that he "travels in a cage under a spell because [of] the envy and deceit of [an] evil enchanter" Sancho Panza tells him that he isn't "under [the influence of magic] at all" (432, 437).

When Don Quixote feels the urge to urinate but cannot because he is encaged, Sancho Panza says that his wish to pee is proof positive that he is not enchanted at all because "people who don't answer the call of nature [may be] enchanted, but not people who feel the urges that [his master] feel[s] and who drink when they are given a drink, and eat, when there's food to be had, and reply to everything they're asked" (449). When Don Quixote believes that a wicked magician transmogrified the beautiful Dulcinea into an unattractive simpleton, Sancho Panza is "amazed that, in defiance of the truth" he could suppose such a thing, especially because he, Sancho Panza, knows, that there is no Dulcinea just a pretty local woman named Aldonza Lorenzo that Don Quixote idealizes into a princess (724, 725).

Evidently, Sancho Panza's perceptual identifications alter Don Quixote's external projections to such a degree that by book-end Don Quixote recovers his extrospective faculty altogether. To elucidate this point consider part one of the book in relation to part two of the book. In part one of the book Don Quixote mistakes: a group of muleteers for a band of iterant knights; a gang of silk merchants for a crew of insolent knights; forty windmills for forty giants; a Basque rustic for a fiendish ravisher; Yanguasian mule drivers for low-born pretend knights; groups of sheeps for hordes of opposed warriors; litter-bearing priests for bier-carrying squires; a basin headed barber for a gold helmeted knight; a skein of red wine for an evil monster; officers of the Holy Brotherhood for enchanted ghosts; and, lastly, a procession of penitents for shadowy enchanters. Evidently, the Don Quixote of Part I experiences intense mental delusions that make him attack innocent people, often out of anger. In part two, however, Don Quixote does not confuse people's identities as much, nor does he initiate so much needless conflict; rather, he identifies people for who they are (or who they pretend to be) and fights only when he feels he must. For example, when Sanson Carrasco, a young graduate student, pretends to be the Knight of the Forest then the Knight of the White Moon, Don Quixote feels he has no choice but to respond to

95

his challenges and insults with combat. So he jousts Sanson Carrasco not out of a sense of blatant misidentification or out of a sense of unprovoked anger but rather to gain honor and glory for himself and for Dulcinea. Thanks to Sancho Panza's matter-of-fact identifications, Don Quixote's perceptual hallucinations are greatly diminished as a result. So much so, in fact, that not only does he recognize inns as inns rather than fortified castles but he also repents on his deathbed for his chivalric misidentifications. In brief, Sancho Panza's realistic interventions sharpen Don Quixote's mind's eye to the degree that he can perceive the external world of concretes by their inherent perceptual qualities.

In return for Sancho Panza's perceptual corrections, Don Quixote helps him improve his public speaking skills. This, he does, by correcting Sancho Panza's misspeech, expanding his conceptual vocabulary, and, above all, teaching him to use a precise economy of words so that he formulates what he is going to say with concision. When Sancho Panza, for example, confuses one word for another, or uses one term in place of another, or expresses a mismeaning, Don Quixote detects these verbal mistakes, right away, and corrects them fast. For instance, when Sancho Panza says *handful* and not *handle*, Don Quixote says: "I think you mean to say *handle* not *handful*" (175). Later, when Sancho Panza says that his wife is "*designed*" to let him go Don Quixote supplies the right word "*resigned,*" (527). Even though Sancho Panza objects to Don Quixote's linguistic corrections by saying: "I've already asked you once or twice not to correct my words if you understand what I mean by them," eventually he agrees that it would save them both time-and-effort if he willingly "accept[ed] everything" said to him to "learn" what he is "taught" (527). As the story progresses, Sancho Panza is more receptive to verbal correction for he "promise[s] to [consider his speech] before utter[ing] a single inappropriate or ill-considered word" (696). So when Don Quixote swaps "*proportion*" for "*abortion*" "*resolve*" for "*dissolve*" "*palfrey*" for "*poultry*" "*critic*" for "*cricket*" and "*longinquity*" for "*longdrinkity,*"

Sancho Panza either agrees with what he "ought" to "have said" or asks for the definition of a new concept to learn its' precise meaning (528, 536, 547, 612, 683). After learning what "eructate" means, for example, he uses "eructate" instead of "belch" (771). This, then, is how Sancho Panza not only learns to use the right words in the correct order but this is also how he broadens his vocal range of speech.

Besides enhancing the content of Sancho Panza's speech, Don Quixote decreases its amount in six ways. By 1) enforcing a speech ban on him; 2) diminishing his use of proverbs; 3) encouraging him to not joke so much; 4) admonishing him when he tries to be too clever; 5) criticizing his volubility, and; 6) dismissing his irrelevant inquiries. To reduce Sancho Panza's thoughtless talk, then, Don Quixote tries to establish a respectful distance between himself and his squire by pointing out that "in all the books of chivalry [he has] read, never [has he] come across any squire who talk[s] to his master [so much]" (164). In fact Don Quixote "considers" Sancho Panza's over-speech to be "a great fault in both" of them; in Sancho because he "show[s] [him] scant respect" and in himself "because" he "does not make [his squire] respect him more" (164). So he imposes a de facto silence-ban on his squire that: stops him from "speak[ing] while his master is speaking;" forbids him from "concern[ing] [himself] with [other people's] business;" and encourages him to curb his enthusiasm (563, 206). Evidently, Sancho Panza learns when he should speak-up and when he should be quiet, as well as what must be said, and how, for he tells Don Quixote to not "worry about [him] getting out of control, or saying anything but what's spot-on, because [he hasn't] forgotten [his] advice about speaking a lot or a little, well or badly" (697). Similarly, when Sancho Panza attaches long sequences of irrelevant proverbs to their conversations, Don Quixote encourages him to: "not be so prodigal with [his] proverbs; [to quote only pertinent] proverb[s]; to make his point[s] clear [with] plain straightforward language without complications; [and to] not slip [a plethora of maxims] into [his] message[s]" (943, 966, 688). Clearly

Don Quixote wants his squire to connect his points to apt sayings that "fit the matter in hand like a ring on a finger [because] proverbs are brief maxims derived from [the] experience of wise men of former times [not] absurd [irrelevancies that are] drag[ged] and force[d] into [one's] discourse [to illustrate their erudition]" (943). As "long as [his] proverbs are appropriate, timely [and are] brought to bear on [what has been] said" Don Quixote "tolerates" them but "loading everything that [he] says with [proverbs] and stringing them together without rhyme or reason" is unacceptable to him (743, 723, 772). After Don Quixote admonishes Sancho Panza for his overuse of faulty proverbs, Sancho Panza promises to "mend [his] ways if [he] can [by] not com[ing] out with" inappropriate aphorisms all the time "because [well chosen speech] is golden" (966, 774). Second, Don Quixote tries to eliminate Sancho Panza's insensitive speech, especially in the form of personal abuse. For instance, when he insults Donna Rodriguez by asking her to stable his donkey, by calling her old, and by disparaging her dress-style, Don Quixote criticizes him for "daring to speak such [insults] in the presence of such [an] illustrious lady" (695). Again, when Sancho Panza calls Dorotea and Luscinda two "whores," Don Quixote silences him by asking how he can allow such insolent indecencies into his "disordered imagination" (695). Moreover, Don Quixote asks Sancho Panza if he "considers it correct to insult a duenna [a farmer's daughter, and an aristocrat] who [are all personages] worthy of respect" (695). Even though Sancho Panza makes it clear that he did not mean to offend Donna Rodriguez but only asked her to care for his donkey because he "thought there wasn't any kindlier person [he] could entrust it to" Don Quixote encourages him to "steer clear of [oral] pitfalls, for he who stumbles as a talkative and funny fellow will soon [put] his foot [in his mouth] and fall headlong as an unfunny buffoon" (694, 695, 696). Evidently, Don Quixote wants Sancho Panza to "put a brake on his tongue [to] consider and chew over [his] words [carefully] before [they are spoken] and to bear in mind that" in high-society one should observe speech protocol (696). Therefore, when Sancho Panza steps out of line, Don Quixote tells him to "hush [up] [to] not answer back [to] keep his mouth [closed] to be quiet to keep [his peace] to come with him to do as he is told [and to mind his] own business" (739, 187, 881,206, 617 (X2), 206). Chastened by these reproaches, Sancho Panza "keeps quiet, gives his master a cloth and doesn't open his mouth to speak" (591, 884). Moreover, when Sancho Panza tries to be wittier then he is Don Quixote tells him that "[he is] a dim-witted chatterbox [who] tries to be too clever by half" (215). In fact when Sancho Panza talks too much Don Quixote ironizes his speech by saying that he is either: "talking away without anyone to stop [him, therefore he should] talk on [and] say everything that comes into [his] head and mouth;" Or, that he "is better at loosening his tongue to babble mischief than at tightening a girth to secure a saddle" (645). In fact Don Quixote says that he "shall pay [no] attention to [his squire's] words [because he] know[s] him [well]" (679). Besides using humor to silence Sancho Panza, Don Quixote mocks his redundant speech as follows: "I know nothing about that [and] anyway the enquiry is irrelevant" (639). Also when Sancho Panza speaks in anger Don Quixote asks him if he is: "quite finished [with his] harangue for [he should be quiet sometimes]" (623). For this reason, the earlier Sancho is very different than the later Sancho in that the earlier Sancho says whatever comes to mind—even if his speech challenges Don Quixote's authority in public or makes fun of him in front of others—while the later Sancho controls what he says a bit better. In sum, by criticizing Sancho Panza's screeds, by reproaching him when he jokes too much, by urging him to think about what he is (or is not) going to say before he says it, and by inciting his squire to know himself well, Don Quixote hones Sancho Panza's speaking skills so that he can express himself with appropriate concision.

Though Sancho Panza is silenced by Don Quixote, he also defends his right to free speech so that he is permitted to say what he likes, when he likes, and how he likes to say it—so long as his speech is polite and respectful. For example, when Sancho Panza asks Don Quixote to "give [him] permission to say a few words [because the] order of silence [his friend] imposed on him" is stifling, Don Quixote listens to his complaints with a will (170). Again when Sancho Panza protests that "[not] speaking to [Don Quixote] when [he] feel[s] like it is the same as burying [him] alive," his silence ban is lifted. Because Don Quixote "understands [that] Sancho Panza [is eager] for [him] to [ease] the [restraint he] placed on [his squire's] tongue [he tells Sancho Panza that he] can speak as much as [he] pleases, [provided] that the lifting [of the ban] only lasts for as long as does [their] wandering [in] the Sierra Morena" (205). Good thing Sancho Panza is allowed to speak in the Black Mountains, too, because when Don Quixote goes crazy there, his squire pacifies him by volunteering to deliver a message to his beloved Dulcinea. Additionally, Sancho Panza asserts his right to free-speech, quite vigorously, when he says: "I'll speak now [with or without your permission]; or I've spoken before now [therefore] I can speak any time in front of anyone [whomsoever I please]" (563). Sancho Panza even reminds Don Quixote about their contractual free-speech agreement when he says: "If you happened to have a good memory, [which you do] you might have remembered the clauses we put in our agreement before we left home this last time, and one of them was that you'd let me talk as much as I liked, so long as I didn't insult anyone or undermine your authority" (617). Due to Sancho Panza's insistence on "free-speech," Don Quixote lets him talk at a roadside tavern by telling him that "he may say whatever [he] pleases so long as it is not his intention to strike fear into him with his words [because he needs all of his courage to fend-off the Holy brotherhood] (428). At times, Sancho Panza says what he thinks despite Don Quixote's anger. For example, when they converse about the happenings in princess Micomicona's kingdom, Sancho Panza contradicts Don Quixote by saying that "there's more going on" there "than folks know about" (428). Even though Don Quixote gets upset at his uninvited speech Sancho Panza speaks-up nonetheless: "If you're going to get cross [should] I keep quiet about what it's my [responsibility] as a good squire to tell you, and what any good servant should tell his master?" (428). Evidently, Sancho Panza thinks that he should not restrain his thoughts so much, especially when his ideas seem reasonable to him. At such times, Sancho Panza says that: "if [he were] allowed to talk as much as [he] used to, maybe [he'd] say that which would make [Don Quixote] see how wrong [he is]." (166). But Sancho Panza does not go too far in his criticisms for two reasons: One, because he does not want Don Quixote to go berserk at his behest; and two, because he does not want to point out too many of Don Quixote's mistakes, mainly out of courtesy deference. Therefore, either he remains strategically silent, saving his ideas for a better occasion, or he waits for Don Quixote to "start a conversation" so that he can guide the flow of ideas in a more favorable direction (204). As this tactic might suggest, when Sancho Panza speaks with intelligence, Don Quixote tells him to "speak on [for he is] in sparkling form today" because, sometimes, Don Quixote admits, his squire voices good reason (528). Thus, when Sancho Panza is rational he may "say whatever he likes" (528). Sancho Panza even defends his untimely speech bursts when he says: "everyone has got to speak up about his needs wherever he is" (694). The Duke of Aragon agrees explicitly: "Sancho's quite right [therefore] he is in no way to blame" (695). In fact, his wife, the Duchess, concurs, because on multiple occasions she allows, even encourages, Sancho Panza to speak freely, even in Don Quixote's presence. For example, when traveling to Aragon "the Duchess orders Sancho to ride with her because she simply adore[s] listening to his clever conversation." Or, when Don Quixote says that Sancho Panza should be removed from the Ducal dinner table because he is likely to "put his foot in his mouth" the Duchess orders "Sancho [to] not move an inch from [her] side" (692). When Don Quixote tells Sancho Panza to keep his narrative "brief," the Duchess retorts "He most certainly shall not keep it brief if he wants to please me, on the contrary he must tell it in his own way" (698). It is in this manner that Sancho Panza is not absolutely silenced from speaking when he has thoughts he wants to express.

Another way Don Quixote and Sancho Panza complement one another is by spurring each other to be brave yet not rash, cautious yet not pusillanimous, bold yet not reckless, so that one partner does not risk himself unnecessarily, while the other partner is not scared unreasonably. For example, after Don Quixote is knocked senseless by a "hailstorm" of rocks thrown by "twelve" ungrateful criminals, Sancho Panza reminds him that: "withdrawing isn't running away [because] when danger outweighs hope the wise man saves himself for tomorrow and doesn't risk everything on one day" (176, 186, 187). Evidently, Don Quixote agrees that caution is sometimes merited for when he is amidst a troop of musketed donkey brayers intent on doing him harm, he takes "to Rocinante's heels and [rides] off as far as necessary for him to feel safe" (667). Likewise, when he is surrounded by "more than forty live bandits he [thinks] it best to fold his arms, bow his head, [and] save himself for a better opportunity" (893). After these confrontations Don Quixote explains that "courage which is not based on prudence is called [rashness]" and its opposite bravery "[is] situated between two extremes, the vice of cowardice and [the vice of] foolhardiness" (599). It is in this way that Don Quixote becomes a brave knight, not a reckless knight; for, as Sancho Panza reminds him: "There is a time to attack and a time to retreat" (512). In contrast, Don Quixote teaches Sancho Panza to be brave when his squire is paralyzed by fear: like when he sees a wild boar gnashing his teeth; like when he hears hammers pounding a stone slab in a fulling mill; like when his skiff floats towards a water mill; like when he sees two pretend demons driving a cart of death; like when he observes an ominous funeral procession travelling at night; like when he rides a supposed flying steed. Specifically, when Sancho Panza "trembles for his life Don Quixote barks at him in fury: What are you afraid of, you cowardly creature? What is it making you blubber you butter-hearted baby? Who is pursuing you, who is hounding you, you mouse-spirited wench" (683). This reproach quiets Sancho Panza down. Likewise, when Sancho Panza quails atop Clavileno "and beg[s] everyone in the garden to help him in his plight," a mortified Don Quixote calls his squire a "spiritless animal" who should "cover [his] eyes" and "not allow the fear that fills [his] body past his lips" (759). At this rebuke Sancho Panza takes heart by "blindfold[ing] [his] tender brimming eyes" to ready himself for the ride (759). Don Quixote also emboldens Sancho Panza by inspiring him with words of encouragement: "Hold on tight, brave Sancho banish your fears my friend everything is going just as it should" (760). He even inspires Sancho Panza by being brave himself. For instance, when Don Quixote confronts a solemn funeral procession of corpse bearing priests "it [is] wondrous to behold the agility with which he attack[s] them and knock[s] them off their mules" (149). To explain, these reproaches, encouragements, and examples of actional bravery, inspire Sancho Panza to take heart, which newfound courage he displays adventures. For instance, when "a goatherd leaps upon Don Quixote, seizes him by [the] throat," and begins to choke him to death Sancho "grab[s] the goatherd by the shoulders, flings him down on [a] table [and] pounds [him with his] feet" (468). In sum, when Don Quixote and Sancho Panza listen to each other they are not rash or craven but brave and steadfast.

Besides pushing each other to be bold when facing their enemies, yet careful with their lives, Don Quixote and Sancho Panza enjoy a plus-up knight-to-squire relationship in that Don Quixote is: cared for when wounded; nursed when sick; dressed when naked; saddled when horsed; armed when unprotected; brought food when hungry; given drink when thirsty; kept company when alone; rested when tired; shielded when attacked; freed when entangled; calmed when upset; and gladdened when sad. In return, Sancho Panza is: paid when required; helped when entangled; refined when rude; excited when bored; emboldened when scared; wisened when ignorant, and hardened when soft. One instance of Sancho Panza caring for Don

Quixote's injuries comes when a group of shepherds "smash two of his ribs crush two of his fingers [and] take out three or four of his teeth, as well" (143, 142). At this time Sancho Panza "looks in his saddle bags for something with which to [tend to] his master's wounds" (144). In another instance, after a Basque thrashes Don Quixote with his own lance, Sancho Panza finds "lint and white ointment" to field-dress his injuries (79, 80). Still, at other times, Sancho Panza lavishes medical attention on Don Quixote. For example, when Don Quixote is lying in bed recovering from his second sally Sancho Panza does not "leave his side," rather he cares for him, nurtures him, and lifts his spirits so that he recovers quickly. Sancho Panza also provides sartorial services for Don Quixote. For instance, when he needs items of dressware, like "his riding boots, helmet, or armour," his squire fetches the appropriate articles (590, 601, 781). Sancho Panza also cares for Don Quixote's horse and maintains his chain-mail armor. For example, when Don Quixote is sitting atop Rocinante he "checks" the nag's "girths" to make sure they are tight and secure; or he "slips armour over his master," like his helmet, for instance, or he hands him offensive-and-defensive weapons like his pointed lance or broad sword or round shield (266, 585). At other times, Sancho Panza relieves Don Quixote of his accoutrements by placing his knight's "helmet on the front pommel of his donkey's saddle tree" so that his knight can breathe freely on the road without lugging around heavy objects (585). Also, Sancho Panza makes sure that Don Quixote's horse is fed, stabled, and looked after. This is why he either asks a stable boy for "some barley for Rocinante;" or releases Rocinante to graze in pasture; or takes Rocinante to a verdant meadow to "munch on green grass;" or arranges for Rocinante to be given "the best manger and the best stall [available] in the stable" (227, 551, 653). Moreover, Sancho Panza ensures that Don Quixote has both enough food to eat, and enough liquid to drink, by supplying him with "onions" and "cheese," "bread" and vegetables, "acorns and medlars, nuts and raisins, bacon and goat meat," and water and wine.

(81, 82, 84, 886). Sancho Panza also provides emotional support for Don Quixote by cheering him up when he is sad. For instance, when Don Quixote is dejected by Dulcinea's elusiveness, Sancho Panza gives him hope by telling him that tomorrow, in the light of day, they will find her "palace or castle" (544). Likewise, when Don Quixote is "plunged into dejection [because he thinks] enchanters turn[ed] his lady Dulcinea into the vile shape of a peasant wench" Sancho Panza tells him to "snap out of [his gloom] and come to [his] senses, and pick up Rocinante's reins, and wake up and cheer up and show some of the dash and spirit that knight errants are supposed to show" (551). Again when Don Quixote "stay[s] in bed for six days, dejected, depressed, broody and in the worst of spirits, turning the disastrous events of his defeat over and over in his mind," Sancho Panza tells him to "hold-up that head of [his] and cheer up, too, if [he] can, and give thanks to heaven that [he] didn't break any ribs [when he] tumbled to the ground because we can all expect to be given a dose of our medicine every so often [but that should not incite us to get down on ourselves so]" (931). Sancho Panza also checks Don Quixote flagging spirits when he says: "you mustn't let yourself be affected by these combats and these thumpings, because he who is down one day can be up the next [as long as he] plucks-up fresh courage for fresh fights" (932). In fact Sancho Panza channels Don Quixote's flow-of-thoughts in a more positive direction by inspiring him with a bucolic vision of how they may become romantic shepherds together:

> Come on lets go off into the countryside dressed up as shepherds as we said we would and amuse [ourselves] in the solitude of the fields, where [we can] give free rein to thoughts of love [to] practice [the] virtuous way of pastoral life [where we] carve the names [of our lady loves] on trees and construct pastoral verses or courtly verses or whatever verse best suits our purposes, to keep us amused in [desolate] places

(979, 973, 974).

Also, Sancho Panza cheers Don Quixote up by being a chipper companion to talk to about: life-and-literature; drama-and-poems; law-and-politics; Christianity-and-Islam; farming-and-shepherding; herding-and-agriculture, and many other topics. Sancho Panza also ensures that Don Quixote is well-rested after his numerous physical exertions. For example, after he waltzes at "a ball with Don Antonio's wife, Sancho deposits his knight in bed, covering him up to make him sweat out the chill he'd caught dancing" (910). Sancho Panza also protects Don Quixote from physical attack. For instance, when Don Quixote is bested by a goatherd who tumbles him to the ground Sancho Panza beseeches the offender "to not hit him again [because] he [is] only a poor [delusional] knight who [has] never done any [intentional] harm [to] anyone in all the days of his born life" (471). Not only does Sancho Panza protect Don Quixote from taking a beating, he also frees Don Quixote from imprisonment. After his second sally, for instance, when he is encaged by the civil authorities, Sancho Panza unlocks his metal cage so that he can get out. Sancho Panza also stops Don Quixote from harming himself. For example, when Don Quixote strips naked "from the waist down," performs "somersaults and handsprings," runs around wildly, smashes his head against stones and tears at trees, Sancho Panza tells him to "be careful how [he] go[es] dashing [his] head [about] because [he] could pick on such a rock and hit it in such a place" that could do permanent damage to his cranium (212, 220). In fact, he encourages Don Quixote to "dash his head against water, or something soft like cotton" so that he does not knock his brain about (212). Not only does Sancho Panza restore Don Quixote's mental balance when he goes berserk in the Sierra Morena but he also removes him from the brown hills by creating a plausible scenario where his knight thinks that his love-suit for Dulcinea is going to be accepted after all. So he tells Don Quixote that he will travel to "El Toboso [to transmit to Dulcinea] such stories about [his great love for her that] will make her as sweet as a nut" (213). He even offers to take a letter to her from the Don, to convey his master's great love. In all these ways, and more, Sancho Panza pacifies Don Quixote's angry spirit so that he cools down, recovers his reason, and stops performing inane acts of madness.

In return, Don Quixote enhances Sancho Panza's material livelihood, social respect, physical toughness, existential security, emotional well-being, and intellectual cultivation, as follows: First, he pays him: with treasure; with donkeys; with a bequest; and with a fixed salary. This is why when they find a dead donkey lying in a stream with saddle-bags stuffed with "gold escudos Don Quixote [tells him] to take the money and keep it for himself" in payment for his many services (188). In another instance, when Sancho Panza protests that he has not received a fixed wage for his squiring, Don Quixote says that since he is "carrying [his] money [he should] work out how long it is since [they] left [their home] village and how much [he] can and should earn per month, and [to] calculate pro-rata [what he is] owe[d]" so that he can be his "own paymaster" (679). Likewise, when Sancho Panza's donkey is stolen by a picaroon named Gines de Pasamonte, Don Quixote writes a warrant for three of his own donkeys in recompense. Also when Don Quixote composes his last will-and-testament he stipulates that: "it is [his wish] that in respect to certain monies in Sancho Panza's possession if anything remains after he has paid himself what [he is] owe[d] it should all be his" (978). Besides paying his squire for services rendered, Don Quixote also frees him from entrapment twice: Once, he "unhooks Sancho" from a dangerous near ground position so that he is not gored by a boar. Likewise, when Sancho Panza falls into a hole atop dapple, Don Quixote vouches to "bring [helpers] to pull [him] out of the [chasm]" (721, 862). Also, Don Quixote teaches Sancho Panza to respect his elders by diminishing his hostility for them. For example, when his squire is "amaz[ed] that [Don Quixote] didn't jump [an] old [man] and kick all his bones to pulp and yank out his beard till there wasn't a single hair left in his chin" Don Quixote reproaches him gently by saying: "No, friend, it would not have been right for me to do that, because [we should] treat [risible] elders with venerance" (643). Also, Don Quixote introduces a bit of adventure into Sancho Panza's hum-drum life by: taking him value-questing around Spain; introducing him to admirals and viceroys aboard a Spanish Galleon; bringing him amidst a band of brigands where he holds his own; enabling him to meet judges and nobles and returning Spanish soldiers; putting him in a position to become a quasi-pretend governor for ten days; and mingling him with a wide array of witty maidens, beautiful damsels, refined princesses, and noble lords. In short, all of Sancho Panza's wacky adventures with Don Quixote are preferable to farming a small plot of Mancheagian land in a dusty backwater somewhere under the blazing heat of a summer sun, especially since "it's great to be waiting to see what's going to happen next as you ride across mountains, explore forests, climb crags, visit castles and put up at inns as and when you like" (474). Don Quixote also teaches Sancho Panza that he should get used to difficult circumstances as a prospect knight for: "easy living, luxury, and repose was invented for effete courtiers, [but] toil, disquiet, and arms were created for those the world calls knights errant" (96). For this reason, Don Quixote wants Sancho Panza to toughen himself—mentally, physically, and emotionally—because "the life of a knight errant is subject to a thousand dangers and misfortunes" (119). As such, Don Quixote encourages Sancho Panza to search "for adventures by night and by day, in winter and in summer, on foot and on horseback, thirsty and hungry, in the heat and in the cold, subject to the burning rays of the midsummer sun and [subject to] ice [cold] winter blasts [because] prospect knights [who] endure all" of this are rewarded by by fame, glory, and money (134, 521). Don Quixote also reminds Sancho Panza that "its' hard business to go about looking for adventures your whole life long [therefore] squires must face up to a lot of hunger and bad luck, as well as other things its' better not to talk about." (204). In fact, Don Quixote says that an ideal knight errant is "patient and long-suffering in the face of toil [and] imprisonment [for] knight errant[ry is about] sleep[ing] in the open fields, exposed to all the inclemency of the heavens, fully armed from head to foot" (458). Therefore, suggests Don Quixote, "knights errant [should get used to] sitting side by side on the hard ground accompanied by the solitude [of] the damp night air" (458, 521). Chivalric knights, says Don Quixote, must also make do with little amounts of food because "there are times when they go for a day or for two days without ever breaking fast" (564). Given that Sancho Panza is used to overeating Don Quixote trains him to ingest "herbs growing in the fields, [because] unfortunate knight errants like [him should deploy their ingenuity to] make up for [a] lack of food in fixes like this" (145). Don Quixote also deprives Sancho Panza of the creature comforts of a cushy lifestyle. Since Sancho Panza likes living a life of "plenty [and opulence] [in] Don Diego's house" and since Sancho Panza enjoys Basilio and Quiteria's hospitality "for three whole days," his master shows him that one should not indulge in life's luxuries for too long. Therefore, he makes Sancho Panza leave Don Diego's house after "four days" and the Duke and Duchesses castle after "a week" (607). In fact when they leave "the highway [to have] a late and inadequate supper [Sancho Panza is] reminded of all the hardship [that] knight-errants [endure] in the woods and the hills, even though on occasion there [is] abundance in castles and houses" (943). Evidently, this is how Don Quixote teaches Sancho Panza to steel himself for the trials, the tribulations, the challenges, and the difficulties, that are part and parcel of exercising the "honourable profession" of knight errantry (739). Don Quixote also enhances Sancho Panza's wisdom by imparting the following advice: "there is a remedy for all things but death; a man is known by the company he keeps; he who reads and travels, sees and learns; let us march on with a firm foot and honest intentions; they who live the longest see the most; a good name is better than great riches; our thoughts and our eyes must be kept aloof from everything lewd and obscene; patience often fails when it is overloaded with insults; good hope is better than bad holding; a good [mind] conquers ill fortune;

[when one lives] there is hope; well begun is half done; the honest truth will prevail over any lie; a jest that hurts is no jest; and, lastly, no sport is any sport if it damages others" (545, 659, 669, 705, 717, 890, 931, 732, 749, 757, 831, 840, 890, 906). This, then, is how Don Quixote refines Sancho Panza's awareness, so that he acquits himself well—both as an ordinary person in his day-to-day life and as a professional squire in a career setting. But this is not the only way Don Quixote and Sancho Panza enhance one another's awareness for they also teach each other the wisdom that they have learned in life—one from reading books, the other from listening to stories.

Don Quixote is literate and therefore gets his knowledge from book lore, while Sancho Panza is illiterate and therefore gets his knowledge from folk lore. They, in turn, share this knowledge with one another during their time together, thus enhancing each other's understanding of the world. First-off, Don Quixote is steeped in chivalric reading for his library consists of the four books of Amadis of Gaul, the very first chivalry tale to be printed in Spain, the exploits of Esplandian, a chivalric epic that explores the deeds of Amadis's son, Amadis of Greece, the sequel to Amadis of Gaul, the Knight Plantir, an old book of knight errantry, The Knight of The Cross, a Holy title that depicts the bravery of a daring Christian Knight, and The Mirror of Chivalry, a story about European chivalric nobility. Besides having these chivalric titles in his library, the narrator tells us that Alonso Quixana "took to reading books of chivalry with such relish and enthusiasm, [and] was so absorbed in these books, that he hardly slept, reading from sun up to sun down" (26, 27). This sentiment is echoed in Part I, chapter XVIII, when the narrator recounts that "Every minute of every hour his imagination was filled with those adventures, extravagances, loves and challenges that books of chivalry recount, and everything he said, thought or did was channeled into such affairs: battles; challenges; wounds; sweet nothings; love affairs; storms; and impossible absurdities" (139). Due to his intense reading, and rereading of chivalry books, he can recount the characteristics of knight's errant – the difficult situations they surmounted – the deeds that they performed – what they did or did not look like – their physical attributes, and, finally, their personal dispositions. Besides being immersed in chivalry books Don Quixote is well-read in poetry for he has studied Diana, one of the "best books of poetry" in Spain, "The Ten Books of Fortune and Love, written by Antonio de Lofraso, [as well as] The Nymphs of Henares, along with, The Undeceptions of Jealousy, The Treasury of Divers Poems, [and] Galatea" (56, 57, 58). During his adventures, Don Quixote draws from these, and other, poetic folios to amplify his points. For example, when Don Quixote is undressed by two maids at an inn he recites Sir Lancelot's ancient ballad about maidens and princesses serving a brave knight errant. Likewise, when Don Quixote overhears a tale about a beautiful woman who disguises herself as a shepherdess, he recounts a lyrical ballad "so well known and so highly praised in Spain [about] the smooth and gentle deeds of love and war" (34). Similarly, when doubts are cast on Dulcinea's "lineage and ancestry" Don Quixote recites a well-known poem "challenging all doubters [to] battle him" (96). Also, Don Quixote draws from his book knowledge to impart wisdom to others. For example, when the Duchess asks "what Demosthenic rhetoric is," Don Quixote replies that "Demosthenic rhetoric means the rhetoric of Demosthenses, just as Ciceronian rhetoric is the rhetoric of Cicero" (706). Or when Sancho Panza recounts an "old ballad," Don Quixote tells him that he sings about "a gothic king who went hunting and was eaten by a bear." (722). Also, Don Quixote has read many picaresque tales, like Lazarillo de Tormes, for example, the first such novel in Spain, in which a poor boy, Lazaro, describes his services under seven successive lay and clerical masters. It is also evident that Don Quixote has read, and watched, a good number of plays because he comments on: the nature and purpose of a fine play; what audiences frequent what sort of plays and why; the optimum structure and plot of high-quality plays; the function of drama in well-ordered societies; why dramatists

111

create the sorts of plays that they do; the motivation of playwrights when depicting certain events; the qualities of a devotional play, a religious play, a poetic play, and a courtly play; what the rules of artistic creation are when applied to dramaturgy; and, finally, the qualities of plays written for the general public versus plays written for the nobles. Don Quixote also comments on history books by delineating: the qualities of a good historian; the attributes of a good history tome; what history is and is not; how history books should or should not be organized; what makes for true histories; false histories; botched histories; tedious histories; inaccurate histories; real histories; popular histories; reliable histories; exulted histories; and, finally, the deeds of historical knights. But history is not the only type of writing Don Quixote is familiar with for he has read so many pastoral epics that he can realistically pretend to be a shepherd in love, which he gathers from rustic novels like: "The Garden of Flowers; Don Olivante de Laura; Palmerin of Olivia; Palmerin of England; Montemayor's Diana; The Shepherd of Iberia; The Shepherd of Filida; and The Book of Songs," to name just a few (53, 55, 56, 57, 58). So steeped is Don Quixote in pastoral verse that he imagines he will become "a shepherd for [a] year, and amuse himself in the solitude of the fields, where he [can] give free rein to his thoughts of love [and] practice a virtuous pastoral way of life" (973). In fact Don Quixote creates an entire pastoral microcosm drawn from his reading of idyllic books. Next, he devises a simple pastoral system where shepherds honour their shepherdess-ladies with free flowing verses of high praise, with carved tributes of their enduring love, and with plain salutations "that come printed in books like "Phyllises, Amaryllises, Fleridas, Galates, [and] Belisardas" (973). Don Quixote even says that "the custom of shepherds in love," according to pastoral books, is for each "to choose the name of the shepherdess he's going to honour" and then to embellish her name and sing her praises, for if a "shepherdess happens to be called Ana, [Don Quixote will] sing her praises under the name of Anarda; if she's francisca, [he'll] call her Francenia; if she's Lucia, Lucinda; etc.. And if Sancho Panza is going to join the club, he can sing his wife's praises with the name Teresina" (974). Though these literary names are appropriate for shepherds with obliging ladies, Don Quixote says that he has "no need to search for the name of a fictitious shepherdess, because [he] already [has] the peerless Dulcinea del Toboso, the glory of riverbanks, the ornament of meadows, the mainstay of beauty, the cream of grace, and, in short, one worthy to receive all praise, however hyperbolic it might [seem]" (974). Besides envisioning an elaborate pastoral romance drawn from reading various bucolic books, Don Quixote quotes great historical minds like: Aristotle; Augustus Caesar; Julius Caesar; Octavian; Alexander the Great; Helen of Troy; Hector of Troy; Achilles; Hauser; Homer; Virgil; Marco Polo; Hector; Aeneas; Ulysses; Methuselah; Zoroaster; Friar Puck; Prester John; Osiris; Charlemagne, Godfrey; Joshua; David; Judas; Magellan; Cato; King Arthur; Reynald de Montalban; El Cid; Don Galaor; and The Duke of Alba. Moreover, Don Quixote quotes Greek and Roman Gods like Apollo, Zeus, Diana, Hercules, Dido, Juno, Pegasus, Vulcan and Mars. Again he shows his vast reading when he paraphrases Religious saints like: Saint Thomas Aquinas, Saint Bartholomew, Saint George, Saint James, Saint Paul, Saint Martin and Saint Basil, to name just a few. In fact Don Quixote speaks with such eloquence, elegance even, that Sancho Panza praises his mental lucidity, rational penetration, and intellectual scope of knowledge by saying: "when he starts stringing his words of wisdom together and giving his advice, he could [not] only take up one pulpit in his hands but two on each finger [for] he says things that are so clever and to the point [that besides illuminating] chivalry doings he sheds light on many other subjects as well" (632, 714). Evidently, Don Quixote has such depth-and-breadth of encyclopedic book-learning that sometimes "Sancho [is] lost in admiration for his erudition and [thinks] that there [can't] be a single history or incident that he [hasn't] got at his fingertips and stamped on his [fine] memory" (876). Awed by Don Quixote's mental prowess

Sancho Panza expostulates: "[gosh] what an incredible master I've got! Is it possible for a man [to] say all of those brilliant things" (653). This, then, is how Don Quixote widens his squire's scope of knowledge through book learning.

In exchange, Sancho Panza enhances Don Quixote's mental outlook by: reciting verbal proverbs; transmitting oral folk-tales; and relating natural observations derived from spoken oral legends. For example, when Don Quixote and Sancho Panza do not know what to make of the noise made by six alternating fulling hammers, Sancho Panza thinks of "the lore [he] learned as a shepherd" which says that "dawn [is just] three hours away, because the Little Bear's mouth is on top of its head" (155). Even when Don Quixote questions Sancho's ability to tell "where [the] mouth of a small bear is so dark is the night," Sancho Panza says that he can still see stars "up in the sky [for one] only needs to use [his] head to realize that it isn't long until daybreak" (156). By rational tabulation of objective cosmic knowledge gained from transmitted oral wisdom, Sancho Panza reasons his way into understanding when a natural phenomenon will occur, so the pair can investigate, by dawn's early light, the source-origin of the ominous thumping. Besides referencing constellations to estimate the movement of cosmic orbs, Sancho Panza recounts a series of folksy proverbs to make a sequence of rational points. Examples of his moral maxims include, but are not limited to, the following: "A man is known by the company he keeps; you [cannot] cage in the sky [so] the sparrows will fly; a good heart conquers ill fortune; from now until tomorrow the hours are many and in any one of them, or in just one moment, [a person's life can change]; he who gives quickly gives twice; a word to the wise is enough; not who you are bred with but who you are fed with; a man who rings the alarm puts himself furthest from harm; out of sight out of mind; [others] help those who help themselves; a bird in the hand is worth two in the bush; danger lies in delay; anyone who can see a mote in another's eye better see the beam in his own; silence is golden; no man is better than the other unless he accomplishes more than the other; [in certain situations] a clean pair of heels is better than a good man's pleas; [those who] gossip about God who won't they gossip about; naked I was born and naked I remain; where there isn't any bacon there aren't any hooks to hang it from; the hare leaps up were you least expect it to; between a woman's yeah and a woman's nay I wouldn't try to put the point of a pin; do as your better says and sit down with him at table; a good name is better than great riches; a good payer's a good pledger; if I do what I ought to do and my intentions are good, I'm bound to govern like an angel; oh yes, they can come and stick their fingers in my mouth they can, and they'll soon see whether I bite or not; [since] gifts break rocks I will not accept any unmerited help; [and finally] it's all a question of starting to get the luck coming your way" (644, 206, 544, 612, 731, 945, 772, 943, 966, 772, 775, 774, 174, 943, 206, 544, 612, 682, 718, 723, 731, 829). These aphorisms convey to Don Quixote that the quality of person's character can be judged by the excellence of his associates; that a creature's need for freedom cannot be suppressed; that one can surmount any difficulty by being driven, hopeful, and optimistic; that a person can improve his, or her, life circumstances at any moment in time; that instant generosity given with a free-will amplifies one's munificence; that a relevant point made once is appreciated by intelligent others; that a person becomes friends with those he chooses to dine with; that a person who signals danger removes himself from hazard; that a person will not think of what is out of sight and out of mind; that a person who takes proactive, self-reliant, actions will move himself into a favorable position where others want to help him; that a person should be happy with what he has, not what he unrealistically thinks he can get; that a person should take a course of action that he knows is beneficial; if a person sees character flaws in others he better see realistic perfections in himself; that sometimes wisdom lies in knowing what not to say; that personal achievement distinguishes people from one another even if they are born equally; that when one is beset by irrational men intent on doing one harm it is wise to escape to safety instead of trying to reason with them; that one's values are sacred and should not be disrespected through speech; that a human being is born in a natural state and should die in a natural state too; that if prosperity is absent, signs of prosperity are absent as well; that a person can advance to life-success when one least expects him to; that once a woman's mind is made up it is difficult to change; that when one's superior makes a wise suggestion it should be followed; that one's virtue, one's honor, and one's innocence is of greater value than making money in a devious way; that people who make good on their promises abide by their pledges; that people who have the strength-of-character required to achieve a worthy goal will govern their interests well; that people who provoke simpletons will soon discover how their taunts are responded to; that firm principles can be adhered to if people only accept payment for their real output; and, finally, to succeed in any new initiative one must begin with intelligence. Through this collection of short, witty, sayings, Sancho Panza shares with his knight the ingenuity of Spanish folklore. In short, Sancho Panza is a member of the folk, who shares his oral wisdom with Don Quixote, while Alonso Quixano is a member of the nobility, who shares his written wisdom with his squire. As such, the former is practical and realistic, while the latter is theoretical and idealistic.

Being of common stock, Sancho Panza is shrewd, pragmatic, and cunning, while Don Quixote, being an aristocrat, is refined, idealistic, and principled. When it comes to money, for instance, Sancho Panza is very practical for he: demands "fixed wages" from Don Quixote; negotiates the back-pay he is owed; wants to be made an earl so that he can gain income from his lands; searches Cardenio's saddle bags to discover hidden treasure; hopes to sell a hunting outfit for cold, hard, cash; reminds Don Quixote to give him a governorship that will enable him to earn a steady income; and takes "foals born" of Don Quixote's "three-mares" over promises of forthcoming spoils (528, 679, 547). Also he has a practical, working, knowledge of foreign languages, like Italian, for example, which he uses to gain intelligence from pilgrims he meets when venture questing. This is why he greets strange travelers with salutations like: "Bon compagno, Jura di!." His life experiences also show his practical side because being "a steward in a confraternity back home" has prepared him to equip, keep track of, and dispense, the provisions that they need to survive (773). Moreover, because he "was a beadle" trusted with keeping order in his local village parish he is able to enforce the law during his town patrols of Barataria (175). Other practical jobs he had "as a little lad" range from farming to goat herding to tending "geese [and] pigs" (763, 716, 768). These pragmatic experiences prepare him to partake in an elaborate fantasy about shepherding. Above all, though, he, himself, acknowledges he is practical by saying "I'm so practical" (527). Don Quixote, on the other hand, is not practical at all. Not in the least. Since he is a hidalgo living on a ready income, he does not work for a living. Rather, he spends his free-time coursing with a mangy grey-hound and reading many books of chivalry. In fact, Don Quixote is so absorbed in the theory of knight errantry that "he almost forgets about hunting [altogether or even] running his property" (26). So consumed is he with abstract reasoning that when he visits inns he does not pay for his room or board. Nor does he pay for the straw or barley that his emaciated horse eats. And when money is demanded of him he says that since "knight errants did not pay for their lodging or for anything else at an inn where they stayed [and since] whatever hospitability they receiv[ed] [was] due to them as a right and a privilege" he too shall not pay (134). Jail-time is insignificant to him. In fact it does not apply to him. Therefore he frees a group of prisoners on their way to the galleys, unconcerned with the Holy Brotherhood's retaliation. It seems that this rural police squad is nothing more than a minor annoyance to Don Quixote to be bested by his mighty arm, not a formidable fighting force capable of swift reprisal. What's more, Don Quixote often acts out of idealism and righteousness, without much regard for practicality. For example, when he threatens to "exterminate and annihilate a burly farmer" for whipping a farmhand who asks for his back-wages, he trusts the farmer's sworn promise to pay his day laborer for services rendered (42, 43). Since Don Quixote thinks that his stentorian commands, coupled with an oath given in the style of chivalry, will be enough to ensure instant obedience, he departs before money exchanges hands. Later, we discover, that when Don Quixote leaves the wood, Juan Haldudo (for this is the farmer's name) "tie[s] [Andres] back to the same oak tree [and gives] him a fresh flogging cracking a joke [with every lash] about how he was making a fool of Don Quixote" (287). Even though Don Quixote acknowledges that "he should not have departed [in the first place because] he knows from long experience, that [a wicked] peasant [will not] keep his word if he thinks that breaking it will profit him" – he does so anyway despite his [better] judgement" (287). But the fact that he trusts a tricky farmer to follow through on a promise conveys his practical naivety. Though Don Quixote is theoretical and abstract without much regard for practicality and Sancho Panza is practical and hard-nosed, without much regard for theory, together they become a complete unit through a synergy of character traits.

To start with, let us recount how Sancho Panza complements Don Quixote through his practical sense of survival, particularly in the unforgiving world of hard reality. First, he teaches Don Quixote that if he wants to avoid being accosted by innkeepers, or enjailed for dereliction of payment, he should compensate landlords for his stay at their motels. After his first sally, for example, when Don Quixote travels alone and does not pay for his overnight "stay, supper, bed, straw and barley" he takes his neighbor Sancho Panza along with him, who, in turn, carries hard-currency in his saddle-bags to pay Don Quixote's way (332). Without the presence of a practical person, like Sancho Panza, to handle all of Don Quixote's fiscal transactions, it is likely that Don Quixote would have been arrested and sent to debtors, prison. Second, Sancho Panza is sometimes allowed to guide

Don Quixote to an appropriate shelter point away from the wilds of the Spanish countryside so that the pair can avoid lurking dangers such as: wild beasts; passing storms; hidden bandits, and the like. This point is stated explicitly when Cervantes has Sancho Panza "choose [suitable] lodging[s]" for the night (145). Left to his own devices, Don Quixote would probably plop down at the first convenient place even if it was located in a hazardous geographical region. Third, if Don Quixote was left to decide what they should and should not eat and in what amount, the duo would probably starve to death. Rejecting Don Quixote's claim that they can live on wild herbs and roots, and the occasional natural nut, Sancho Panza produces real food from his saddle bag pantry, like: chunks of goat meat; lumps of cheese; nuts-and-raisins; feathered provisions, and loaves of white bread. Without his ample larder of provisions, it is likely that Don Quixote would be too weak to battle. Fourth, absent Sancho Panza's practical presence, Don Quixote would push himself too hard by not resting and gathering his strength when adventuring along the highways and byways of Spain. This is why after the pair is trampled by a drove of raging bulls, Sancho Panza wisely suggests that Don Quixote "lay himself down on [a] green mattress of grass [to] have a little nap" (884). Moreover, if Don Quixote decided what to do, or not to do, it is likely he would have tried to venture along the road to Barcelona, despite being sore wounded. In short, Sancho Panza's common sense pragmatism which he derives from living in the real world of harsh survival, renders him able to calculate how the pair will gain what they need to survive. It is in this way that Sancho Panza acts as a counterbalancing foil to check Don Quixote's quixoticism.

In reverse, Don Quixote's abstract sense of idealism and morality guides Sancho Panza to realize that life is not just about fulfilling one's practical survival needs it is also about fulfilling one's higher spiritual moral needs such as "righting wrongs; correcting injustices; relieving the needy; defending maidens; protecting widows; succoring orphans; avenging the offended; punishing treachery; assisting the helpless; redressing grievances; succoring the wretched; favoring the oppressed; defending women's honor; upholding promises; protecting wards; punishing insolence; redressing outrages; remedying distress; forgiving the modest; destroying the cruel; and observing the will to do good to people of all kinds" (36, 85, 111, 134, 139, 150, 177, 183, 205, 284, 584, 643, 701, 739, 840, 879, 887). By way of example, Don Quixote teaches Sancho Panza that he can create the world anew by generating good-will between and among human beings. For this reason he compels, or at least tries to compel, a "rich farmer [from] Quintar" to pay the back wages he owes a farm laborer working for him for "nine months" (43). Don Quixote also upholds the principle that one should pay for received services by "persuading four men" to pay for their stay at an inn. He is so convincing, in fact, that with his "fine words" the muleteers consent to "pay their bill in full" (414,416). Generosity is another primary virtue that Don Quixote enacts when he gives a lion keeper "two ducats to make amends for" battling his lions (597). Indeed by being true to his word and by following through with his promises Don Quixote tries to instill a sense of honesty in Sancho Panza. Accordingly he jousts the Duke's lackey Tosilos to make him keep his word to marry Donna Rodriguez's daughter. Destroying the wicked is yet another principle Don Quixote enacts when he vouches to slay an evil usurper giant named Malumbrino who disenfranchises the Princess Micomicona from her inheritance and birthright. Fighting for people's freedom is another ideal that Don Quixote foreswears when he battles to rescue Melisendra from the Moors in Spain. Through, it is true, many of Don Quixote's deeds, thoughts, sayings and doings are misguided, delusional even, it is also true that he is always well-intentioned, and occasionally, he creates real benefits for distressed people. In turn, because Sancho Panza witnesses Don Quixote's sense of justice, generosity, chivalry, and bravery, he begins to act on a long view of morality. As such, he is no longer motivated solely by a short term practical desire to gain material goods, rather he is actuated by a long term theoretical need to live according to an abstract moral code. This is why Sancho Panza translates principles of quixotic moral leadership into real world tangible benefits. The most striking example of Sancho Panza turning idealism into realism occurs when he becomes governor of Barataria for ten days. During his time in power he: judges legal cases according to principles of objective fairness; monitors a whole host of merchants so that they are honest with their customers; enforces security and stability in Barataria by prosecuting criminal predators; teaches the populas how to farm so that they can produce comestibles; gives his superiors a clear account of what he did during his incumbency, and rejects all manner of bribes, solicitations, loans, and other temptations. The earlier Sancho Panza would probably have collected his money happily with little or no regard for who suffered as a result. Yet thanks to Don Quixote's influence he learns to live morally. In sum, Don Quixote's more intellectual and abstract approach of moral living balances Sancho Panza's more practical survival approach of concrete existence. Thus, Cervantes balances idealism and morality with realistic practicality in such a way that readers, by default, learn to harmonize these two vital elements to succeed in life.

In conclusion, since Don Quixote needs Sancho Panza to operate in the real world of concrete existents and Sancho Panza needs Don Quixote to function in the realm of abstract ideals, together they form a constructive synergy where both partners merge their life skills into a cooperative union of sorts. This is why Don Quixote and Sancho Panza's goal in life is to revive the forgotten code of knight errantry by fusing the moral and practical together to enact virtue effectively. Without one the other would be lesser yet together they synergize into a moral-practical unity that is *sui generous* in creative literature. It is for this reason that Don Quixote and Sancho Panza embody the essence of what idealism and realism mean in carnal form. And it is for this reason, and for this reason alone, that we not only associate idealism with Don Quixote De La Mancha but practicality with Sancho Panza the squire.

Essay 4

Good Politics in Sancho Panza's Governorship: *How an Intelligent Commoner Refines Into a Great Governor Through A Series Of Jokes That Turn Earnest.*

Sancho Panza becomes a great governor of a town called Barataria, on the island of Baratario, because people around him teach him: how to be a fair judge of character; how to be true to himself; how to maintain his integrity; how to perpetuate his identity; how to introspect; how to budget his time; how to read; how to write; how to speak; how to eat; how to dress; how to practice good hygiene; how to carry his body; how to oversee merchants; how to treat Baratarites well; how to deal with gossip; how to deal with laziness; how to deal with malingerers; how to encourage productivity; how to view his ancestry; how to view other people's descent; how to enact virtue; how to discard vice; how to repel frontal military assaults; how to repel hidden clandestine attacks, all so that he has a guiding moral sense of how a refined town governor should live not only carrerwise, in his professional life, but also personally, as a living, breathing, human-being intent on living a good life.

While many prominent people teach Sancho Panza many significant leadership lessons from without many of his mental attitudes come from within and are only drawn forward and intensified during his governorship. Phrased another way, before becoming governor Sancho Panza's views are in a latent, underdeveloped, unexpressed form, yet when he becomes governor, his ideas become more specific. By thinking about how he should allot entrusted financial resources; how he should form justice during his town patrols; how he should reform jailed criminals; how he should exercise shrewdness when judging townsmen; how he should provide food to energize people; how he should neutralize organized predators who try to bilk citizens out of their money; how he should refine his wife so that she leads well; how he should illustrate loyalty for his civic mentors, his ideas in all of these areas become more exact. So while Sancho Panza uses other people's guidance to take-on a refined set of moral virtues for himself he also has many latent characteristics deep within him which he self-amplifies to realize an honorable mode of mental functioning that helps him understand who he is, what his end-goal should be and how he can get there. What's more, all of Sancho Panza's experiences as a governor (i.e. the responsibilities, the obligations, the tests, and the challenges of his office) actualize a specific set of character traits within him through a process of humor that turns earnest.

So no, his governorship is no mean-spirited joke, staged by two depraved aristocrats, to get a laugh at a rural peasant's clumsiness: Rather, it is Cervantes's way of shielding himself against negative repercussions he would have faced if he told pointed social truths in a more straightforward way.

Cervantes hides serious social criticism of the clergy, of aristocracy, and of society by being purposefully vague, which he expresses through talk-around terms couched in irony and sarcasm and humour. In effect Cervantes wrote in a joke-disguised style because he not only wanted to publish and circulate his novel in Spain but also because he wanted to protect himself from personal reprisals – physical, mental, and existential. Therefore, to guard against sudden execution; physical compulsion; perpetual exile; or the confiscation of his wealth, Cervantes used a technique of soft humor to blunt his social jabs. In this way he moderates a serious critical-sting with a series of funny light-hearted jokes to get society to laugh at his book and accept it into their midst instead of rejecting it outright. So all this business of a bunch of idle aristocrats, abetted by their servants and lackeys, to stage a comical farce, to get a laugh at Sancho Panza's funny rural ways, is a mistaken interpretation that mischaracterizes Sancho Panza's governorship because what begins as a joke soon turns serious.

Although the Duke, the Duchess and their servants joke with Sancho Panza by duping him into believing that he is governor of Barataria—when, really, his civil-power, his abundant attentions, and his exaggerated loyalties begin as an elaborate hoax to get a laugh at his personal botchery—his tricksters, to wit, are genuinely surprised by the mixture of his intelligent behavior, and simple naïveté, and wonder if they themselves are being fooled, in the process of their foolery, and if, somehow, Sancho Panza has the inherent potential to be a good governor if he is led by others to reform his moral character. In effect, what makes Sancho Panza's jesters analyze his basic mindset is his mixed mode of conduct which combines wise sayings, sage doings, incisive penetration and witty candor, on the one hand, with silly speech, foolish deeds, and obtuse density, on the other hand, or a method of operation that is, on balance, both positive and negative, at the same time. This flitting back-and-forth between two opposite poles of conduct makes Sancho Panza's jokers question whether their quips have great, or small, impact on his governorship; if their buffoonery combines with other factors to influence his rule and if their jokes accelerate, or retrogress, his transformative process of adapting to office. By the end of Sancho Panza's governorship it becomes clear to his jokers that their quips remove his faults, at least in part, so that he takes on the virtues of a purified character. In essence, then, what begins as a light-hearted jest to see how Sancho Panza will act as a pretend-governor turns into a stead-fast effort to groom him into a civil leader.

As part and parcel of this transfigurative effort, the Duke and Duchess of Aragon kid with Sancho Panza to amuse themselves, yet their actions soon become pursuant to his gubernatorial actions in that they want to see what he does as a leader, establish why he does it, and determine its overall political impact on the town of Baratario. Hence, the Duke "giv[es]" Sancho Panza a "round and well-proportioned, fertile walled town of about five thousand inhabitants nam[ed] Baratario [on] the Island of Barataria [with] the Duke's, very intelligent butler in [overall] charge of [the] operation [of] handling Sancho Panza [who, in turn, is] coached by his master and mistress" (766, 777, 785, 825, 828). Because royalty senses that they "ha[ve] such a suitable subject who [will] take their jests in earnest [they] tell their servants how to behave to Sancho [Panza] during his governorship of the promised island" (766, 777). In this way aristocracy monitors how Sancho Panza acts in a variety of staged township scenario's ranging from courtroom dramas to street patrols to market inspections to private audiences to elaborate feasts to other secular activities. During these scenes they test his leadership qualities to see if he has the ability to govern well, or not. In addition, royalty holds out beguiling but harmful allurements like bribes, for example, or other more subtle forms of influence peddling, like flattery, for instance, to see if, and how, Sancho Panza overcomes temptations. By experimenting with him in this way, royalty tries to determine whether Sancho Panza is worthy of taking the reins of civil command, or not. In other words, because royalty thinks that Sancho Panza is on the cusp of generating a self-initiated change of mind and heart, they erect a gubernatorial training exercise to get him to stop acting foolishly. Hence, they test him out, through humor, to see if he can be a good governor.

Although officialdom casts a mock gubernatorial simulation designed to build Sancho Panza's managerial ability, other people, who are not in the know, believe that his governorship is real—like his erstwhile acquaintances, for example, or innocent townspeople, for instance. Therefore, during Sancho Panza's governorship, many different kinds of people "who aren't in the secret" treat his rule as if it were real (786). These individuals include: two old men who quarrel over a debt; a woman who brings forward a rape charge; a herdsmen who claims he is innocent of rape but guilty of prostitution; a farmer who objects to a tailor's undersized clothing; a tailor who resents a farmer for stereotyping his profession; a girl who runs away from an overprotective father; a brother who helps his sister escape from home; a lad who loiters on the streets in defiance of authority; a gambler who feels he is right to keep his money; a knifer who robs a gambler for retaining his winnings; a market-woman who cheats her customers with faulty goods; Sancho Panza's fellow villagers back home along with his wife, his daughter, and his son. Many of these people, though surprised, think that his governorship is legitimate: Hence, by word, by action, by saying, and by doing, they help him transform from a simple country farmer to a sometimes wise governor of one of the Duke's "most important towns" (785). In brief, since many Baratarites think that Sancho's governorship is real his administration takes on a generative life of its own.

Jokery aside, then (which is a safety valve mechanism to amuse the casual reader) Sancho Panza's ten-day governorship focuses on him training for and growing into the office of a judge; a legislator; a marshal; a deputy; a jailer; a warden; a market inspector; a commercial attaché; and a civil administrator who, in effect, is invested with inferred representative powers to act and speak independently on behalf of the Duke and Duchess "of Aragon" via their primary, mouth-piece, emissary—the wily, though sometimes wise, Don Quixote de la Mancha (890). In essence, then, part II, book chapter XLII through book chapter XLVIII, is not merely an episode of light-hearted entertainment written to amuse the noncritical reader, but is actually Cervantes's way of preparing the overall mind-state of a civil governor, so that he is fit to represent the people and think on their behalf in matters of civil law, market economics, and moral ethics, and who thus, by dint of his abilities, earns the right to be entrusted plenipotentiary powers to overwatch executive civics. Most importantly, though, Sancho Panza's governorship focuses on the operations of Don Quixote's mind and proves that when he thinks of matters other then chivalry he is quite logical.

In an effort to improve Sancho Panza's critical thinking skills (so that he becomes politically *fool-proof*) Don Quixote suggests that he have a reliable starting point of thought to base his system of governing ideas upon because "a fool knows nothing, either in his own house or in another's for on a foundation of folly no edifice of good sense can ever be constructed" (775). This quote suggests that because items of knowledge stand in a certain relationship to prior items of knowledge Sancho Panza should construct his gubernatorial ideas on a realistic base of thought, so that his concepts ring true and clear. Judging by Don Quixote's oration "thanking heaven" for "turning [a] fool into a man of good sense;" Sancho Panza transforms his mind by the end of his governorship (834). In this sense, Sancho Panza's tomfoolery is reversed, at least for a time, by dint of Don Quixote's advice giving coupled with Sancho Panza's remedial efforts, as well.

Besides being lead to form his ideas on reasonable grounds, Sancho Panza also turns the tables on his jokers through his words, deeds, and actions, which makes people wonder if his governorship is somehow real. Early in his term, for example, he is aware that certain people are trying to fool him: "Oh yes, they can just try pooh-poohing me and calling me names [but] if they think they're coming out to shear me they'll find themselves going back shorn" (773). Later in his governorship, after he penetrates a ruse designed to "make fun of him" Sancho Panza advises his jokers to not "try to pull the wool over [his] eyes" (812, 813). Surprised, the "very intelligent" butler, one of the Duke's wisest servants, "writes to his master and mistress about what Sancho Panza said and did, as amazed as [he was] at his sayings as at his doings" (773, 831). He even wonders if somehow he is being tricked himself for he exclaims: "In this world everyday brings new surprises; jest turns into earnest, and jesters find the tables turned on them" (814). This, then, is how Sancho Panza's governorship turns real, at least in the mind's of some; like the Duke's page, for example, who believes that "Senor Sancho is a genuine governor, and [that his] master and mistress the Duke and Duchess have given him the governorship, [in which post] he is performing most admirably" (830). Most importantly, though, in the process of their buffoonery, some of the Duke's servants either become the butt of their own jokes, so smart is Sancho Panza, or end-up believing that his governorship is genuine. Therefore, while Sancho Panza's kidders test his resolve through humor, their japes create a positive governmental momentum in the town of Baratario.

Sancho Panza takes to mind-and-heart his newfound leadership responsibilities, especially with regard to preserving a governor's lifestyle requirements, screening out importunities on his time, and setting up formal audiences to transact town business, all of which he speaks on thusly:

> Aren't we governors, we judges, men of flesh and blood, who've got to be allowed to rest for as long as we need to – or do [people] think we're made of marble. Now I really do see that governors ought to be and need to be made of bronze so as not to be worn out by all the [questioning] from these folks who come on business and expect you to listen to them and deal with them at all hours of the day and night. So, all you [people who] come on business don't be in such a hurry wait until the proper time fixed for audiences
>
> (800, 812).

In the above excerpt, Sancho Panza feels that certain categories of unthoughtful people intrude on him at the wrong time and in the wrong way, and are insensitive to his requirements – not only as a governor responsible for managing the town's affairs but also as a living, breathing, human being, who needs to eat, sleep, and rest to relax and restore his mental and physical functions. Therefore, he "says to everyone present [in] the hall [to not] come when its' time for [him] to be eating or sleeping because [he] must give to nature what nature naturally needs" (812). He even intends to "put the screws on some people [who] come on business, so busy [is he] with all the things [he] must deal with" (800, 836). During one episode, for example, a tricky farmer comes to Sancho Panza, at an inappropriate time, asking him for a letter of marriage recommendation and "six hundred" ducats in dowry. Sancho Panza flatly rejects his request on the grounds that his story is a "lie" and that he cannot "afford the [prohibitive] expense as a new governor" (803, 804). He even urges the farmer "to get a move on [because] this is a time for sleep not for business" (802). By vocalizing his dismissive authority in this way, Sancho Panza emphasizes his privacy concerns to the public in the hopes that eager favor seekers will get the message and not importune him in an unwelcome way. Here we see Sancho Panza prioritize his efforts and budget his time so that he attends to and completes his obligations in a professional manner, especially given his post of official responsibility, which requires that he determine the order of magnitude of the civil-business presented to him so that he can implement a job task with hierarchical efficiency.

To make good use of his time, Sancho Panza wants to get to the heart of matters quickly, render his decisions swiftly, and then move on to other important public affairs. He exemplifies this brevity when a young girl and her brother recount a longwinded story about how they snuck out of their father's house in disguise to avoid detection. During their explanation of events he does not waste time contemplating their drawn-out tale nor does he delay to unravel their circumlocutions; rather he is clearly "in despair at the way the girl was spinning out her story, and he told her to relieve [him] of [his] suspense, because it was late and there was still a lot more of the town to patrol" (820). After the girl crystallizes the gist of her adventure, (without fanciful exaggerations and weeping hysterics) Sancho Panza says:

> To be sure, my young friend, this has been a very childish prank, and to explain this silly escapade of yours there wasn't any need for all that stalling and sighing and sobbing, because if you'd just said, "[I'm] so-and-so and so-and-so, and [I] left [my] parents house to have a bit of fun, in [this] disguise, just out of curiosity, without any other thought in mind, that would have been that, without any whining or blubbering or going on and on and on

(821).

In mediation of the youth's transgressions, Sancho Panza tells both siblings that their actions have caused "no harm" and even offers to take them home, provided that they "don't behave like little children in the future" (821). In this instance, he eases the conscience of youthful minds by being gentle and kind, yet, at the same time, he suggests that the youngsters should act like mature adults by crystallizing their narrative explanations with concision, especially in consideration of their governor's time. Evidently, the content and shortness of Sancho Panza's response to a child's excited, yet improvable, explanation of events, shows readers that he not only wants to distill the truth of matters quickly but that he can mobilize the appropriate reaction to maximize his time-effect as a governor.

Although Sancho Panza does not waste time as a governor he does not rush to error for efficiency's sake nor does he construct an argument precipitously. Rather, he takes time to determine what happened, why it happened, and what to do about it. For instance, when he asks "a woman wearing man's clothes who she [is] where she [is] going and what made her dress up like that" and she gives a false identity, "the daughter of Pedro Perez Mazorca," and claims that she is "an unfortunate young girl driven by jealousy" to seek her lover, Sancho Panza points out that her story is inconsistent because "Pedro Perez Mazorca hasn't got any children" therefore she should "not be afraid to tell [him] what really happened" (818, 819). Before she responds, the butler tells Sancho Panza that her "widowed" father keeps his child "shut away" without "even giving the sun a chance to glimpse her" (819). After "comforting [the girl] with the best words he [can] find [Sancho Panza] asks her to tell" him, in her own speech, "what happened" (819). She replies:

> The fact is gentlemen, ever since my father laid my mother in her grave [he] has kept me [under house arrest]. Being locked up like this and never allowed to leave home, not even to go to church, has been making me feel depressed for a long, long, time; I wanted to see the world, or at least the town I was born in, and I didn't believe this wish infringed the decorum that young ladies of rank are supposed to observe

(819, 820).

Instead of making a snap absolute decision based on false criteria and in lieu of penalizing a "sixteen" year-old for her fibs, Sancho Panza "puts [her] curiosity down to her youth" and escorts her home in the hopes that "maybe [her] father hasn't missed her" (821, 822). Evidently, rather than acting with rashness because he is lied to Sancho Panza crystallizes a girl's real motivation for flying to the streets before he makes a decision and follows through with it. It is in this manner that Sancho Panza registers the facts methodically.

Besides teaching Governor Panza to use his time in reception of the facts, Don Quixote also teaches him to objectify his examination of a legal case to determine: what did and did not happen; who is innocent and who is guilty; what is an appropriate and inappropriate sentence; how the verdict should and should not be delivered, and, most importantly, what *life-effect* his decision has on the people involved. Therefore, to get his squire to engage in a case-by-case decisional process of fact gathering and data analysis Don Quixote propounds the following judicial precepts:

Never make your whim the measure of the law

(769).

Let the poor man's tears move you to greater compassion, but not to greater justice, than the rich man's allegations

(769).

Try to discover the truth as much among the rich man's gifts and promises as among the poor man's sobs and entreaties

(769).

Whenever leniency can and should play its part, do not apply the full rigour of the law to the delinquent, for the cruel judge does not enjoy a better renown than the compassionate one

(769).

If you do bend the rod of justice, let it not be with the weight of a gift but with the weight of mercy

(769).

When you have to judge a case involving one of your enemies, forget all about your grievances and concentrate on the facts of the matter

(769).

Do not let your own feelings blind you to others'
claims; for most of the mistakes that you make will
not be reversible, and if they are it will be at the cost
of your reputation or even of your pocket

(769).

If a beautiful woman comes to seek justice, turn your
eyes away from her tears and your ears away from her
lamentations, and ponder over the merits of her plea,
unless you want your reason to be drowned in her
tears and your integrity in her lamentations

(769).

If you are going to have a man punished with deeds,
do not batter him with words, because the suffering
the wretch is to undergo is enough, without the
addition of any vilification

(769).

Think of the culprit whose case comes before you
as one worthy of pity, and as far as you can, without
prejudice to the contrary party, be compassionate and
lenient

(769).

All of the above stated veridical standards are aimed at making
Sancho Panza realize that a judge must thoroughly cogitate and
carefully deliberate when making legal decisions; that a judge must
not only make a fair-and-balanced legal decision based on a clear
line of reasoning but he must also match his objective judgments
with dispassionate emotions. Additionally, Cervantes shows readers
that a judge must illustrate a fair sense of mercy in cases where

clemency is possible and moderation is appropriate; that a judge must render decisions based on the facts and merits of a case; that a judge must utilize a dispassionate process of adjudication, no matter what is being judged or who is being judged; that a judge must display a proper degree of severity, not less than is warranted and not more than is necessary, and finally, if a judge chastises a man with punishing actions then he should not reprove him with reproachful words as well. As we see, here, this psychological legal counsel encourages Sancho Panza to account for case facts, to figure out the relationships between those facts, to form those facts into a whole picture, to determine who is telling the truth, who is lying, what decision should be reached, what sentence should be passed, how it should be passed, and to what effect. Evidently, Sancho Panza consults and implements Don Quixote's legal theory when he judges individual cases.

As a civil judge, Sancho Panza enacts Don Quixote's judicial advice when he settles personal legal disputes. For instance, in Part II, chapter XLV, when he first "takes control" of Barataria people come to him with differences of opinion, some of whom are truthful and honest in their claims for restitution, while others are less than candid in their assertions (786). During one period of debate, for example, "two old men" present competing and contradictory claims about a debt (787). The plaintiff claims that he lent the defendant "ten gold escudos, as a special favour, on the condition that [the other party] repays [him] when [he] asks" (787). He then claims that when he asks "again and again not only does [the defendant] not repay the debt, he says that he never borrowed the ten escudos in the first place" (788). As public arbitrator of this disagreement Sancho Panza "considers the patience of the plaintiff," notes the objections of the defendant, and, then, thinks back, retrospectively, to a time at the beginning of the trial, when he asked the defendant to swear an oath "on" his "staff of office" averring that he never lent the plaintiff the money in the first place, or, if he did, that he "returned the money" to him long ago (788). When the plaintiff promises the court that the debt never existed, Sancho Panza recalls that before oath-swearing he "handed the other man" a cane to "hold" (788). After considering this fact and pondering the claimant's character types, Sancho Panza gives the plaintiff the cane to hold and orders that it be "split open" and lo-and-behold, out pops ten gold escudos (789). Thus, we see, here, that Sancho Panza exercises his legal acumen to expose the ruse of an old man who does not want to pay back his debt, who evades the truth to hide his lie, and who deludes himself, on the basis of a specious technicality, into the false-belief that his conscience is clear. In this instance, by carefully sorting out case-facts for relevancy and then pondering those items with quick deliberation, Sancho Panza judiciously solves a civil dispute; and, in the process, he accomplishes two goals: he avoids creating unnecessary trouble between two disputing parties and he prevents a needless waste of the court's time by rendering a swift and accurate summary judgment that is fair and reasonable and that applies and upholds the law.

Besides forming justice in a debt dispute Sancho Panza reproves that he "has what it takes to govern a kingdom," when he arbitrates another disagreement between a farmer, on the one hand, who overreaches by asking for too many hoods to be made from a single length of cloth, and a tailor, on the other hand, who seems to comply with a farmer's material request only to produce "five tiny hoods on his fingertips" in court (787, 789). As presiding judge, Sancho Panza delivers this judgment: "I don't think there's any need for long delays in this case – what's needed is an on-the-spot commonsense verdict, so my decision is that the tailor will forfeit his pay and the farmer his cloth, and the hoods will be given to the prisoners in jail, and there's an end to it" (787). This decision not only chastens a farmer for his prejudice against all tailors, and, therefore, his assumption that a particular tailor will "try to filch some cloth" for himself, it also admonishes a tailor for cheating a "suspicious" farmer when he should have diminished his distrust with frankness (787). Most importantly, by delivering this verdict Sancho Panza teaches the farmer that instead of stereotyping the tailor because of his past experiences with other tailors he should treat each and every tailor as a unique individual; he teaches the tailor that he can refute the farmer's typecast of him by not playing into his personal prejudices; he teaches the farmer and the tailor to extend a degree of goodwill for one another (at least, at first, until and unless that respect is defaulted on by the other person's speech or actions) and, lastly, he delivers justice to the farmer and the tailor with fairness. Besides doing all of this, Sancho Panza's decision hastens the court's docket, confers rehabilitative benefits to penal detainees, and delivers the message that prisoners who are trying to be good and are making headway in that effort will have their loads lightened by their governor.

In an attempt to rehabilitate criminals so that they are fit for society Sancho Panza holds out hope to lawbreakers to inspire them to reform. During one instance, for example, when a constable approaches him "clutching a young man" by the collar, instead of finding him guilty of wrongdoing and enjailing him, Sancho Panza questions him to find out why he ran from the law, what he was doing out on the streets and what his trade-craft is (816). The youth replies that he ran away "to avoid answering all of the questions the authorities always ask;" that he was outside to "take the air" and that he "weaves iron lance heads" by profession (816). Sensing that there is more to this "clever young lad's story" then his witty answers Sancho Panza threatens to "take him to where he will see with his own two eyes how wrong he is" (817). To avoid jail the boy asserts:

> let's be reasonable and come to the point. Suppose
> you have me taken to prison, and there they clap me
> in fetters and chains, and stick me in a [lightless]
> dungeon, and threaten the jailer with an enormous
> fine if he lets me out, and then suppose he obeys all
> of his orders – regardless of all that, if I don't want to
> sleep, and I decide to stay awake all night long without

> closing an eye, will you be capable, with all of your
> power, of making me sleep if I don't want to?

In light of the young man's age, for the "good straight answers that he gives," because he is innocent of any egregious guilt, coupled with the fact that he is honest, at least, and fairly "witty," too, Governor Panza releases him with a stern-warning "that from now on [he mustn't] make fun of the authorities [because] other [police officers] that [he] comes across [may] make [him] pay for [his] japes with a cracked skull" (816, 818). Besides administering judicial clemency here, Sancho Panza inspires model prisoners to reform their characters by giving funds to the repentant so that their time in rehabilitation is eased a bit. This, he does, by adding "thirty [extra reals to a gambler's fine] for penniless prisoners" (815). Moreover, to lighten the load of reforming criminals, Don Quixote counsels Sancho Panza to "lead [model inmates] to expect an early release" for good behavior and to "visit the prisons" often for "prisoner comfort" so that with constructive attention deserving convicts are fitted for freedom (835). These penal actions prove that while Sancho Panza is prepared to enforce the full rigor of law, especially if lied to, he can still be merciful, at times, if the occasion suits clemency. In sum, Sancho Panza has some sympathy for repentant prisoners hence he appeals, at times, to their better angels, by being merciful.

Because lawman Panza treats prisoners with punishment, yes, if necessary, but also with moderation, if warranted, and because judge Panza adjudicates many cases with well-reasoned theory and swift practical dispatch he inspires "all those present [with] astonishment," like, "the man, [for example], who was recording his words, deeds and movements [and] couldn't make up his mind whether to regard him as a simpleton or as a sage:" Or, another man, for instance, who was "struck with amazement at his new governors verdicts and decisions" (789, 791). Even the Duke's butler is "astounded to see that a man as untaught as [Sancho Panza] can make so many observations full of wise maxims and good counsel, so different from what is expected from [his] mind" (814). Besides drawing forth "amazement [from] all those who know [him]" induced from hearing him "speak with such elegance," a messenger, too, is astonished by Sancho Panza's trenchant mind and exclaims: "It is precisely as my lord governor says and as far as a full understanding of the case goes, his account leaves nothing to be desired or open to doubt" (812, 833). Such startling personal reactions to Sancho Panza's character and decisions refutes his widely held popular reputation as a doddering country bumpkin thereby earning him the startled esteem of witness onlookers, of all stripes and varieties, who witness concrete and significant evidence of his quick and accurate mental judgment.

In keeping with his newfound status, Sancho Panza exercises flashes of penetration when he foils the designs of people who try to deceive him. When a "farmer [for example] a man of [seemingly] good presence" recounts a rambling, ponderous story about a "pock-marked girl" named "Clara Perlerina who lives in the same village as his son," Sancho Panza asks him "what [he] wants" and to "come to the point [of his tale] without beating about the bush or sidestepping, without cutting anything out or adding anything on" (802, 803). So compelled, the farmer quickly asks him "for the favour of writing a letter of marriage recommendation to her father" and requests "six hundred ducats in dowry towards setting up his house" so that the couple can "live on their own" (803). This response angers Sancho Panza who "fum[es] with rage at [the] wheedling portrait painting farmer." (804). Greatly upset, he asks him "where [he] expects a day-and-a-half-old governor [to get] six hundred ducats from" swearing on "the soul of [his] master the Duke" that he is a "scoundrel sent from hell to tempt [him]" (812, 803). Cowered by this fulmination, "the farmer leave[s] the hall with his head bowed and look[s] frightened that the governor might turn his fury into action, because the rogue played his part with great conviction" (804). Later, we discover that the "farmer [was] coached by the butler, who in turn was coached by the Duke, [to make] fun of him; but Sancho Panza held his own against them all" (812). In short, by being a shrewd judge of character, Sancho Panza upholds his Ducal oath to "do [his] best to be a [good] governor despite all of the rogues standing in his way" (766).

What accounts for Sancho Panza's penetration flashes are the principles, the rules, and the instructions that Don Quixote gives him to purify his values, remove his abuses and correct his faults which Sancho Panza takes-in, makes his own, and acts upon. To prove this claim, let's think about Sancho Panza's mental focus when he first hears Don Quixote's gubernatorial instructions. During this time he "listens to his master's advice with rapt attention, tries to store [it] in his memory, because he is determined to follow [it] and with its help bring the pregnancy of his government to a successful delivery" (770). True to his word he vows: "Honestly sir I'm planning to keep [your advice] in my memory [and] I can well see that everything you said is good and holy and helpful" (771, 773). Thinking that he will need a written storehouse of information to supplement his oral memory Sancho Panza asks Don Quixote to put his advice "in writing" so that he can recollect it "when needed [for] what is [it's] use [he asks] if [he] can't remember any of it?" (773). Ever happy to oblige, Don Quixote hands him a "written version" of his instructions "so that he can get someone to read it to him" frequently (777). Besides giving his squire live-advice, in person, he often writes his friend long distance letters to jog his memory: like a message, for instance, that says: "Consider and reconsider, think and think again about the advice and instructions I wrote out before you left for your governorship, and you will see that you can find there, if you heed them, a contribution towards [enduring] the trials and tribulations that beset governors at every turn" (835). It is in this manner that Don Quixote tries to impress a receptive Sancho Panza with basic principles of moral conduct so that he uses his knight's ethical compass to guide to his thoughts and motivate his actions.

Evidently, governor Panza applies Don Quixote's wisdom by reason especially during legal difficulties where a man's life hangs in the balance. For example, when he is consulted by a group of perplexed judges about a nettling case involving "a great river [that] divides a lord's estate into two parts [with] a bridge that [crosses] the river [and] a gallows [at one end] and some sort of a court house in which sits four judges to administer [an] imposed law" that says:

> [If] anybody [wishes] to cross this bridge [he] must first state under oath where he is going and for what purpose; and if he tells the truth he is to be allowed to cross it, and if he tells a lie he is to be hanged on the gallows that stands there, without any possible reprieve
>
> (832).

But when "one man takes his solemn oath and then states that his purpose is none other than to die on those gallows standing there;" instead of being thrown into a mental quandary over whether to "allow this man to go free and cross the bridge" Sancho Panza refers to Don Quixote's advice to resolve this "complex and puzzling" case (832). Thus, he delivers this legal advice to a group of judges: "the reasons for condemning [this man] and for acquitting him balance each other out, [so] he should be let free to cross the bridge, because doing good is always more highly praised than doing harm (833). Not only is he lenient here, as per Don Quixote's advice, he also credits him for his decision when he says "what came into my mind [when deliberating] was one of the rules that [my] knight Don Quixote laid down for [me] on the night before [I] came to be governor of this island, and it was that when there are any doubts about justice [I] should go for leniency and mercy" (833). This example proves that Sancho Panza not only pays careful attention to Don Quixote's leading wisdom but also strives to implement, with full sincerity, the rules that his knight defines for him.

Another instance of Sancho Panza enacting justice a la Don

Quixote's advice, occurs when a woman claims that a "wealthy herdsmen used her body as if it were a dirty rag when [she tried] to keep her most precious asset in tact;" while the accused claims he "paid [the woman] the usual amount [to] lie [with her; and] she's lying [when] she says [he] raped her" (790). To determine if the woman is truthful in her rape charge or if the herdsman is truthful in his denial of it, Sancho Panza "orders [the defendant] to produce his purse and give it to the plaintiff" (790). Then he tells the hog driver to "take [his] purse off her" (790). Finding that taking back the money is impossible "so tenacious [is] the woman's defense;" coupled with her claim that she would "sooner let him take [her] life then [her] purse," Sancho Panza delivers this verdict: "My good woman [if] you'd shown the same grit and spirit defending your body as you have in defending your purse all the strength of Hercules couldn't have raped you. Off you go you fraud, you swindler, you brazen little hussy!" (791). Despite a woman's plea for "Justice, justice everyone" Sancho Panza does not let his reason "drown in tears [and his] integrity in lamentations" as Don Quixote suggests earlier (769). This example proves that from the outset of his governorship, and during his civil rule, Sancho Panza brings up in his mind and acts upon Don Quixote's wisdom, so that he knows what to do, how to do it, and why to do it, for which logic he receives fortifying, quixotic, recognition.

To positively reinforce Sancho Panza's reckoning accuracy; a letter comes from Don Quixote expressing praise and admiration for his gubernatorial conduct. In this missive, Don Quixote opines about Sancho Panza's actions: "Whereas I was expecting to receive news of your negligence and your blunders friend Sancho, I have had reports of your intelligent behavior [and] I am told that you govern like a man" (834). Clearly, Don Quixote is pleased with his squire's smarts and tells him so to praise him in areas where he deserves credit and recognition; to reinforce his confidence and consciousness; and to bolster his real-time decision making skills. It is in this manner that Don Quixote solidifies his previous advice, offers new counsel, and brings forward in his liege's mind object-lessons of morality, all to enhance his personal leadership command qualities.

Other people, besides Don Quixote, also groom Sancho Panza for political office; like the Duke, the narrator, and a random stranger, for example, who reinforces his memory and sharpens his general understanding. This, they do by verbal encouragement, by intellectual mnemonics, and by psychological repetition, so that he not only improves his rate of mental retention but also so that he learns to bring forward the right data point, at the right time, in the right way. An example of their coaching occurs when Sancho Panza seems unsure about whether he will remember the "ABC's of good governorship" (766). Observing his hesitation, the Duke not only reassures him that "with such a good memory [he] can't possibly go wrong;" but he also compliments his "fine understanding;" by saying that he will be "as good a governor as [his] sound sense promises" (766). To supplement the Duke's praise, the book's narrator and a random stranger also complement Sancho Panza's "fine memory" and "incisive mind" (789, 832). This, then, is how other people improve Sancho Panza's rate of mental retention during his "ten-day" governorship of Barataria (850). Besides improving his memory by mental exercises, other people teach Sancho Panza to avoid libel, slander, and other forms of gossip mongering while in office.

To enhance Sancho Panza's ability to repel "idle-talk" spoken by the fray of thoughtless Baratariaites; and, similarly, to get his squire to rebuff conscious slander designed to attract his attention and distract his concentration, Don Quixote counsels him to not only practice the virtues of a refined moral character, so that he brings about, by illustrative example, the morality in others, but he also advises him to develop the intellectual armor he needs to repulse all canards, innocent or sinister. Therefore, to get his friend to lead by good example, and thus to rebuff external weak-point attacks, Don Quixote, in a letter, writes: "A father to virtue [should not be] covetous, a womanizer, or a glutton, because as soon as the people and those who have dealings with you discover your weakness, they will concentrate their attacks on that point, until they topple you down into the depths of perdition" (835). Here, Don Quixote advises his squire to free himself from jealous grasping, skirt chasing, and sensuous overindulgence so that he not only "delivers [himself] from slanderous gossip from which no station in life is exempt:" but also so that he denies his backbiters the intellectual ammunition they need to fuel their libel (768).

Taking heed of Don Quixote's advice, Sancho Panza, and his family, repulse slander in two ways: One, they identify gossip for what it is thereby denying detractors the legitimacy they need to launch their verbal assaults; and, two, they off-put critical cynics by ignoring their ill-founded chatter, altogether. A case of slander identification comes when Sancho Panza speaks about hearsay as follows: "if [a] judge doesn't listen to [people] and deal with them because he can't they soon start cursing him and gossiping about him and backbiting him, and [they] even go into all sorts of detail about his family" (812). Here, Sancho Panza points-out gossip to make people aware that he is aware of the specific form of their oral sniping so that those same slanders think twice about spreading false rumors about him, especially for fear of public exposure. Sancho Panza's daughter Sanchita, also comments on extricating herself from gossip: "A thousand plagues on all the gossips in the world who cares if they all laugh and mock" (829). This speech indicates that Sancho Panza and his family not only seek to develop thick-skin so that their minds are well-balanced (despite thoughtless speech) but it also signifies that Governor Panza tries to focus the bulk of his psychological energy on running Barataria.

To perpetuate his personal integrity as a measure of his leadership, Sancho Panza is led to adopt ethics in his practices by rising above corrupting temptations and entrapping advances in the form of money-payoffs and other dubious favor persuasions. Thus he emphasizes his probity as follows: "If you think I'm going to sell my soul to the devil for the sake of being governor let me tell you I'm more interested in going as Sancho Panza to heaven than as a governor to hell [therefore] as I govern this island, all bribes I'll refuse but insist on my dues, and everyone had better watch out and mind their own business" (775, 813). This sentence indicates three things: that Sancho Panza intends to reject unearned material gifts in exchange for his favor; that he demands adequate monies for governing sensibly; and that he warns intrusive interlopers to not meddle in his affairs. Evidently, he remains true to his resolve for later in his governorship he sends a letter to Don Quixote that says: "So far all bribes I've refused and I haven't caught sight of any dues" (837). This sentiment is echoed at the end of his incumbency when he declares: "all the other governors that came to this island take lots of money from the islanders in gifts or loans even before they arrive [but I on the other hand] hadn't got a penny when I was made a governor and I haven't got a penny now I'm stopping being one, very different from governors of other islands" (837, 849). Don Quixote makes a similar point when he says:

> Others bribe, importune, solicit, rise-early, entreat, persist, and still do not achieve their aim; and then along comes some other fellow and, without the faintest idea about how it has happened, he finds himself occupying the position that so many had been seeking

(767).

Evidently, this quote applies to Sancho Panza's official promotion which can be attributed to his "rejection" of shady "money;" his "declination" of dubious "gifts" and his "rebuffing" of coaxing "loans" made by eager "favor-seekers" rapt on getting their way. Most importantly, though Sancho Panza's ethical behavior illustrates that he will not trade his moral integrity for access to powerful individuals, he will not trade virtue for vice, he will not yield to beguiling but harmful allurements of seeming expediency, and, lastly, he will not succumb to the corruption of others, hence combining, with other elements, to win him the town's moral approval. Besides gaining popularity by exercising steady principles, Sancho Panza adopts other good will measures to boost public morale.

Sancho Panza seeks to gain Barataria's sincere trust by being gracious to all, by ensuring a stable food supply, and by issuing a few laws needed for the town to flourish. Don Quixote echoes this point when he reminds Sancho Panza that "To gain the goodwill of the people [he is] to govern there are [three] things [he] must do: in the first place, [he] must be polite to one and all; secondly [he] must try to ensure a plentiful supply of food; [and thirdly he] must not publish too many edicts ensuring that those [he does] publish are good ones that are observed and obeyed" (834). Evidently, Sancho Panza is courteous to all for he addresses people in respectful terms such as: "my good woman, my good man, my friends, my lad, my young lady, my young friends, my dear master [and] kind friend" (791, 799, 803, 814, 816, 821, 836, 837, 848). He also shows respect for others when he asks his escritoire to read him an urgent letter. Finding that his secretary is "Basque" he exclaims "with that tagged on you could be secretary to the emperor himself." (799). Sancho Panza also tries to maintain an abundant food supply for the populas by discoursing on "ploughing and digging" by expounding on "pruning and layering vines" and by lecturing on exercising a "reapers sickle" which, he infers, are necessary agricultural measures required for the town to produce food (849). This, he does "because nothing wearies the hearts of the poor as much as hunger and deprivation" (834). Also as need arises Sancho Panza publishes a set of specific by-laws that stipulate three primary measures: "if anyone waters [wine] down or passes it for another type he will pay [dearly]; no blind man can sing couplets about miracles unless he has solid evidence authenticating them as true ones; [and] feigned mutilations and false sores [as a cover] for thieving arms [along with] sound bodied [public] drunkenness" are hereby outlawed (838). In this passage, Cervantes highlights a few limited laws needed for Barataria to function properly because if Baratarites are to respect and love their governor they need to have certainty in their lives and stability of long-term action so that they can work towards their goals, hopes, and aspirations in peace.

All of these goodwill measures create positive affections in the minds and hearts of Sancho Panza's team of subjects, like his steward, for example, who says: "Truly, my lord governor, what you say is quite correct, and I hereby offer all islanders on this island to serve you with all diligence, love, and goodwill because the mild style of government that you have adopted leaves no room for doing or thinking anything that could redound to your disservice" (813).

After issuing a few well-reasoned laws, after showing a willingness to enforce those laws, and after providing basic life staples, like food, for example, Sancho Panza turns to other problems that need to be addressed and resolved in Barataria, like out of control gambling, for example.

To punish and preclude extortionate money-stripping—especially when it tricks middle-to-lower income wage-earners out of their livelihoods—Sancho Panza is, by and large, anti-gambling and anti-speculation because he believes that chanceful betting, at best, or cheatful trickery, at worst, does not contribute anything new to civilization. Rather, he believes, it degrades society's moral fabric by rewarding dicey behavior, by generating greedy vice, and by creating devious deception. So, to send a powerful message to degenerate gamblers that financial duplicity does not pay, Sancho Panza shows no mercy to a gamer when he comes to his attention: "You the successful gambler, whether a good man or a bad one or an indifferent one, will give your knifer here a hundred reals" (815). By severely chastising a card-sharper, even when deadly force is perpetrated against his person, Sancho Panza makes it clear to him, and to other financial-speculators, that if they cheat to earn a living then the law will not protect them. Besides this specific anti-gambling example, Sancho Panza also proclaims a general desire to "shut these gaming houses down, because, to [his] mind, they do a lot of harm" (816). During a town patrol for law breakers, for example, he is told by his clerk that he can start to game-bust by "flexing his muscles on lesser gambling dens [because] they're the ones that do the most damage and cover up the most iniquities" (816). This statement suggests that because lower-level betting establishments, such as "a tradesmen's place," are less regulated, not as well-monitored, and empty of oversight, they attract the treachery of organized predators who conspire to "trap a poor wretch in the small hours and flay him alive:" Whereas, "in the houses of high-ranking gentlemen and nobles, famous card-sharpers don't dare get up to their tricks" for fear of being caught (816). Thanks to his Basque clerk, Sancho Panza sees "that there are a lot of ins and outs to this [gaming] question" and tries his level-best to eliminate the "vice of gambling" (816).

Besides repelling financial speculators who extort the town's money through fraud and deception, Sancho Panza freezes other human parasites in their tracks, like transient bums, for example, or slothful slouches, for instance, or criminal mooches, worst of all, who brain-drain the mental and physical products of Baratario's human resources thereby diminishing the town's full productive potential. Thus, to halt all parasitic activity in Baratario Sancho Panza announces the following intention: "I'm planning to rid this island of all sorts of rubbish and tramps and idlers and layabouts, because I'll have you know, my friends, that, useless, lazy people in a society are like drones in a bee hive, eating up the honey that the worker bee produces" (814). True to his word he expels a loafer involved in a knife fight: "you without a job or an income, scrounging your way through life on this island, will take these hundred reals, and tomorrow without fail you will leave this island, under sentence of banishment for ten years on pain of [death] if you violate it because I'll hang you from the pillory or at least order the executioner to" (815). Not only does Sancho Panza assert a general will to boot out layabouts for their pestilence he also follows through by ostracizing a criminal parasite caught in a violent stick-up act.

Although Sancho Panza expels vagrants from Barataria's citizenry, he also gives redeemable cases another chance to live in Barataria because either they show some quality of character, however faint, that promises a change of reform or because borderline cases shape-up quick by acting with a level of vigor that accords with their ability. To realize this goal Sancho Panza "creates the post of overseer of beggars, not for this official to persecute them but rather to examine them to ensure that they are really unable to work" (838). In addition to launching an overwatch authority figure and empowering him with the ability to prevent pretend sicknesses used as an excuse to shirk work – Sancho Panza also infers, with subtle discretion, that he wants to get rid of dead weight, either completely, if sluggards are impossible to correct, or, wholly, if non-workers are notoriously difficult to develop; but, at the same time, if people hold real promise of positive reform, and make a real effort to tap their creative abilities, Sancho Panza thinks, presumably, that such people can develop their own productive capacities, through their own individual efforts, so that they contribute to their own personal sense of well-being and fulfillment, through which they can then add to civilization's true growth. This, then, is the full implication of Sancho Panza's actions vis-à-vis productiveness and, by and large, he establishes enduring laws and takes other material steps that enable Barataria to thrive, especially, as we shall see, in the trade realm.

To enforce trade rules that reward the creation of original goods and the production of quality-merchandise, Governor Panza sets "by-laws" that facilitate "the smooth running" of the town: like the pronouncement, for example, that "no food be sold by anyone other than its producer:" Or, the order "that wine be permitted to be brought from all parts [of the kingdom] provided that the place of origin is declared so that a price can be [determined] according to its popularity, quality and reputation" (838). Thus, to ensure that articles of trade meet certain quality standards, Sancho Panza "visit[s] the markets" regularly to value test merchandise (837). During one evaluative inspection, for example, he "come[s] across a stallholder selling" what she claims are "fresh hazelnuts" but finds instead that she "mixed a bushel of new nuts with a bushel of old ones, empty and rotten" (837). Sancho Panza immediately "confiscates [the hazelnuts] and sentences [the] market-woman to not set foot in the [bazaar] for a fortnight" to spread the message that merchants who cheat their customers with faulty goods will be temporarily prohibited from earning their livelihoods (835, 837). For a similar reason, Sancho Panza is told to "visit the Butcher shops [often] for a Governor's presence is a boogeyman for the butchers who have to use accurate weights for a while" (835). These steps are taken to not only set-out honest advertisement as essential for free enterprise, but these measures are also adopted to reward people who produce and exchange material commodities, with value for their time and money.

Besides policing merchants to bring about the characteristics of a "good tradesmen," Sancho Panza also aids workers earn a decent living wage so that they, in turn, can afford staple items, like decent shoes, for example. Therefore, to do this, "he establishes the limits of servants wages [and] lowers the price of all footwear" (844, 838). By setting income levels to a fair-rate of work-return and by decreasing shopping expenses to offset the cost-of-living he ensures that people are able to afford everyday life-supporting stables. In sum, by writing fair trade rules into Barataria's constitution, Sancho Panza facilitates the lawful commerce of goods; transparent trade dealings with others; quality merchandise and just salaries, too, thereby enhancing Barataria's overall living standards.

One last thing that Sancho Panza does to establish a wholesome air in Barataria is to "impose [restrictive] penalties on anyone singing lewd or disorderly songs by day or by night because he considers that most of the miracles that blind men sing about are fictitious and bring about discredit on the true ones" (838). By discouraging miraculous lyrics and imagined divinations, Sancho Panza tries to staunch the spread of patent falsities that could, if unchecked, morally degrade the town. Instead he encourages an innocent method of singsonging and the dissemination of verifiable truths. In sum, then, Sancho Panza institutes, in the town's charter, legal repercussions for civil misdemeanors to punish wicked conduct, that he thinks disables Barataria's smooth functioning, and, conversely he "reward[s] virtuous" behavior—which he thinks enables the town to thrive (814). In short, "Sancho [makes] such excellent by-laws that they remain in force in the town to this day and they are called **The ordinances of the great governor Sancho Panza**" (838).

Since these bylaws come at the end of Sancho Panza's reign, he has to first reach the mind state necessary to grasp and implement these practices: So, to get him to think about himself, his thoughts, his actions, and their effects, Don Quixote shares with his squire his own introspective wisdom: "You must always remember who you are, and try to know yourself, which is the most difficult knowledge of all to acquire. Knowing yourself will stop you from puffing yourself up" (767). Thus to prompt Sancho Panza to actualize, in his psyche, an appropriate sense of rational egoism, Don Quixote advises him to "temper the solemnity appropriate to his position with a gentle mildness, exercised with prudence [so that he] is not always severe, or always mild, but a middle way between these two extremes" (768, 799). Since true self-knowledge is a prerequisite for self-mastery, Don Quixote encourages his squire to conduct a radical process of evolutionary self-analysis through which he will learn how to act well in formal court society. In this sense Don Quixote encourages Sancho Panza to hold himself accountable for his behavior by reminding him to "always act as one would expect a man [of his] caliber to act" (835). By counseling governor Panza to observe his mind's interiority in this way, Don Quixote encourages him to be cognizant of his personality so that he attains (and retains) an accurate conception of himself; so that he understands what thoughts, feelings, and emotions drive his actions, and ultimately; so that he realizes an appropriate sense of self-respect; a self-conception that is free from overblown vanity and overexaggerated bluster, yet, at the same time, is self-respective, self-dignified, and self-proud. It is in this manner that Don Quixote tries to trigger in his squire an introspective process of realizing the tranquility of mind and the calmness of emotions that he needs to achieve a virtuous conception of himself.

In addition to guiding him to introspective self-mastery, Don Quixote counsels Sancho Panza to develop the moral character of his wife, so that she not only improves her person in her own right but also so that she enhances her husband's intelligent powers, as well. At the same time, however, Don Quixote allows that if the moral improvement of a leader's spouse proves impossible, for whatever reason, that leader should choose "a better wife" because "a governor's wife occupies a position of great importance" and should be fitted to lead well otherwise she will not be happy and her people will be poorly taken care of (768). To obviate this scenario, Don Quixote suggests that if Sancho Panza "takes [his] wife along with [him] (*because it is not a good idea for those who govern for long periods to be without wives*) [he should] teach her, instruct her, polish all that coarseness of her, because everything that is gained by an intelligent governor is often lost and wasted by a [thoughtless] wife" (768). This quote suggests that because the company of a good wife is needed for extended political leadership Sancho Panza should develop the moral powers of Teresa Panza so that she can help him rule. Despite Don Quixote's drive to improve Teresa Panza's ethical character he also embraces the possibility of a connubial separation because "if by chance [Sancho Panza] is [naturally] widowed, something that could well happen, [then] thanks to [his] high office [he] can acquire a better wife" because the responsibility of a "judge's wife" is included "by her husband [in his] life and the final account of his doings" (768, 769). In sum, while Don Quixote explores the possibility of a marital divorce, he gives priority to revivifying Sancho Panza's wife, so that she is fit for civilian rule.

Besides these hortative efforts, other people, like the Duchess, also prepare Teresa Panza for political life.

The Duchess grooms Teresa Panza for political life by: writing her a warm letter of friendship; giving her several good will gifts; inquiring after her person; asking about her "village;" expressing gratitude for the "excellent" governance of her husband; articulating a will to match her daughter, Sanchita, with a becoming gentlemen of some "rank" and stature; and, lastly, inviting her to write back (824, 825). This is why the Duchess writes a letter to her vassal to assure her of the following: that her "husband's most excellent qualities of goodness and cleverness" are most appreciated by "the Duke [who] find[s] [him] a most able governor;" that she, the Duchess, bestows her favor, materially, by enclosing "a string of corals with gold Paternosters," that Sanchita, her daughter, should "be held in readiness for marriage to a man of high rank;" that their relationship should be continued by method of the reception of a bunch of "fine fat acorns to be had in [Teresa Panza's] village" with a penultimate inquiry about "how [she] is" followed by a solicitation that "if there's anything [she] needs she only has to say so, and [her] every word will be the [Duchess's] command" (825, 826). This letter thanks Teresa Panza for bearing the absence of her husband, shows special praise by gift-giving, and invites Mrs. Panza to partake in an open relationship with her ladyship by expressing her own well-being; her daughter's state of "readiness;" and the town's existential state, as well (825). Ultimately, the Duchess's epistle is designed to begin a symbiotic friendship with Teresa Panza where her grace benefits by linking with the loyal wife of an effective governor and Teresa Panza benefits by receiving the Duchess's royal favor in spiritual, material, and moral terms.

Evidently, the Duchess's political outreach efforts begin to take positive effect on Teresa Panza for she dictates a return letter to the Duchess to: cement the bonds of their opening friendship; show heartfelt appreciation for the Duchess's patronage; report the town's happiness at Sancho Panza's governorship; and, lastly, express Sanchita's gratefulness for being thought of in fond terms. In this missive she informs the Duchess that she was "really, really happy to get the [original] letter from [her] grace" (842).

Teresa Panza then thanks her "for [the] very fine string of corals" as well as her "husband's hunting outfit" (842). Later, she not only reports that "everyone in the village is cheered up [to] no end [with] Sancho [being] made governor" but also she expresses gratitude on behalf of her "daughter Sanchita who kiss[es] the Duchess's hands" with affection (842). In further appreciation, Teresa Panza "sends [her] grace about a half gallon of acorns" along with a fine "fat cheese [that] the Duchess [is] delighted to receive" (843, 845). She then ends her letter with five goodwill compliments: First, she wishes "our Lord to look after [her] Grace;" second, she pledges "allegiance" to her "ladyship" for her benefaction; third, she "promises to give her news from the town;" fourth, she implores her grace to not "forget" about her; and fifth, she signs-off that Teresa Panza is her "most grateful servant" and that she is "keen to see" her "Ladyship" in person and will, in the future, "write" again (843). Above all else, the tying together of her excellency, the Duchess, and her liege, Teresa Panza, enhances, by default, the natural graces of Mrs. Panza so that she is a credit onto both her lady's regional administration as well as her husband's localized governorship.

Ever "pleased" that his wife is treated well Sancho Panza extends his patrons a fitting degree of courtesy and respect, especially those who promote him in rank and stature, like the Duke and Duchess, for instance, or those who help him govern well, like Don Quixote, for example. Therefore, in obeisance, he pledges his fidelity to these people by material acts of loyalty (837). Textual evidence of his goodwill not only comes when Sancho Panza "kisses the Duke and Duchess's hands" and accepts, with gratitude, "his master's blessing" but also comes in a letter to his superiors in which he vouches that "the Duke's orders will be obeyed exactly as issued" and that he'll "take good care to serve [the Duchess] with everything in [his] power" (800). Included in this missive are instructions to give a "hand kissing [to his] master Don Quixote so that he can see [that Sancho Panza is] a grateful servant" (800). Sancho Panza even offers "to send [him] something [like] some enema tubes, [for example] for us[e] with bladders" in appreciation (837). Pleased with his friend's loyalty Don Quixote reminds him to "write to [his] patrons [often] to show how grateful [he is] for a person who is grateful to those who have done him favors" generates reciprocal goodwill (835). In response, Sancho Panza swears he will "try to show [the Duchess] how grateful [he is] when the time comes and [affirms] that her kindness isn't going to slip [his] mind and [he'll] give her proof of that [because] its only right and proper [says he] for those who've been done a kindness to show that they are grateful" (837, 869). In brief, all of Sancho Panza's pledges, sayings, thinkings, and doings, not only illustrate that he is loyal to the Duke, the Duchess, and Don Quixote but also that he appreciates their patronage and backing.

Besides showing a proper measure of respect for his civic mentors, Sancho Panza illustrates that despite his new found authority; he is the same as he ever was, in many important ways.

Even though Sancho Panza becomes a high-ranking governor, he does not let power change him nor does he let the importance of his office inflate his ego unrealistically. One early sign of his modesty comes from his belief that basic traits interconnect all people, high and low, young and old, "rich and poor," because "when we are asleep we're all [similar] great and small" (775). Likewise, when the Duke recommends that a governor of "sound sense" should wear "the proper uniform" of his office, Sancho Panza says that even though his outer wardrobe changes his inner nature remains the same: "They can dress me up as they please whatever clothes they put me in I'll still be Sancho Panza" (766). Later, when his butler tries to prefix a Don to his name he insists that "plain Sancho Panza" is fine because that "was what [his] father was called and what [his] grandfather was called before him, and they were all Panza's without any Dons tagged on in front or behind" (786). When he is offered gourmet foods to eat he says that he "can stay alive on bread and onions just as well as [he] can as a governor on partridges and capons" (775). During a subsequent scene when a farmer fawns over Sancho Panza by begging him "for his hand so that he can kiss it, Sancho Panza refuses, and tells him to get up and say what he wanted" (801). When he is leaving Barataria people offer him "anything" that comes to mind "for the well-being of his person and the comfort of his journey" (850). Modestly, he says that he "only wants a bit of barley for his donkey and half a cheese and half a loaf for himself, because his journey [is] a short one and he [doesn't] have any call for more or better provisions" (850). Evidently, Sancho Panza preserves the continuity of his identity by not adding a superflux of titles to his name; by not letting his clothes define his person; by not altering his eating practices and routines to the point that he is gastronomically inflexible; by not accepting an overabundance of gifts and favors when he does not need them; and, lastly, by not receiving profuse compliments, in the form of excessive attentions that slow state business. Most importantly, though, Sancho Panza illustrates that even in high office he creates a channel of real understanding between himself and his constituents, (without fussy obsequies, or other needless preliminaries) so that supplicants can bring important matters to their governor's time and attention quickly without feeling that they must first show an abundance of gushing respect for his person or that talking to him frankly is somehow inappropriate given his stature. In short, even as a high-powered governor there is something deep within Sancho Panza that does not change.

Although Sancho Panza is a modest governor he is also firm and self-confident in his decisions so that he inspires respect for, and agreement with, the actions that he takes. For this reason, Don

Quixote counsels his friend to "oppose the humility of his heart for the sake of the dignity of his position [because a] person in a post of great responsibility must accord with the requirements of this post" (834). The Duke reinforces this quality of leadership by saying "it's a splendid thing to issue orders and to be obeyed" to which Sancho Panza replies "it must always be good to be in charge" (766). Later, when the town is under pretend attack, Sancho Panza becomes a guide and captain, in difficult times, by rallying his troops and issuing orders: "Here, boys here, this is where the enemy's pressing hardest! Guard that gate, shut that other one, prise those ladders off the walls! Bring fire-pots, pitch and resin in cauldrons of burning oil! Barricade the streets with mattresses!" (847). Given his directorship role and given the general effects that his decisions have over the lives of the people, Sancho Panza takes command to figure out what defensive actions will protect the town; how those tactical actions rebuff offensive advances; when to marshal concrete gains; where to deliver battlefield advantages, and how, stylistically, to transmit his field orders.

Besides erecting a hypothetical frontal assault on the town to test Sancho Panza's battle readiness, the Duke also sees if Sancho Panza can protect himself against subtle clandestine attack. Hence, he creates a mock assassination scenario designed to persuade his governor that murderers are plotting to kill him and spies are trying to subvert his government. Thus, he sends "Don Sancho Panza" a letter warning him "that four persons have entered the town in disguise to take [his] life because they are afraid of [his] intelligence" (799). Therefore, he should "keep [his] eyes open, [he should] be careful about who comes to speak with him [he should] not eat any food that is given to him as a present [and, above all, he should] stay alert, so as not to be taken unawares" (799). Though, "astonished" by this news, Sancho Panza vows to "see off all the spies and killers that come pitching into [him] and [his] island" (800). As a safety precaution, he orders his page to "tell [a farmer] to come in, but [to] check [him] first to make sure he isn't [a] spy or a killer" sent to gain information or to end his life (800, 838). In care of his physical health, then, Sancho Panza advises his trusted steward to "let [him] have a [loaf] of bread and [some] grapes because [given their self-contained nature] there can't be any poison in them" (800). One further security step Sancho Panza takes is to alert his staff that his "lord the Duke wrote to him the other day warning [him] that some spies [have] come on this island to kill him" so that his team of assistants are aware of a potential danger and take countermeasures to neutralize the threat (836). Forewarned, his staff bands together to ward-off intruders—like his butler, for example, who says: "have no fear" because "we're all here with you;" or his steward, for instance, who protects him from food poisoning by suggesting "that [he] shouldn't eat any of the food on this table because it [is] a gift" (800). By being cautious, Sancho Panza protects himself against perceived bodily hazards because, ultimately, he wants to make it "safe and sound out of his governorship" (800). Besides prompting him to self-defend against pretend spies, fake assassins, and false attackers, Don Quixote counsels him to have the intellectual firmness to follow through on a prospective course of action: which mental efforts, Don Quixote suggests, could earn him, personally, and his office, too, earned financial income.

Before Sancho Panza becomes governor of Barataria, Don Quixote advises him to discreetly inquire about what monies are due to him in his new position and if he determines that his pay is sufficient to meet his own needs, and the needs of his subjects, he should allot earned income, fairly, in a way that not only rewards good work with a fitting salary but that also creates an environment of fiscal discipline in Barataria. This is why Don Quixote counsels Sancho Panza to: "Put out discreet feelers to discover what [his] new position might be worth: and if it will allow [him] to give [his] servants liveries, let them be modest and practical ones, not spectacular and showy" (771). The full implication, here, is that if Sancho Panza apportions his finances according to the real level of his staff's output—he will not only satisfy his subjects financial needs but he will also create a general atmosphere of thrift in Barataria by matching skill and ability with a fair outlay of finances. In effect, then, through the vehicle of developing Sancho Panza's sense of budgeting state revenues appropriately, Don Quixote grows his squire's moral character because a "new system of giving livery is one to which the vainglorious cannot aspire" (771). In short, Don Quixote instructs Governor Panza to spend the capital he is entrusted with in a manner that fits the town's needs, his requirements, and those of his assistants.

In addition to giving Sancho Panza fiscal advice about income assignment, Don Quixote prepares him to self-govern his self-grooming practices. This is why Don Quixote counsels his friend to:

> Walk sedately, speak with deliberation, but not so he seem[s] to be listening to himself; for affectation is always bad; [to] be temperate in [his] drinking, and bear in mind that wine keeps neither secrets nor promises; [to] moderate [his] sleep; for he who does not rise with the sun does not enjoy the day; and [above all to] remember that diligence is the mother of good fortune, [and] its opposite, sloth, never attained any worthwhile goal.

(767, 768, 772, 770, 771).

In this speech Don Quixote gives Sancho Panza "instructions for the embellishment of [his] body" so that he moves calmly, speaks honestly, orates carefully, moderates his drinking, is not lazy, does not oversleep, keeps trusted information to himself and has the good sense of mind to pursue a useful objective, which, according to Don Quixote, requires Sancho Panza to modulate his wake/sleep cycles with normal regularity so that he is brisk, alert, and alive with vigor, especially during the day (770). To this end Don Quixote counsels his sidekick to:

be clean, cut [his] fingernails, [and to] not let them grow long; [to] not eat [too much] garlic or onions; [to not] chew on both sides of [his] mouth at the same time; [to] not eructate when in company; when [he] ride[s] on a horse, [to] not lean back in the saddle, or stiffen and stretch [his] legs so that they stick out from the horses flanks, but [to] not relax so much, either, that [he] look[s] as though [he was] riding [his] donkey

(770).

It is in this manner that Don Quixote urges Sancho Panza to adopt a neat mode of personal hygiene, a choice selection of gastronomic foods, a refined manner of winsome eating, a considerate respect for other people, and an elegant style of horsemanship, so that he strikes a perfect balance between dignified composure, on the one hand, and relaxed comfort, on the other. Evidently, Sancho Panza retains some of this counsel for he claims that "one of the pieces of advice that [he's] planning to keep in [his] memory is that one about not belching, because it is something [he] often do[es]" (771). Here Don Quixote tries to instill, and draw forth, in Sancho Panza's mind and emotions, the self-sanitation practices of a clean character, the refined politeness of an effective governor, and the winning graces of a civil leader; all of which, he suggests, if adopted, will not only provide him with a sovereign sense of self-respect in his own eyes but will also inspire his subjects, his peers, and his superiors, alike, with an overarching sense of value for his person.

With this aim in mind Don Quixote and Dr. Aguero moderate Sancho Panza's food intake, aid his digestion, and sharpen his mental and physical functions via a strict-purification, pseudo-starvation diet, which although, at times, is passed-off as a big joke, is actually regimented to get the message through to Sancho Panza that his health of body and longevity of life require that he trim his waistline to an appropriate size, so that he has the physical capacity of body and the bio-cognitive sharpness of mind to reign with the intelligence of an astute governor. To this end Don Quixote (senior partner) helps Sancho Panza (junior partner) cultivate his will to lose weight by advising him to consume only a moderate amount of food: "Eat little for lunch and even less for dinner, because the health of the entire body is forged in the smithy of the stomach" (771). In supplementation of this dietary advice, Dr. Aguero introduces himself as a physician-nutrionist:

> I, sir, am a doctor and I am employed to take care of governors, and I take care of their health [much more] then my own, studying by night and by day, and gauging each governor's constitution so as to be able to cure him when he falls ill; and my main task is to be present at all of his lunches and dinners, and to allow him to eat that which appears to me to be suitable, and to take away that which I believe to be injurious to his stomach because as our master Hippocrates, the light and guide of medicine, says in one of his aphorisms, *Omnis saturatio mala* [or] all excess is bad
>
> (797).

This glib introduction establishes the tone, sets the aim, and commences the direction of Dr. Aguero's seemingly draconian but actually beneficial dietary regimen, which is proscribed to settle Sancho Panza's stomach, help his digestion, and "conserve and fortify his health," so that he is well-nourished, not too heavy, and used to a moderate amount of food (798). To this end, Sancho Panza's "steward," coached by Doctor Aguero, "place[s] [many] different food[s] in front of him but before he [can] taste or even touch them, they are tapped by a pointer and removed" (796). To further cement Sancho Panza's gastronomic resolve to eat only the appropriate amount and type of food, Doctor Aguero compels him to drop his gluttony, choose his foods wisely and shed extra weight all by placing him on a mandatory diet consisting of "a hundred wafer tubes, thin slices of quince jelly, candied fruit and iced water" and not much else (798, 831). During his sudden swift-diet, Sancho Panza grumbles and complains and accuses his doctor of wanting him "to die of hunger" (836). He even tries to break his fast by requesting his medician to not "bother giving him choice foods or dainty dishes, because that would only unhinge [his] stomach [when] it's used to goat-meat, cow-meat, fat bacon, salt beef, turnips and onions "(812, 813). In response, doctor Aguero insists "that at governor's tables all must be elegance and delicacy;" yet he does ease up a bit by "allow[ing] him to eat some dinner that evening" (813). The butler also moderates his diet by arranging for his "lord and governor to eat a lunch that he will greatly enjoy because he thinks it unwise to starve such a wise governor" (834). Bottom line, as severe as Sancho Panza's diet is, it is partially eased by others, and is designed by doctor Aguero to quickly burn his excess fat stores along with his unused energy deposits so that he balances his body's ratio of lean-muscle mass and nutritive-bone with his natural flesh and needed soluble fats at a healthy and stable level. In brief, through a series of humorous jokes doctor Ageuro prescribes a very frugal, and therefore, restraint enhancing diet so that Sancho Panza loses weight at a rapid pace and does not "get ill in the first place" (836).

Besides his new diet benefiting his bodily health, there is also clear and compelling evidence that Sancho Panza becomes a smarter governor as a result of his food limitation. First, the narrator tells us that: "a tiny amount of delicate food sharpened his mind [and] this [is] what [is] needed by people appointed to govern and fill positions of responsibility in which it is not so much their physical as their mental powers that they have to employ" (831). Later, this sentiment is echoed during the seventh night of Sancho Panza's governorship when "he [is] lying in bed sated not with bread or with wine but with sitting in judgment and giving opinions and making decrees and by-laws in spite of his hunger" (845). Evidently, doctor Aguero's sudden food cut-off prevents Sancho Panza from stuffing his body to excess with all types of unwholesome comestibles, thus he shrinks his stomach, decreases his weight, and sharpens his mind as a result. In sum, Sancho Panza, a rather "fat" governor, is compelled to lose extra weight via the firm dietary intervention of Doctor Aguero, whose efforts result in Sancho Panza integrating his mind with his body in biophysiological terms (775). Luckily, the Duke entrusts Sancho Panza to a good doctor—who uses strict, but justified, tactics to reduce his weight—yet, by opposite contrast, as we shall see, another type of doctor comes into view.

During his ten-day governorship of Barataria, Sancho Panza comments on the basic nature of good-and-bad medical doctors to distinguish between two different types of health professionals: Doctors who practice medicine in the best health interests of their patients, by prescribing what is necessary, and only what is necessary, to treat, and perhaps cure, real-and-pressing health concerns, and, alternatively, wicked doctors, who purposely peddle quack cures for a quick buck. One example of a bad doctor is brought to Sancho Panza's attention by a farmer who recounts that "an incompetent doctor killed [his wife] by purging her when she was pregnant" (801). This speech reinforces the concept that people are ill-effected, in many significant ways, by legitimate medical malpractice. Besides this glaring example of a bad doctor, Sancho Panza highlights a qualitative disparity between two different types of health practitioners by voicing his approval, or disapproval, of them. For example, in Part II, Chapter XLVII, he expresses a firm desire to honor "wise, prudent, and sensible doctors for their wholesome advice" but "swears by all that is holy to grab a cudgel and thump every single ignorant doctor off this island" (798). Similarly, he believes that "good doctors deserve palms and laurels" and "bad doctors" deserve blame and banishment (812). Furthermore, on a doctor's instructions, Sancho Panza tells his steward to "take very good care over what [he and his] dun [are] given to eat" (813). Later, during a formal conversation, Dr. Aguero highlights qualities of a sensible health prescription by telling

Sancho Panza that "simple medicines are more highly regarded than compounds, at all times, in all places, by all people, because with simple medicines one cannot go wrong whereas with compounds one can, by erring in the quantities of the ingredients" (798). So, we see, here, that Sancho Panza shows good will and receptive grace to doctors who prescribe simple restorative medicines that aid his health and conversely he demonstrates hostility for doctors who ill advise and maltreat him. Besides evaluating the qualities of character that make for a good doctor, Sancho Panza's moral developers counsel him to wear good clothes that synchronize with the office of a governor.

In terms of gubernatorial uniform, the Duke guides, and Don Quixote advises, Sancho Panza to dress situation appropriate, so that he, as lord-governor, is not only well-prepared, in dress-wear, for the different circumstances at hand (like his formal honorary coronation to his official civil parade to all manner of state functions) but also so that he inspires a certain measure of respect in the conceptions and perceptions of the town's civil inhabitants. For this reason, he advises Sancho Panza to "not go around with [his] clothes loose and flapping about [him]; for untidy dress is a sign of a lackadaisical spirit" (770). Conversely, he suggests that Sancho Panza "wear good clothes that his office requires ensuring that they are clean and tidy" (834). Because Don Quixote believes that Sancho Panza's dress style signals his psychology, his civility, and his dignity, he explains, in detail, what clothes Sancho Panza should and should not wear: "As for clothes, you should wear full breaches, a long coat, a somewhat longer cloak; knee breaches most certainly not, because these are suitable neither for knights nor for governors" (773). Even the Duke amplifies Don Quixote's dress-wear advice when he says: "one's clothes must suit the position that one occupies, because it wouldn't be right for a lawyer to go around dressed as a soldier, or a soldier as a priest" (766). Thus, to prepare Sancho Panza for the wisened and militaristic role he is to fulfill as a governor the Duke counsels him to dress "half as a scholar half as a captain, because on [his] island arms are needed as much as letters, and letters as much as arms" (766). In dress-terms, then, the Duke trains Sancho Panza to be both a political intellectual, who signals his learning by the items of his civil wardrobe, and a military commander, as well, who indicates his marshal position by the composition of his civil uniform. Essentially, the Duke gives these sartorial instructions so that Sancho Panza's identity is apparent, at a glance, to all people, both within the town's internal hierarchy of domestic personnel and to foreign chains of command, as well. Thus, to identify Sancho Panza to all interlocutors so that they know how to treat him "The Duke [tells] Sancho to dress [as] a governor" (765). On cue, Sancho Panza follows the Duke's clothing instructions by "dress[ing] in a scholar's clothes [consisting of] an ample topcoat of tawny watery camlet with a cap of the same material" (777, 778). Moreover, Don Quixote tells Sancho Panza to dress simply, "not [with an overabundance] of trinkets and regalia" mind you but with "the fine apparel worn by a person in a post of great responsibility" (834). In brief, Sancho Panza is led to take pride in his dress by not only practicing earnest care for his external appearance but also by following the mental discipline of orderly habiliment, all so that his outward wear signals the organization of his mind and the order of his thoughts. This, then, is precisely how the Duke and Don Quixote want Sancho Panza's dressware to signal the dignified poise of an incumbent governor.

As a soon-to-be secular leader Sancho Panza is counseled to not only gain political office through the practice of his individual merits but also to take pride in his heritage so that rather than his lineage being a barrier to his progress it is a catalyst that pushes him to excel. For this reason, Don Quixote advises Sancho Panza to exercise a fitting reverence for his ancestry; an overarching sense of pride for his kinship relations; an avoidance of enmeshing himself in blood feud entanglements; a respect for other people's background, and, lastly, an initiative-based sense of qualified individual self-elevation, all accomplished, according to Don Quixote, by practicing the twin-virtues of honesty and integrity, all of which he speaks of as follows:

> [As regards your background] do not be ashamed to say that you descended from peasants; because when people see that this does not embarrass you, nobody will try to make you embarrassed about it. [Also] you must never become involved in arguments about pedigrees, not at least when they are being compared to each other, because in such comparisons one family is bound to emerge as superior, and you will be hated by the family that you disparage, and you will not be rewarded in anyway by the family that you exalt. [Furthermore] take pride in being a virtuous man rather than a lofty and sinful one [for] there are innumerable men who, born of low stock, have risen to the highest positions, both pontifical and imperial. For look here Sancho, if you make virtue your method, and you take pride in doing virtuous deeds, you will not have to envy those descended from lords and noblemen; because blood is inherited and virtue is acquired, and virtue has in itself a value that blood lacks
>
> (770, 771,772).

This passage strongly suggests that Sancho Panza should not be ashamed of his ancestral roots of origination – of his blood-line tree of descent – of his family relations – and of his genetic background because "not all governors are descended from kings" and though he is "not of noble extraction" if he is not embarrassed by what other people think or say about his blood ties, then good-natured people will not tease him about his progeny (768). Also, Don Quixote counsels Sancho Panza to not partake in comparative arguments about his ancestry because if he avoids blood quibbles altogether he will not draw scorn from touchy families downgraded, in conceptual terms, in both rank and position. Most importantly, though, the above passage explains to Sancho Panza that it is better to be in a lower social position yet to retain the integrity of one's character coupled with the virtue of one's honesty then to be in a higher civil-station but to be morally corrupt. In closing, this sanguinary advice nudges Sancho Panza to realize that the advancement of his rank, the attainment of his office, and the enhancement of his social position can accord with his ability, his drive, his determination, and his commitment to self-actualization, and, that, ultimately, his dedication to the integrity within him determines his good standing as a human being, and not, solely, the bloodline from which he was spawned.

To honor himself, his kith, and his kin, Don Quixote suggests that Sancho Panza speak like a governor with well-chosen words so that he says what he means, means what he says, knows what he is talking about and is verbally persuasive as well. For this reason he advises his friend to use precise terms that correspond to particular concepts in his mind to simplify his language by omitting unnecessary jargon to orate clearly by choosing intelligible speech; and, most importantly, to match his words with his audience's mental level, which, Don Quixote says, requires that he "not mix [a] multitude of proverbs into everything [he says]; for although proverbs are brief maxims loading everything that one says with them, [and] stringing them together without rhyme or reason, makes one's discourse flimsy and vulgar" (771, 772). This verbal counsel suggests that effective speech consists in using the correct words in their correct context to express an idea as clearly and as concisely as possible (in full-keeping with its background relevancy), which can be achieved, says Don Quixote, by Sancho Panza not "dragging" inappropriate proverbs "in so that they seem like [mere] nonsenses" (771). For this reason, Don Quixote urges Sancho Panza to not revert to his long-standing habit of cramming his speech full of rambling proverbs that "come crowding into [his] mouth when [he] is talking" (772).

Besides honing Sancho Panza's communication skills, theoretically, he often checks his speech defects, practically: Like, for example, in Part II, chapter XLII, when they are discussing literacy and Sancho Panza spouts "proverbs and more proverbs," Don Quixote reproaches him for "the [irrelevant] speech that comes to [his] mind:" or, for instance, when Don Quixote queries "where he finds all of [his proverbs and] how [he] brings them to bear on what [he is] saying when [he] has to work and sweat as if he were digging a ditch to use one in an appropriate way" (772, 774). Besides rebuking his squire for using inappropriate "proverbs" in the negative, he also prompts his friend to use appropriate proverbs in the positive by pointing out when certain "proverbs are relevant and to the point" (767, 772). In short, Don Quixote trains Sancho Panza to "say [mottos] that go well with the gravity of his [job]" and sometimes to say nothing at all because "silence is golden" (772, 774). It is in this manner that Don Quixote not only forbids Sancho Panza from cobbling together a splutter of chattery proverbs that crowd-out his self-expression but, conversely, he urges him to express himself simply, lucidly, and directly, especially because his job as a governor requires eloquent verbal expression.

For this reason, Don Quixote teaches Sancho Panza to read, write, and expand his conceptual vocabulary so that he can absorb information through writing, so that he can express himself on paper, so that he enhances his database of verbal concepts, and ultimately, so that his language processing ability, both written and oral, is sharpened. This is why he emphasizes that it "ill becomes a governor not to be able to read and write [therefore he] should like [his friend] to [learn] to sign [his] name," to which Sancho Panza replies that "[he] can sign [his] name all right" (773). During Don Quixote's second set of instructions it becomes clear that his squire does not "know what eructate means" (771). Don Quixote explains that "eructate means to belch" and "if certain others do not understand [this word] it does not matter much because usage will make [it] more and more familiar, so that [it] will be readily understood and this enriches the language" (771). Later, when Sancho Panza reverts to his use of the term belching, Don Quixote repeats: "Eructating Sancho, not belching" (771). Sancho Panza responds: "Eructating is what I'll say from now on and I promise I won't forget" (771). Apparently, he remembers this vital lesson for "he tells [his] secretary to write down what he dictated, without adding or taking a word away" (836). It is in this manner that Don Quixote encourages Sancho Panza to learn to read and write per the requirements of his gubernatorial office.

During Sancho Panza's governorship many Spanish citizens grow to like him as their leader for his blunt no-nonsense penetration, for his wise veridical judgments, and for his willingness to act on principle, even if he is not always polite in speech or always politically correct in action. In fact people develop such a fondness for his person that when Sancho Panza leaves Barataria "They all embrace him and, weeping, he embraces them all, and he leaves them in amazement, at both his words and his firm and wise decision" (850). Most importantly, though, many of Sancho's fellow townsmen develop a bond of affection for him because they profit, in real terms, by his real actions. This is why when he leaves Barataria the townspeople not only "offer him their company and anything else he [may] need for the well-being of his person" but they also reaffirm his personal value by exclaiming: "We shall be sorry to lose you because your fine mind [makes] us want you to stay" (850). After the people proclaim that their governor's intelligence is an endearing character quality of his, Sancho Panza says that "Since [he is] leaving empty-handed no further proofs [are] needed to show that [he] governed like an angel" (850). Since he does not govern solely for money but rather manages civil affairs for the weal of his constituents he wins the love of the people he leads. In fact so conscientious is he during his incumbency that when he is told "that every governor, before he leaves the place he has been governing, must give a [reckoning] of his administration" he, instantly vouches to perform this obligation by "going to see [his] lord the Duke [to] give him a full account" of his ten days in power

(850). In conclusion, Sancho Panza's candor of official conviction coupled with his noble human impulses, earns him the people's moral sanction.

After guiding Sancho Panza with the good-sense, the wisdom, the knowledge and the experience that he has accumulated in his lifetime Don Quixote offers his boon-mate this pithy summary conclusion:

> [I have] done my [best to] advise you as sincerely and as sensibly as I can; and so I have discharged my obligation and kept my promise. May [reason] guide you, Sancho, and govern you while you govern. I think you are worthy of being [a great] governor [because] you're a good-natured fellow, and, without that, no amount of knowledge is of any use. Try not to err in your main resolve; what I mean is that you must always set out with the clear objective of doing right in every matter with which you deal, for heaven always favours good intentions
>
> (775).

So, basically, Don Quixote feels that he has aptly fulfilled, to the best of his ability, the responsibility of mentoring Sancho Panza's behavior; and that, ultimately, his friend has the intrinsic merit to govern well, so long as he controls his mind, checks his emotions, and matches his ideas with his feelings. Above all, though, Don Quixote suggests that if Sancho Panza "follows [honor generating] rules and [stability creating] precepts [his] life will be long, [his] fame eternal, [his] rewards abundant, [his] happiness indescribable; [he] will marry [his] children to whomever [he] pleases, [his] children and [his] grandchildren will have titles, [he] will live in peace and enjoy everyone's approbation; and as [he] comes to the end of [his] days death will overtake him in [his] tranquil, ripe old age, and [his] great-great-grandchildren will close [his] eyes with their tender, delicate little hands" (770).

During Sancho Panza's provisional governorship, Don Quixote mentors his friend's moral character by teaching him to control and direct the force of his mind, by guiding him to calm and focus his emotions, by coaching him to take good care of himself, especially in matters of self-government, personal maintenance, and individual judgment, so that he qualifies to lead civil life by exercising the keen wits of good political government. To this end, he teaches Sancho Panza to develop the sober-gravitas of a firm ruler yet also to temper his stern seriousness with the receptive approachability expected of a leader and motivator of men. To give permanent form and definite shape to these leadership standards of thought and action, Don Quixote counsels Sancho Panza to develop a serious disposition of demeanor, a prompt habit of attitude, while also, at the same time, a generous receptivity to the serious and worthy concerns of the people. Thus, to develop a delicate balance between strength and resolution, on the one hand, and receptiveness and approachability, on the other, Don Quixote encourages Sancho Panza to achieve, in his identity, the gravity of high office harmonized with the *noblesse oblige* befitting a leader and judge of men, so that he learns to exact both a proper degree of distance and respect from his subjects—so that they are not overly familiar with their governor; and, so that they do not concern him with micro-issues of minutia that are not important enough to be brought to his time and attention, yet, at the same time, still feel that they can approach their leader, openly-and-freely, with either general matters of township business or smaller exigent issues, worthy of being contemplated and decided by their governor.

In conclusion, by developing and guiding Sancho Panza's leadership qualities, intrinsically, in relation to his internal thought process, and, by sharpening his command authority, extrinsically, in relation to his external actions, Don Quixote, with the occasional aid of the Duke, the Duchess, and their assistants, refines Sancho Panza's essential character so that he leads well. For this reason, his benefactors help Sancho Panza realize the personal qualities requisite to not only rule himself well but also the practices of action that are likely to draw both his own self-esteem and the first-hand respect of the people so that the town truly looks up to their leader for the achievements of his person, for the integrity of his speech, for the wisdom of his suggestions and for the good sense of his judgments, and are willing to follow his lead out of a sense of self-interest, concord, and concurrence. It is in this manner that Don Quixote tries to draw forth and inspire, in Sancho Panza's mind and heart, worthy and serviceable life lessons that embody the qualities of an exemplar lord-governor, which, Don Quixote suggests, consist of: An abiding sense of virtue that motivates his actions; the honesty to follow the dictates of his inner conscience; the courage to follow his candor of belief; the self-trust to follow his rational judgments; the wisdom to follow his natural inclinations; and, finally, the firmness to follow his true-convictions. Put another way, all of Sancho Panza's moral and ethical developers aim to enhance the mental focus of a developing people's governor by highlighting first-rate qualities of character that an emerging leader must have if he is to rule wisely: Like a keen sense of moral rectitude that forms and guides one's thoughts; or a willing ableness to think in terms of principle when making serious decisions; or, most importantly, a realistic conception of the best course of action given the different alternatives at hand. It is in this manner that Don Quixote cultivates Sancho Panza's internal frame of reference and refines his external actions, so that he is truly looked up to by wise others for the content of his character for the respectability of his thoughts for the nobility of his feelings; and, most importantly, for the rectitude of his actions. To this end, Don Quixote advises Sancho Panza to exercise an abiding sense of conscious virtue, the *noblesse oblige* of natural honesty, and, above all, a rational moral sense of what is right and wrong, especially because his decisions effect the public's general well-being. In other words, Don Quixote advises Sancho Panza to refine his core competencies so that he can smoothly run, efficiently execute, and optimally administrate the town's civil affairs with the strength of belief, the power of character, and the quality of temperament that a leader must have if he is to govern with the proper philosophy and serious gravitas of a formative civic mentor.

It is clear, then, that during this part of the story, Don Quixote conducts himself with a coherent and rational mind, evidenced by his reasonable explanations of governorial do's and do not's given to his friend and developing assistant Sancho Panza the squire. Even the narrator notes Don Quixote's "ready wit in [his] instructions" and asks: "Who could have heard this discourse of Don Quixote's and not considered him to be a man of sound mind and excellent disposition?" (770). This rhetorical question is designed to get the reader to pause, think, and conclude that there is more to Don Quixote's core character then his chivalric bravado and more to his actions then wistful chivalric dreams. Evidently, then, when Don Quixote focuses his mind on a rational sense of life he is rather lucid for it "has so often been pointed out in the course of this great history, [Don Quixote] only talked nonsense when people led him on to the subject of chivalry, and when discussing all other matters he showed a clear and confident understanding" (770). In essence, then, *Don Quixote De La Mancha, Part II, chapters XLII-LII*, highlights Don Quixote's sometimes sanity via his cogent speech, eloquent letters, and intelligent thoughts. This coupled with the narrator's insight into his character signals that he has mixed cognitive habits of mental operation that enable him to perceive existence when he takes his mind off of the extravagances of chivalry to focus on reality.

Essay 5

How a Female Peasant Makes Good In Society: *Dulcinea as a Model of Inspiration For Aldonza Lorenzo and A Source of Encouragement for Don Quixote.*

Dulcinea's characterization illustrates that a strong, smart, able, and attractive woman can gain social prominence by virtue of her own efforts, and not due to her lineal pedigree, social connections, material wealth, or any other reason other than who she is, what she wants, and how she plans to get it. In other words, Dulcinea's rags-to-riches story presents a new type of empowered female: a self-made woman who rises by dint of her own merit, determination, and energy even within a classist society dominated by concepts of social determinism. Contrary to the stagnant class structures of 17th Century Spain—where the poor remained poor while the rich got richer—Dulcinea exemplifies a new paradigm of female social agency where one's objective self-worth becomes their criteria for advancement, nothing less, nothing more. By presenting Dulcinea to be a wholly self-made character who relies on her own individual effort to excel, Cervantes shows readers that a lady's objective self-worth is the primary criteria for consideration; not her circumstantial background or her connection to those in power.

Since a confident, independent, upwardly mobile woman was unusual in 17th century Spain, Cervantes message about feminine self-determination was made on an implicit conceptual level not an explicit observational one. If Cervantes presented the idea that a female peasant could better her station directly, without the mediating influence of humor, he would have been punished by the Holy Inquisition, swiftly. Afraid of a severe clerical reaction to his ideas, Cervantes protected himself against official reprisals by disguising his thoughts with a variety of tactical devices—like easy opposite interpretations; hard to pin-down double meanings; humor; madness; unreliability; and mistaken identification. All of these smokescreens are Cervantes way of getting around the Holy Censors of his times so that he could argue for civilizational change without appearing to do so. Thus he had to be purposefully vague, otherwise the authorities would have muzzled him, discredited him, tortured him even, to get him to conform to their will. Thus Cervantes's book lends itself to a variety of logical interpretations so that those who wanted to keep things the same could say that *Don Quixote* maintained the status quo while those who wanted to improve society could say that *Don Quixote* voiced social change. In other words, since, Cervantes's portrayal of Dulcinea defies official permissible thought, the author took great pains to hide the notion that a female peasant can improve her educational level, her material wealth, and her moral character, to become a refined noble woman. In fact his verbal artistry is so effective that to this day critics have misunderstood Dulcinea's literary significance. To understand why Cervantes obfusicates *Don Quixote's* meaning, some historical context is necessary.

In 17th Century Spain there was an entrenched social aristocracy that frowned upon, limited, even blocked upstarts from gaining rank by their own efforts. Since parvenus challenged the automatic clout of the nobles, aristocrats had to suppress virtue in society to maintain their top-class position. To perpetuate the status quo, unorthodox, unconventional, atypical individuals, like Dulcinea, were suppressed by upperclassmen so that high society could continue to dominate Spain. So King Phillip the III deployed the

Spanish Church to perpetuate the status quo. Thus, to maintain frozen class structures, the inquisition thwarted virtue altogether by keeping peasants in their place, even if those peasants deserved to be nobles themselves. Cervantes knew all of this. Yet he also knew that to beat the holy inquisition's censors he had to confuse them greatly, which he did by writing a very complicated book. Said differently, since he needed to get his work published, he had to dilute his controversial opinions with a blur of off-putting confusion so that the content of his book would not be deemed transgressive, outlandish, or in any way blasphemous. Otherwise, the papal authorities would have punished Cervantes, severely, by excommunicating him, by torturing him, even by killing him. Since Cervantes did not want to be burned at the stake for being nonconformist he had to be careful about how he expressed unorthodoxy lest he suffer a bad end. Hence, themes of social mobility, especially in regard to a female peasant's social agency, are tamped down by Cervantes because he did not want to be chastised for having controversial thoughts. Remember he was already in jail for losing state funds; he did not need any more problems. Therefore, to comprehend the nature of his book, one has to tease out, very carefully, as it were, Cervantes controversial message about feminine social mobility, lest they miss this theme altogether.

Despite little direct evidence of Dulcinea's self-made success, Cervantes suggests, in rather subtle ways, that she can elevate her civil station by advancing under the radar, so to speak, even within a social world designed to block her progress. To fully understand how Dulcinea improves her being, first we must understand her depiction within the novel (i.e. what she means within Cervantes's fictional world). To begin this project, we will analyze how she rises up to achieve greatness by unpacking all of the biographical, existential, and ideological material about Dulcinea identity, nature, and actions. Then we will make a variety of logical inferences about the small body of evidence there is.

First, to understand who Dulcinea is, what her qualities are, and where she is going in life, one must comprehend that though she is a quasi-embellishment of our knight's imagination she is modeled on "a good looking peasant girl" named Aldonza Lorenzo whose father is "Lorenzo Corchuelo" and whose mother is "Aldonza Nogales," (29, 214, 100). Born of real parents, Aldonza Lorenzo is real, too—at least in Cervantes's fictional world. Who then is Dulcinea? According to the book, Dulcinea is partly-true partly-fictional. Partly true because she is modeled on a woman who Don Quixote has encountered in his own life; and partly fictional because she represents the distilled essence of a variety of characters he has read about in his chivalry books—like Queen Guinevere, princess Micomicona, and princess Melisendra, for example. Since Dulcinea combines the qualities of a simple farm girl with the qualities of a high-minded literary queen, she represents reality and fiction blended together in symbolic narrative form. In this sense, Aldonza Lorenzo is a real flesh-and-bones person while Dulcinea is a projection of what a perfect woman would look like. Though Don Quixote "has never seen [the] lady Dulcinea" it is also true that Dulcinea comes from a real character named Aldonza Lorenzo (707). As such, Dulcinea del Toboso is Aldonza Lorenzo yet better since she takes on all of the charms and perfections of a woman's highest attainable standard without embodying any feminine flaws. Accordingly, Cervantes depicts Dulcinea's realistic, yet essentilized, character traits through the ideal lens of Don Quixote's mind. Ergo, since Dulcinea's characteristics are semi-real, the virtues that Don Quixote gives her are semi-real too; in that they exist here on earth, in carnal, tangible, form. If we accept this to be the case, it can be reasoned that a perfect woman, like Dulcinea, can exist in reality because she comes from reality. As such, Dulcinea is a fictional representation of all of the qualities a woman must have if she is to be a great lady. This is why Cervantes says she is "virtuous, peerless, graceful, delightful, urbane, chaste, continent, illustrious, fair, merry, wise, pure, the acme of intelligence, a treasury of fine wit, dignified with due pride, amorous yet modest, gracious from courtesy, courteous from good breeding, courtly [in] bearing, incomparable [in] constancy, energetic [in] mien, [full of vigorous] spirit" and, in short, "exactly as a lady ought to be" (708, 710, 785, 647, 709, 504, 406, 636, Prologue: (2x), 708, 23 (2x), 215, 784, 476, 643, 707). Evidently, Cervantes lists Dulcinea's personal merits because he wants his female readers to adopt her characteristics for themselves so that they take-on the virtues of a purified soul. This is why Don Quixote "see[s] her as being exactly [what] a lady ought to be if she [is to] possess all the qualities needed to make her famous throughout the world" (707). So great is Dulcinea, in fact, that she inspires Spanish women, like lady Oriana, to match her example: "O Dulcinea, I so wish I could adorn my body and my soul with what you are, and what you long for, too, and watch the famous knight whose heart you won win some famous battle for you" (Prologue). By having Lady Oriana express high praise for Dulcinea, Cervantes relates the idea that since one of his characters wants to be like Dulcinea maybe the reader should too. In brief, Dulcinea expresses Cervantes's conception of what it means to be a perfect lady so that other women strive to match her example.

Clearly, Dulcinea's feminine qualities evoke Don Quixote's loyalty, monogamy, and constancy, since he rejects various love-suits from women like Altisidora; since he turns down perceived advances from females like Donna Rodriguez and Maritornes; and, generally speaking, since he repeatedly professes his fidelity to her during his many different adventures. One example of Don Quixote's fidelity to Dulcinea occurs when a "fourteen year old" maiden named Altisidora pretends to woo him as part of a royal joke to get a rise out of him (784). To Altisidora's great surprise, however, her joke turns serious when she develops real feelings for Don Quixote because his loyalty to Dulcinea is attractive to her. Accordingly, when Altisidora serenades Don Quixote from a garden courtyard below his room, he voices commitment to Dulcinea by saying: "for Dulcinea alone [he is] puff pastry and almond paste, and for all other women [he] is flint" (784). Undaunted by the denial of her love-song, Altisidora re-tests Don Quixote's fidelity by continuing her suit. This time she "pretend[s] to faint" in a castle hallway (702). Then has her "friend" Emercia "unlace her bodices," so that Don Quixote will rush-up and display concern for her health (792). To make clear to Altisidora that he loves Dulcinea and no other woman Don Quixote asks Emercia to place "a lute [in his] room, to console this afflicted maid" because "when love is dawning, to be undeceived is the best cure" (792). That "night" he sings a "ballad he'd composed [during the] day [that says that]: Sewing and embroidery and ceaseless occupation are the antidotes to the virulence of amorous inclination [for] Toboso's Dulcinea is indelibly portrayed upon the canvas of [his] heart and never will she fade" (793, 794). He then concludes his sonnet by saying: "True constancy in love is what all lovers prize: It makes Love work his miracles and raise them to the skies" (794). Don Quixote's gentle rejection of Altisidora is not "hard-hearted," as Altisidora claims; just the reverse, it is considerate because rather than instilling false hopes by giving her the impression that love is possible between them, he makes it very clear, from the get-go, that he cannot love her because he loves Dulcinea. In other words, rather than allowing Altisidora's expectations to flower only to be dashed, Don Quixote respects her feelings by telling her the truth from the start. Thus, callous, or obdurate, or unfeeling, Don Quixote is not because rather than giving Altisidora false intimations of a love that can never be, he is frank with her from the start so that she knows where she stands. And, even though Don Quixote tells Altisidora that love is impossible between them since "his heart belongs to another" she continues her suit by trying to make him feel guilty for what she thinks is cruelty on his part. This, she does, during the catafalque scene, when she says:

> 'God forgive you, loveless knight, because through your cruelty I have been in the other world for what seems like more than a thousand years. [And there I

have been] tormented for two whole days, tormented by the thought of the severity with which you O callous knight have treated me

(953, 957).

In reply Don Quixote says:

I am sorry you have directed your affectations towards me, because you can expect no response but gratitude from mine; I was born to belong to Dulcinea del Toboso, and the fates (if they exist) have dedicated me to her; and to think that any other beauty can occupy the place that she has in my soul is to think the impossible. This is sufficient disabuse to make you retire within the bounds of your chastity.

(958).

In this speech, Don Quixote encourages Altisidora to direct her affections to another person because true love is impossible between them. This, in turn, hastens her psychological recovery process, so that she can move on with her life quickly. In other words, even though Don Quixote tells Altisidora what she does not want to hear, he spares her much torment in the long run by minimizing her emotional attachment to him. This illustrates Don Quixote's guiding principle that in love affairs it is better to be up-front with a lady by telling her an unpleasant truth, sooner, rather than later, instead of leading her on by delaying what ultimately must be said. Besides loving Dulcinea above Altisidora, another reason why Don Quixote rejects Altisidora's advances is because she is too young for him. She is fourteen years old and he is forty-nine years old. An age difference of thirty-five years marks unequal intellectual outlooks thus signaling, at least to Don Quixote, the impossibility of any romantic relationship growing between them. Since such a wide-gulf of time separates the understanding of these two human beings, Don Quixote rejects Altisidora's love-suit in favor of Dulcinea's adult womanhood. Not only does Don Quixote tactfully reject Altisidora's jejune flirtations he also rebuffs amorous advances from other quarters as well. For example, when two women "flirt with [Don Quixote] on the sly" he insists that impure thoughts will not enter his mind because Dulcinea "is the queen" of his "thoughts" and he "suffers none but her to vanquish" his heart (910). As such, he "repulses" these ladies "flirtations" by "[sitting] down on the [dance] floor" to decline waltzing with them (910). Evidently, he refuses to dance with these women to blot-out their seductive temptations. Likewise, when Don Quixote thinks that other women are trying to suit him, he reiterates his fidelity to Dulcinea. For instance, when he mistakes Maritornes for an Innkeeper's daughter come to make love to him, "he begins to ponder the predicament in which his virtue is in, and resolve[s] in his heart not to betray Dulcinea" (125). Again when Don Quixote thinks that princess Micomicona wants to marry him he claims that "it is impossible for [him] to contemplate marriage" because he must "preserve the fidelity that [he] owe['s] [his] lady Dulcinea del Toboso" (275, 130). He does not even entertain the idea of marrying another person because "Don Quixote [wants to marry] his beloved Dulcinea del Toboso, from whose womb [will] issue cubs" (432). Another instance of Don Quixote "commending himself with all his soul and all his might to his lady Dulcinea" comes when he thinks that the Innkeeper's daughter wants to caress his hand because she is "overwhelmed by her love [for him]" (782, 406). In response Don Quixote says:

> My heart goes out to you, beauteous lady, for having directed your amorous inclinations towards a quarter where it is not possible that they should find the response due to your great merit and grace; for which you should not blame this knight errant, prevented by love from being able to yield [my] heart to any other

than her whom, from the very first moment I saw her, [I] made [her] the absolute mistress of [my] soul. Forgive me, my good lady, and retire to your room

(407).

This is how Don Quixote kindly declines yet another advance. Besides these specific examples of his loyalty, Don Quixote vouches his faithfulness to Dulcinea again and again by saying: "[that] he preserved his chastity for Dulcinea's sake; [that] Dulcinea [is lucky] to enjoy his incomparable constancy; [that] Dulcinea is the sole mistress of [his] most secret thoughts; [that] to be Dulcinea's and no other's nature brought [him] into this world; [that he] owes [his] fidelity to [his] lady Dulcinea; [that he is] no use whatsoever to any woman, thanks to the peerless beauty of [his] lady Dulcinea del Toboso; [that he] needs no greater assurance than [his] own continence and modesty [that he will not cheat on Dulcinea]" (780, 784, 126, 785, 806, 807). So strong is Don Quixote's love for Dulcinea that he does not forget her, even when separated by great geographical distances. This is why he says:

If anyone claims that Don Quixote de la Mancha has forgotten or can forget Dulcinea del Toboso, I shall, with equal arms, force him to acknowledge that he is very far from the truth, because neither can the peerless Dulcinea del Toboso be forgotten nor is Don Quixote capable of forgetting her

(887).

In conclusion: despite being pursued by multiple women who appear to be queens and princesses and damsels in love with him – despite being flirted with and wooed and tantalized in rather persistent ways – despite being separated from Dulcinea by great spatial distances, Don Quixote remains faithful to his partner because "for Dulcinea alone [he is] honey and aloes and [for her] nature brought [him] into this world" (785). In sum, Don Quixote rejects a multitude of female seductions—whether feigned or actual, real or imagined, genuine or not—to maintain his constant monogamy for Dulcinea del Toboso.

Besides inspiring Don Quixote with a sense of constancy for her person, Dulcinea also inspires him with the courage that he needs to perform many brave acts of chivalry. For example, when he battles an enormous windmill-giant he "commend[s] himself with all his heart to his lady Dulcinea [and] charge[s] [forth at] top speed" (64). Again when Don Quixote mistakes the thuds of six-alternating fulling hammers for the plops of an oncoming ogre he "implores [Dulcinea] to favour him in [his] dreadful enterprise" (162). Likewise, Don Quixote conveys his enthusiasm for Dulcinea when he asks Sancho Panza if he "realiz[es] the might[ty] [strength] that [she] infuses into [his] arm" (276). Evidently, Dulcinea's identity heightens Don Quixote's physical strength, and amplifies his fighting prowess, because through bravery he wins her heart, sustains her admiration, and enhances her respect for him. Just thinking of Dulcinea while battling "enlighten[s] [his] mind and strengthen[s] [his] heart, so that [he is] unequalled in intelligence and in courage [because] nothing in life makes knights errant more courageous than being favored by their ladies" (533). Since Don Quixote thinks that success in battle comes not just from the strength with which a force is applied but also the intelligence with which smart-power is exercised, his love for Dulcinea strengthens his muscles and elevates his mind so that he bests his foes with a winning strategy of potency plus reasoning translated into triumph. Put another way, Dulcinea encourages Don Quixote to deploy his muscles and actuate his mind on her behalf to win battles aplenty – even against ferocious beasts. This is why he "freverently commends himself to his lady Dulcinea" to give him the strength he needs to defeat an uncooperative lion (595). Besides Don Quixote's rash, or delusional, or foolhardy acts for Dulcinea, he also performs sane acts of courage for her which have more positive results: like when he frees a poor farmer laborer named Andres from being flogged by his paymaster; like when he jousts Tosilos to compel him to keep his promise to marry Donna Rodriguez's daughter; like when he frees a chain-gang of outlaws who are tortured, lash stroked, and sent to the galleys for minor crimes; like when he brandishes his sword to protect a beautiful shepherdess named Marcela from importunate advances; like when he upholds true-love by battling rich Camacho's friends in favor of poor Basilio's suit; like when he tries to block an armed clash between two villages who feud over a petty, "donkey-bray," misunderstanding. These examples prove that Don Quixote "has performed, do[es] perform and shall perform the most famous deeds of chivalry that have been witnessed, are [now] witnessed and shall be witnessed in the world," all for Dulcinea del Toboso (49). In short, Dulcinea inspires Don Quixote to enact a wide variety of brave feats—some foolish some not—to bring positive growth to Cervantes's fictional world of 17th century Spain.

One reason why Don Quixote performs brave acts for Dulcinea is because he thinks she is beautiful, smells good, and is physically attractive. This is why he says that:

> her hair is golden; her forehead the Elysian Fields; her eyebrows [are] rainbows; her eyes [are] suns; her cheeks [are] roses; her lips [are] coral; her teeth [are] pearls; her neck [is] alabaster; her breast [is] marble; her hands [are] ivory; her complexion snow; and, the parts hidden to human gaze by modesty [words] cannot find comparisons, [only to] extol them

(100).

Obviously, Don Quixote is enamoured by Dulcinea's loveliness because "to [him] she looks like the most beautiful woman in the world" (699). In fact Don Quixote avows that "it is enough for [him] to be convinced that Aldonza Lorenzo is beautiful and virtuous [for he] imagine[s] that everything is precisely as [he] says it is [therefore he] depicts her in [his] imagination as [he] wish[es] her to be, [both] in beauty and in rank" (216). Again, Don Quixote does not invent Dulcinea's likeness out of thin-air because she is based on a real life woman who Don Quixote has encountered "four times [in] twelve years" (214). As such, Dulcinea's beauty is modeled on Aldonza's beauty, who, evidently, is a "good looking peasant girl, with whom [Don Quixote] had once been in love" (29). For this reason, Don Quixote believes that Dulcinea's "beauty is superhuman, for in her all the attributes of loveliness that poets ascribe to their ladies becomes reality" (100). This is why he describes her as "[the] fairest of the fair, wonderful [in her] loveliness, peerless [in her] appearance, [a] flower of [true perfection], [and] beautiful without blemish" (974, 45, 806, 70, 707). Since she "is the most beautiful woman in the world" Don Quixote wants "the fame of lady Dulcinea's [physical qualities to] endure [eternally]" (928). Thus, to immortalize Dulcinea's attractiveness Don Quixote praises her good-looks with "written verse," by asking a student/poet to compose a ballad to her with "one letter of her name at the beginning of each line, so that when the reader reach[es] the end of the poem and put[s] all the first letters together they [will] read: *Dulcinea del Toboso*." (513). By praising Dulcinea's loveliness in iambic pentameter, then, Don Quixote etches her memory in the minds of his readers so that future generations can admire her beauty for centuries to come. Why else does he say that "Helen cannot rival her, nor can Lucretia or any other of the famous women of past ages, whether Greek, Barbarian or Roman" (216). In fact Don Quixote is so taken with Dulcinea's good looks that he "traces a great number of verses in a stream's sandbank to praise her [beauty]" (221). Moreover, when he plays the role of a shepherd in love he declares that there is "no need to search for the name of a fictitious shepherdess [to honor] because [he] already [has] the peerless Dulcinea del Toboso in mind because to him she is the glory of riverbanks, the ornament of meadows, the mainstay of beauty, the cream of all the graces, and, in short, one worthy to receive all praise, however hyperbolical it [may seem]" (974). Dulcinea even smells like tender blooms to Don Quixote for her "sweet odor derives from living among ambergris and flowers" (550). In conclusion, Don Quixote praises Dulcinea's beauty and attractiveness and odor because he needs "a lady of whom he can be enamored: for a knight errant without a lady-love is a tree without leaves or a body without a soul" (29).

Besides waxing eloquent about Dulcinea's beauty, Don Quixote elevates his courage during difficult times by bringing Dulcinea to mind. By thinking of Dulcinea in battle he endures the trials, the tribulations and the hardships associated with hero questing throughout south-central Spain. For instance, when a group of muleteers disturb Don Quixote's arms-and-armour atop a water trough, he fixes his thoughts on Dulcinea and says: "Assist me, dear lady, in this first affront suffered by this breast that is committed to you; let not your favour and your succour abandon me in this first moment of peril" (39). Later on, when Don Quixote "charges at [nearby] windmill[s] [he] begs Dulcinea to succour him in his plight" because defeating a mighty ogre is hard-work (64). Subsequently, when Don Quixote's "ear" is lopped off by a truculent Basque along with "a large part of his helmet," Don Quixote appeals to Dulcinea "to succour [her] knight, who [undertakes many] dire peril[s] to satisfy her great goodness" (70, 77). In this case Don Quixote's hymn to Dulcinea infuses his soul with the strength he needs to rain-down a double-handed sword blow on a Basque's cushioned head with sufficient force to bloody "his nose, [gore] his mouth, and [scar] his ears, [so that from shock-trauma] he slides off his mule," utterly defeated (77). In fact Don Quixote even travels to Toboso to view a peasant girl Sancho Panza claims is Dulcinea because as "long as Don Quixote see[s] [Dulcinea], whether over a wall or through a window, or through the chink of a door or through the railings in a garden, her beauty will enlighten [his] mind and strengthen [his] heart, so that [he] shall be unique and unequalled in intelligence and in courage" (533). One final example of Don Quixote drawing moxy from Dulcinea comes when he fights the Knight of the White Moon. Before jousting him he "commends himself with all his heart to his" lady Dulcinea (928). Besides inspiring Don Quixote's bravery during dark times, just thinking of Dulcinea bolsters his spirit so that he finds the strength he needs to endure a whole host of temporary setbacks. For example, when Don Quixote is stoned and robbed by a band of outlaws and nearly starves to death in the Sierra Morona, he calls on "Dulcinea to consider the place and state" in which he is in and to "grant" him the "prosperity [he] needs" to endure dangerous animals, menacing marauders and lurking bandits that inhabit the desolate gulleys of the Black Hills (211). By calling on Dulcinea's energizing spirit when he is down, Don Quixote musters the strength he needs to traverse miles of hardened terrain – even while injured – to make it out of the desolate wastelands. Throughout the book, when Don Quixote is down in spirit, he ascends in fortitude, by composing prayers to Dulcinea, by imploring her to favour him during difficult times, and by willing him to elevate his intelligence, so that, ultimately, he finds the moral strength he needs to achieve his life's purpose. For example, before Don Quixote descends into Montesinos's Cave he calls on the "illustrious and peerless Dulcinea [to] answer [his] prayers and supplications [by granting] him [her] favour and help, now that [he] stand[s] in so much need of it" (636). Since the mouth of the cave is dangerous because it plunges down into the very bowels of the earth and because the "birds of the night" – like the "bats" and the "crows" – could kill him by knocking him off-balance, Don Quixote steels himself for his underworld descent by delivering a soliloquy to his lady. What's more, since Don Quixote does not know what he will encounter in the murky depths of the yawning abyss he appeals to Dulcinea to bless his dangerous spelunking expedition. In short, by relying on Dulcinea as a source of aid in hard times, Don Quixote musters the spirit he needs to succeed.

After Don Quixote completes several successful adventures in Dulcinea's name, he sends chains of defeated knights to her, so that they pledge their allegiance to her Excellency in modest tones of compliance: just like Sir Lancelot conquered foes for Lady Guinevere, and the Knights of the Round Table. This is why he creates:

> [a beautiful woman] to whom he can send [vanquished foes] as [personal] tribute, so that [they] come before [her] fall to their knees and say in humble tones of submission: 'I, my lady, am the giant Caraculimbro, the lord of the Isle of Malindrania, vanquished in single combat by the never sufficiently praised Don Quixote de La Mancha, who has commanded me to present myself before Your Highness so that Your Grace may dispose of me as you will

(29).

In this sense, Don Quixote creates a circle of good-will trust between Dulcinea and foreign knights by compelling them to submit to her will. Right away he makes a defeated Basque "promise to repair to the village of El Toboso and present himself on [his] behalf before Dulcinea [so] she may dispose of him according to her pleasure" (77). Likewise, after Don Quixote frees a chain-gang of outlaws he says that they should: "set off without delay for the city of El Toboso [to] present [themselves] before the lady Dulcinea [to] tell her that her knight presents his compliments [without reservation]" (185). Similarly, he sends other boon-beneficiaries to El Toboso like a Basque woman he rescues from being ravished by a group of friars. To "requite the benefit [she] receives from [him, Don Quixote asks her] to present [her]self before Donna Dulcinea [to] inform her of what [he] accomplishes [on her behalf]" (69). By doing good onto others, and then sending them to his lady Dulcinea, Don Quixote seeks to impress her by making conquered knights "get down on bended knee in her presence [and] say they've come on [his] behalf to swear obedience [to her ladyship]" (285). In short, one more reason that Don Quixote creates Dulcinea is because he wants a female to fight for, to do good for, and, ultimately, to destroy evil for. This is why Don Quixote imagines that Dulcinea's spirit gives him the resolve he needs to conquer evil doers in order to convert them to the ethical mores of valiant chivalry. As such, he sends strings of defeated knights to his beloved Dulcinea, so that they, in turn, declare their allegiance to her in good faith. In this sense Don Quixote wants to revive the forgotten code of knight errantry so that other knights have the courage to enact great deeds of chivalry; just like he does for Dulcinea. Since, traditionally, knights fought for right honorable justice on behalf of a beautiful and virtuous strong-minded woman, Don Quixote selects a superlative female to inspire other knights to act as he does.

One other function that Dulcinea fulfills for Don Quixote is to soothe his mind when he is mentally upset so that he views events from a healthy perspective; not from a deranged mental viewpoint. For example, when Don Quixote runs around wildly, smashes his head against stones, and tears at trees (in imitation of a crazy man he has read about named Orlando Furioso) Sancho Panza becalms his master by pretending that he has talked to Dulcinea and that she "[told Sancho Panza] to tell [Don Quixote] that she [sends] her kind regards, is keen to see him and beg[s] and order[s] [him] to leave the wastelands [of the Sierra Moreno] and to stop playing the fool and to set off straight away for El Toboso because she wants to see him so much" (208, 282). Soon thereafter, Don Quixote stops doing naked "summersaults and handsprings," tranquilizes his angry spirit, puts his clothes back on, and sets off for Toboso town, where he recovers his wits a bit (212). In this case, thoughts of seeing Dulcinea turns a grief-stricken Don Quixote into a sane person again. Don Quixote even says that Dulcinea "can calm [his soul] by providing rest for his cares [and] rewards for his services" (406). In short, Dulcinea tranquilizes Don Quixote's feverish mind so that he enhances his inner calm.

Cervantes also uses Dulcinea's example to show Spanish women that nobility is not just a question of bloodline or wealth or beauty or genetic background but is also a function of the merit, the drive, and the brio that a female achieves in her being, even if she comes from simple stock. This is why Don Quixote says that in Aldonza's case "the question of lineage is not very important [because] a virtuous person of [modest] extraction is worthier of regard and esteem than a depraved aristocrat" (708). Evidently, even though Aldonza Lorenzo comes from simpletons, Cervantes emphasizes her positive qualities by saying that she is:

> a good-looking peasant girl who pitches a bar as far as the strongest lad in the village; hale and hearty and strong as an ox, [with a] long distance voice [capable of being heard from far away]; [with the grace of] a courtly lass [who] enjoys a [good] joke with everyone and turns everything into a good laugh; [a great] jump[er] [who] can leap from the ground on to the back of a donkey as if she was a cat!

(29, 215, 699).

What's more, since Dulcinea, the noble aristocrat, is an outgrowth of Aldonza Lorenza, the common peasant, Cervantes suggests that modest women can become great through their efforts. After all, how do noble people become noble in the first place? Through their achievements, of course: nothing less, nothing more. This is why "low born people [who] have prospered little by little [can] achieve the eminence of great lords" by meritorious conduct (174). In other words, the lineal virtues ascribed to Dulcinea, like good-standing natural to "high-birth;" like a noble bearing because she is related to all of the "ancient aristocrats [of] Toboso;" like "[the] nobility [that stems from an exulted] pedigree" are all acquired traits that Aldonza can obtain, and pass down to her children, if she elevates her status from a nobody to "a somebody" (708, 710, 708, 174). Also, Sancho Panza's pretense that a simple farm-girl from El Toboso can become a Dulcinea if she tries signals the idea that merit can be rewarded in life. This is why Cervantes suggests that a girl who lives in "a tiny house" who "sieves a bushel of buckwheat" and who can not "read or write" can come to live in a "splendid castle" with "string[s] [of large] pearls [at her disposal]; [to achieve literacy in the verbal arts by crafting] eloquent poetic compositions," sitting atop a "rich dias" (539, 280, 282). Thus, Cervantes's view that an Aldonza Lorenzo can become a Dulcinea is symbolized by her fine mansion, great jewels, and small throne. In conclusion, all of these facts when taken together suggest that a modest country girl can upgrade her net-worth, her intellect, and her circumstances, so that she qualifies to wear minor robes of nobility.

Given all this proof, why, then, does Cervantes not say that a farmgirl can improve her character, knowledge, and understanding directly? What is he so afraid of? Why does he make his points about upward social mobility on an implicit suggestive level and not on an explicit observational one? One answer is because he wrote *Don Quixote* at a time when Spain was highly stratified, thus fluid social mobility, based on individual merit was frowned upon, restricted even, especially for a peasant. As such, Cervantes had to be very careful about how he depicted a peasant girl bettering herself. This is why Cervantes only *implies* that an Aldonza Lorenzo can become a Dulcinea del Toboso instead of saying so outright. Perhaps Cervantes was wise to couch the theme of social mobility in Don Quixote's insanity, because in 17th century Spain the idea that someone could rise from the lowest of the low to the highest of the high through individual self-elevation was anathema, blasphemous even, to the prevalent idea that those born rich or powerful or influential where somehow automatically entitled to rule, even if they themselves were abject villains, or incompetent nincompoops, or low-minded dolts, or some hideous combination thereof, despite having great forebears. As such, the idea that a commoner, like Aldonza Lorenzo, could rise-up in society by means other than some grand hidden bloodline, was distasteful, taboo even. Usually, the high echelons of civilization were solely and exclusively the domain of royal lords who were born to rule, even if they were not qualified to do so. Yet with Cervantes' advent of Aldonza Lorenzo, we see a subtle paradigm shift. No longer is one's station automatically determined at birth by their pedigree. Rather their rank, their status and their class is a logical outgrowth of their intelligent focus coupled with their motivated drive and talented ambition, as well. But since Cervantes wanted his book to be published worldwide he needed a supportive patron to agree with and endorse his work. Therefore, Cervantes articulates a clever side-message about how an intelligent commoner elevates her station only indirectly so that a wealthy sponsor could overlook his written unorthodoxies. Through hidden metaphor, mistaken identity and psychological misapprehension, Cervantes expresses his ideas about class hierarchy indirectly so that casual readers could overlook his written unorthodoxies as products of Don Quixote's delusional folly; while astute readers would understand his points about class status for what they really were. In sum, Cervantes's subtle line of reasoning vis-à-vis Aldonza/Dulcinea suggests that an able peasant can advance in society, despite having modest origins, much like Aldonza Lorenzo transcends her station to become Dulcinea. This, in turn, shows readers that anybody, no matter how modest their background, or how overwhelming their life challenges, can rise to great success through enough smart and hard work sustained over an extended period of time. This is why the author implies that an Aldonza Lorenzo can transcend her anonymous birth to become a Dulcinea of her very own.

Cervantes continues the theme that a woman can reach the sublime heights of civilization by praising Dulcinea's personal merits—for even a princess like Dulcinea can become "a queen [replete] with crown and scepter" if she has the right "qualities [of characteristic] for the merits of a beautiful and virtuous woman extend as far as" her drive takes her (708). Despite her high starting place to begin with, "Dulcinea [has] the makings of a great queen" because she has virtues that "ennoble the blood" like: "intelligence, wisdom, purity, grace, urbanity, modesty, dignity, chastity, continence, good-sense, high-principles, a delightful presence, intelligent conversation, a beautiful bearing, well-deserved fame, an energetic mien, a cheerful disposition, and amorous modesty" (708, 542, 23, 709, 708, 647, 540, 504, 543, Part I Addendum, 708). By giving Dulcinea all of these qualities Cervantes suggests that she can rise to a higher social station by dint of her own will-power because, says Cervantes, Aldonza is a refined human being of self-made soul who "is the daughter of her own works" (708). In sum, by presenting a moving portrait of a mere peasant becoming a rich noblewoman, Cervantes conveys the implicit message that social prominence can be gained by dint of one's own virtue.

Evidently, Dulcinea is Don Quixote's conception of a perfect woman: a lady who inspires him to defend his life, maintain his honor, and uphold his moral principles – a female who encourages him to safeguard his being, defend his possessions, and protect his family – a meritocrat who represents natural law, civil liberty, and social fairness incarnate – a person who inspires Don Quixote to actuate his value quest of generating an ethical Spanish society, despite the danger, the difficulty, and the detriment this entails. Under Dulcinea's watchful gaze, Don Quixote prompts himself to battle all manner of foes: like windmill giants, threshing mill ogres, wicked-smart farmers, contumacious Basques, merciless soldiers, parasitic picaros, snarling lions, foam-spraying boars, crude muleteers, duplicitous lackeys, droves of pigs, and herds of bulls. Even though some of Don Quixote's actions are misguided, silly even, he does what he does to live-up to Dulcinea's high-opinion of him because, ultimately, he does not want to disappoint himself. As such, Don Quixote performs brave deeds, commits strong acts, and endures hard times to revive idealism and nobility and knighthood in a society empty of these precepts. In effect, by equating Donna Dulcinea with Queen Guinevere and the Knights of the Round

Table, Don Quixote tries to resurrect the legend of King Arthur with Sir Lancelot in tow. This is why he sends scores of defeated knights to Dulcinea to swear allegiance to her high-principles. Based on his extensive reading of chivalry tales, Don Quixote even attempts to create a scenario similar to the Arthurian Grail cycle where a brave warrior knight travels far-and-wide, conquers hold-out braves, sends them to a civilized royal court in a great capital city to convert them from serving evil and darkness to serving light and goodness. Integral to this elaborate fantasy is Don Quixote's envisonment of a noble queen (i.e. Dulcinea) who, by virtue of her merit, inspires pugilistic men to gladly fight for her person. Said differently, to inspire other knights to fight for Dulcinea's standard, Don Quixote expresses to them that she has: healthy blond hair; clear sparkling eyes; chalk-white teeth; crimson plump lips; a snow white complexion, and the aroma of fresh roses.

One other point that Cervantes makes about Dulcinea is that she is not simply an embellishment of Don Quixote's overactive mind but rather she is derived from a living, breathing human-being he has met in his own life: a pretty and intelligent farm-girl named Aldonza Lorenzo from the nearby town of El Toboso. By connecting Aldonza Lorenzo's identity to Dulcinea Del Toboso's person, Cervantes shows readers that a Dulcinea can exist in the real world because she comes from the real world. The fact that Don Quixote combines Aldonza Lorenzo's positive qualities with Dulcinea's fictional embellishments expresses his desire to strive for, to fight for, even to die for, a larger-than-life woman worthy of his constant affection. Most importantly, though, even though Dulcinea is partly imagined, partly embellished and partly real, she is a striking fictional example for other Spanish women to match, so that they, like her, take on the qualities of a refined essence. Hence, the virtues ascribed to her (even though amplified for dramatic effect) are drawn from the positive qualities of a real life damsel who inhabits Cervantes's fictional world. What's more, because Don Quixote views Aldonza Lorenzo in such elevated terms, she becomes his supreme romantic value—a person worth devoting his mind, his heart, and his being to. By off-putting many amorous advances from ingénues like Altisidora, or trollops and jokers, like Maritornes, or seductive enchantresses, like Madame Palomeque, Don Quixote counsels easy, or infatuated, or dishonest females to busy themselves in constructive activities apart from love, until they develop the ability to distinguish true-love from false-lust. This, in turn, shows readers that once they spot a companion with true potential they should strive to develop a meaningful romantic relationship with that person if they wish to live a happy and fulfilled mental-and-emotional life. As such, part of Don Quixote's yearning for Dulcinea stems from the fact that he never consummated carnal relations with Aldonza Lorenzo—maybe out of shyness, maybe out of concern for her lesser station in life, or maybe because he could not create a romantic opportunity with her. But this much is certainly true: a real, corporal, physical-woman worth fighting for, even dying for, would have balanced Don Quixote's warlike aggression to settle his mind and his emotions a bit. And we get this impression, at least in part, because when Don Quixote contemplates Dulcinea he regains control of his mind.

Besides tranquilizing Don Quixote's febrile spirit, Dulcinea/ Aldonza is Cervantes's attempt to loosen rigid class structures dominant in 17th century Spain, so that a meritocracy could emerge (i.e. a social system that gives opportunities and advantages to people on the basis of their ability, rather than their wealth or seniority.) In effect, Cervantes uses Dulcinea/Aldonza's person to show all women – high and low, young and old, rich and poor – that the measure of their self-worth is not metered by their blood-line, current rank, or an unearned social status, but rather is determined by their ability, achievement and will to do what is right for themselves and for their people. Given the sensitivities of the times, Cervantes casts only a dim sidelight on a merit-based civil-social order because flooding this theme in full sunlight would have led to dire consequence for himself and his book. Accordingly, he only suggests that an Aldonza Lorenzo can become a Dulcinea del Toboso, which he further obscures with Don Quixote's covert delusions coupled with Sancho Panza's overt subterfuge. By presenting elusive meanings open to double-entendre, Cervantes disguised his book's central message with an array of conceptual ploys so that his novel was not blocked, or expurgated, or stigmatized by the inquisition's Holy censors. If one is able to unravel Cervantes's entire system of off-putting smokescreens, double messages, and unreliable characters, the message of Dulcinea's rise to success is quite clear: obvious even. On a deeper level, however, Cervantes evades the Holy censors of his times by slipping in the idea—under the radar; so to speak—that a woman is a product of her own individual agency. This is why he disguises Donna Dulcinea's true nature through a welter of mistaken identity, doubtful veracity, and outright trickery, coupled with Don Quixote's delusional insanity, as well. Anything too incendiary, or controversial, or blasphemous, especially in regard to a woman's social advancement, would have made his Patron uncomfortable with and therefore likely to reject his book. Thus, to ensure that his novel was published, Cervantes toned down his language about an Aldonza becoming a Dulcinea, leaving it up to the wit of an astute reader to decrypt his hidden message of feminine social mobility.

ESSAY 6

How Cervantes Unites Christians and Muslims in Don Quixote: *Bridging the Gap.*

In *Don Quixote de la Mancha,* Cervantes begins a fictional conversation between Muslims and Christians by creating a Muslim philosopher, on the one hand, who he claims writes the novel in Arabic, while he creates a Christian translator, on the other hand, who steps in-and-out of the tale to speculate about the primary intent of its original Moorish author. By inventing a Moorish narrator, on the one hand, who pens Don Quixote's story, and a Castilian Morisco, on the other, to translate it, Cervantes starts a hypothetical dialogue between Muslims and Christians, where both religions come to understand one another through peaceful, non-threatening, words, not hostile, warlike, actions. Given that Cervantes wrote *Don Quixote* at a time when the Spanish monarchy was at war with the Ottoman Empire, he initiates a fictional exchange between Christians and Muslims in a funny book, so that rational religionists realize that they have more in common than they think. In other words, through storytelling, Cervantes establishes the atmospheric conditions necessary for a religious rapprochement to take place in the minds and emotions of his readers so that tolerance and understanding and peace prevails not narrowness of mind or prejudice or war.

In keeping with *Don Quixote's* theme of religious unity, Cervantes hopes to direct race relations between Muslims and Christians in a more moderate path so that both communities learn to live with one another instead of harboring xenophobic emotions for each other. By intermarrying a Muslim woman with a Christian man Cervantes shows his readers that individuals of two conflicting religions can come together because they love one another. By sparing the lives of two Muslim soldiers provoked into shooting two Spanish shipmen, Cervantes illustrates the concept of forgiveness in action. By having a Muslim elder arrest "his relative and great favorite of his" because he is guilty of assaulting a Christian woman, shows that justice is a trait honored by all people no matter their race, religion, creed, or ethnicity (664). By transfiguring an exquisite Moor named "Jarifa" into a great Christian woman named Dulcinea, Cervantes shows readers that an excellent woman is an excellent woman whether she is a Muslim who prays to Allah or whether she is a Christian who prays to God (49). Together, these examples prove that Cervantes calms tensions between Muslims and Christians, so that individuals of both religions do not confront each other as enemies but instead embrace each other as friends who have a lot to learn from one another.

By voicing a commonality of belief through the words of a Muslim Moorish Philosopher and a Christian Morisco translator, Cervantes suggests that Muslims and Christians are alike in many fundamental ways because: both religions think that holiness is made up of charity, humility, and faith; both religions are monotheistic believers in one true God; both religions believe that special human beings are chosen by a merciful deity to spread God's teachings in the world; both religions hold that there is an afterlife reached by virtue or by sin; both religions think that Heaven is a place of joy and Hell is a place of suffering; both religions believe in the existence of angels and demons who act as messengers of God or harbingers of the Devil; both religions believe that people can come to know God through good deeds; both religions believe in a code of morality that presents sacrifice as the primary virtue; both religions believe that one can generate kinship ties of purity and eternal life through penitence; both religions are concerned with how humanity can save itself from a universal condition of sin and death; both religions believe that human beings must be generous and love one another; both religions offer prayer as a way of communing with God; both religions believe that one's free-will is necessary to chose right from wrong, good from evil, light from darkness; both religions believe in an all-knowing, all-seeing, all-powerful being who controls the universe through His divine will; both religions have canonical books that carry God's authorative word (The Bible for Christians the Qur'an for Muslims); both religions believe in the raising of one's mind and heart to God to request good things of him; both religions organize human life through the ideal of faith and moderation; both religions believe in the cleansing power of virtue and the damning power of sin; both religions believe that people can come to know God by worshipping Him directly; both religions believe that compassion and mercy are the primary virtues of life while cruelty and rigidity are the disvalues of death; both religions provide moral guidance about ethical issues relevant to their social communities; both religions believe in a day of judgment where God decides who has been naughty and who has been nice; both religions stress honesty and candor as a way of reaching Heaven; both religions believe that God has full knowledge and control over all that occurs on earth; both religions believe that all that happens on earth, or has ever happened in this world, has been preordained; both religions assign virtue to alms giving and charity; both religions see the basic unit of society as the family; both religions emphasize poverty, humility, and the avoidance of sin as ways of communing with God; and, above all, both religions have a set of cultural values synonymous with justice and peace. Sometimes directly, sometimes indirectly, Cervantes identifies these common principles in *Don Quixote* so that his readers come to understand that Islam and Christianity are alike in many significant ways.

By way of creating a constructive synergy between Muslims and Christians, Cervantes notes five points of spiritual convergence that signals many mutual principles shared between these two faiths. First, he notes that the state of not having enough money to take care of basic needs such as food, clothing, and shelter is a trait common to many people, whether they are Muslims who believe in Allah, or Christians who believe in God. Second, Cervantes fuses Christianity and Islam together in perceptual externalities by having his Christian characters dress, and act, as Muslims do. Third, Cervantes conveys the idea that a sworn statement is a serious promise, whether it is made to Allah (by a Muslim) or made to God (by a Christian). Fourth, Cervantes logic-chops belief in alchemy or magic or omens or astrology or horoscopes or false miracles or spectral ghosts, to undermine superstitious beliefs associated with a misversion of Christianity and a misversion of Islam. Fifth, Cervantes emphasizes that only through the use of a person's free-will with respect to religion can that person live morally. It is through these five points of agreement that Cervantes shows us that Christians and Muslims are alike in many significant ways.

Cervantes's examination of interfaith synergy begins with his critique of money and charity, where he identifies a willingness to give money, help, and time to less fortunate people as characteristics of holy Christians and devout Muslims. Thus, Cervantes purposely has his characters give alms to the needy. This is why a major Christian character in the story named Sancho Panza, donates money to the poor, especially if he feels that certain individuals deserve his help. An example of Sancho Panza's alms giving occurs when he "feels sorry" that an old man is condemned to the galleys because he is judged guilty of witchcraft and "bodybroking" and therefore gives him "a [golden] real" to ease his suffering a bit (180). Similarly, when a poor farm laborer named Andres complains that his paymaster whipped him for demanding nine months of back-pay, "Sancho takes a hunk of bread and a lump of cheese from his saddlebags and gives it to the lad with the words: 'Here you are, brother Andres" (288). Again when Sancho Panza encounters six Morisco pilgrims who ask him for his help he donates "half a cheese and half a loaf [of bread]" to feed them (851). In fact Sancho Panza rails against not giving money to those in need when he says that "where meanness is king there isn't any room for generosity" (438). Since Sancho Panza says that he is "a good [person] of old Christian stock" he donates food, money, and time to others when he feels that he should (175). But generosity is also shown by a Muslim woman named Lela Zoraida when she gives a Spanish Captain money on several occasions. By repeatedly lowering a "cane [with] a [gold laden] handkerchief," Lela Zoraida exhibits her generosity to Captain Viedma: a Christian bagnio prisoner (370). By emphasizing that prosperous Christians and wealthy Muslims can give alms to the poor if they want to, Cervantes advocates his primary thesis that voluntary charity is a trait that bonds Christians and Muslims together. To encourage pious Muslims, and devout Christians, to assign value to people who lack material goods, Cervantes's original Muslim author—one Cide Hamete El Benengeli— philosophizes on poverty by saying that "from conversations [he has] had with many Christians [he knows] that anybody who can manage to be happy [despite] being poor must have much God in him" (780). Here, Cervantes relates a feeling of impoverished contentment with a feeling of being a good Christian or a virtuous Muslim. Yet, at the same time, Cervantes allows, if the devout have wealth and affluence they can share their riches with deserving others for knowing God is knowing how to "possess material goods as if you did not possess them." (780). This statement suggests that there is a clear difference between goods of the soul, which depend on one's own spiritual morality to find formal expression, and materials of the body, which depend on physical externalities for sustenance. The former, being internal qualities of introspection, are deeply ingrained character traits difficult to corrupt, while the latter, since they are physical objects of the world – like food, clothing, and shelter – can be lost, or taken away, quickly. Therefore, Cervantes suggests, since poor Christians and penurious Muslims are used to material deprivation they have learned to survive with what little they have, whereas rich Christians and affluent Muslims unaccustomed to surviving in times of shortage find themselves hard pressed when impoverished. This is why Cervantes claims that a lack of wealth "batters" Christian and Muslim nobles more than common everyday religionists because they are not used to going from having a lot to not having much (780). In all these ways, and more, Cervantes shows his readers that generous alms giving characterized by a magnanimous and noble spirit is one of the virtues that define practicing Christians and devout Muslims.

Cervantes also unites Christians and Muslims together in perceptual externalities by giving them similar clothing, like body postures, and congruent outward demeanors. For example, when a landed aristocrat named Don Fernando enters a road-side inn he is accompanied by "four [of his Christian servants] riding on horseback [with] Arab-style stirrups" (778). Likewise, when Sancho Panza introduces Don Quixote to a Christian peasant she "jumps onto [her] horse [like an] Arab in one leap" (549). In fact, when this peasant lass finally mounts her steed she seats herself on a "great and tall Arab-style saddle" in Islamic style (551). Cervantes also links Christians and Muslims together in outward deportment by having them perform similar bodily motions. For example, Sancho Panza "bends over in the form of a Turkish bow" to express his respect for Don Quixote (121). Also, when Don Quixote and Sancho Panza meet Don Diego de Miranda, Sancho Panza wants to "kiss" his hands "because" to his "mind" the knight of the green topcoat is "the first saint riding in Arab-style [he has] ever come across in all the days of [his] born life" (586). And when Sancho Panza travels to Barataria to govern his island "he rides a mule with Arab-style short stirrups" (778). By cross-dressing Spaniards and Moors in Arabic outfits—and by giving his Christian characters body postures reminiscent of good Muslims—Cervantes relates Christianity and Islam into a constructive synergy, where their common external appearance signals their mutual internal identities.

Another way Cervantes brings Christianity and Islam together is by highlighting the idea that both religions have ostensible believers who are open to ungodly, irrational, mystical beliefs, which ultimately degrade the quality of their respective religions. To unwind these quasi-religious beliefs, Cervantes logic chops the belief that objects can assume supernatural powers; that happenings in the natural world can take on spiritual significance; that soothsayers can predict the future by referring to the alignment of cosmic bodies; that animals can take on human qualities; and, above all, that dead spirits in purgatory can visit people on earth to communicate mystical messages. First, he refutes the idea that ghosts can exist on earth and do exist in this world by having Sancho Panza insist that the muleteers who blanket tossed him were "not ghosts dreamed-up and imagined [by Don Quixote] but men of [real] flesh and blood" (430). Here, Cervantes undermines a quack version of Christianity and a quack version of Islam, by discrediting the idea that dead spirits can haunt living persons. Next, Cervantes rejects the pseudo religious belief that objects have mysterious pagan powers and can therefore cause magical effects. This is why he has Sancho Panza refute the notion that a wicked enchanter has the ability to transform persons, places, and objects into tangible forms other than what they really are. Evidently, Cervantes connects Christianity and Islam together in concept by voicing a common stand against idol worship. Third, Cervantes believes that people have direct, volitional, control over their lives, and, therefore, cannot be coerced into acting one way or another by a fraudulent pseudo-scientific miracle potion. This is why he has Don Quixote discredit the idea that magic spells can guide a person's choices throughout life for "there are no spells in the world that can control a person's free will (as some simple people believe): for our free will is sovereign, and therefore there is no herb or enchantment that can control it" (180). To amplify this point, Cervantes has Don Quixote expose Charlatans peddling quack nostrums by saying that "what some deceitful rogues do is to make certain poisonous mixtures that they use to turn men mad, claiming that they have the power to make men fall in love, when it is impossible to coerce the will [in this way]" (180). To Cervantes, no potion, however mysterious in nature, or whatever people claim about it, has the power to control a person's free-will, for, scientifically, such a feat is impossible, no matter what a person drinks. Here, Cervantes emphasizes the idea that Christians and Muslims are masters of their own love lives, which, evidently, is another point of interfaith agreement. Fourth, by having Don Quixote express his "unhappiness with [an] ape's power to divine" he undercuts the idea that an animal can foretell the future through mystical premonition (660). By refuting the notion that a travelling puppeteer can train a baboon to prognosticate past or present events, Cervantes brings Christians and Muslims together through a common stand against false divination. Fifth, Cervantes undercuts the notion that an astrologer can foretell the future based on the position of the planets in relation to the sign under which a person was born. Speaking through Don Quixote, Cervantes undercuts horoscopes by saying that he:

> knows of a lady who asked an amateur astrologer whether a little lap-dog bitch of her's would become pregnant and have puppies, and how many and of what color they would be. The fellow cast the horoscope and replied that the bitch would indeed become pregnant and have three puppies, one green, another red and the third a mixture of the two, so long as the bitch was covered between eleven and twelve in the morning or the night, on a Monday or a Saturday; and the outcome was that two days later the bitch died of overeating and the amateur astrologer was exposed as [a fraudster]

(661).

This passage suggests that both Christians and Muslims have the same way of processing mathematical reality, since logical Christians, and, scientific:

> Moors must be confronted with examples that are palpable, straightforward, easy to understand, demonstrable, indisputable – with mathematical proofs that can't be denied, such as 'If equal parts are taken from equal parts, the remainders [must] also [be] equal'
>
> (300).

Why, Cervantes identifies Moors with this characteristic is because, pre Al-Ghazali, when Islamists respected the mind's ability to perceive concrete reality, Moorish civilization was very advanced. Historically, this is evidenced by the fact that Muslims invented algebraic principles, like the concept of the absolute zero, which they applied to invent convex lens for optical instruments, telescopes, and, other, useful astronomic devices. And, since there was scholarly interaction between Christians and Muslims—Christians came from Europe to observe the advanced progress of the Muslim world at the time—there was ideological interpenetration between the peoples and thought-systems of these two great faiths. This, then, is why Cervantes reasons that if

> [both Christians and Moors] can't follow verbal reasoning they must first be shown it all using their fingers and have it placed in front of their eyes.
>
> (300)

This quote suggests Cervantes's disbelief that an astrologer can predict a person's future when the cosmic positions of various stars, planets, and asteroids are in correct alignment. Obviously, many of

Cervantes's Christian and Muslim readers would agree with this point. Another area of thought that Cervantes treats with skepticism is the phenomena of false miracles—like the idea that a marble bust can speak with God's voice to tell the future or that wooden statues can summon rainfall through prayer or that effigies can weep God's liquid tears. To purify Christianity and Islam from irrational mystical notions, Cervantes shows us how supernatural beliefs scandalize these two respective faiths. In fact he derides false miracles altogether by denouncing plays featuring "religious subjects" because such dramas often invent "false miracles [and] apocryphal and misunderstood events" to entertain the theatre going public (445). This is why he describes these plays as ridiculous because:

> they make bold to insert miracles, without any respect or consideration – their only thought is that such and such a miracle or special effect, as they call them, would do very nicely there, to fill the ignorant rabble with amazement and persuade more of them to come and see the play all to the detriment of the truth and to the prejudice of history, and even to the discredit of Spanish writers

(445).

By disputing the notion that apocryphal miracles have a valid place in a rational system of religious belief, Cervantes seeks to unite Christians and Muslims together by opposing them against mysticism. Likewise, magical mysteries, like a future-telling bust, are also discredited by Cervantes when he "explains [that the] magical mystery enclosed within the bust" was not due to God speaking through an inanimate object but "due to an intricate system of tin tubes and marble slabs connected to a room below where an intelligent student was able to hear questions and provide sensible answers" (913). As such, the clergy politely requests that "[Don Antonio Moreno] dismantle his statue, and never use it again, to prevent the ignorant rabble from being scandalized" (914). Besides undercutting false miracles that debase Christianity and Islam, Cervantes discredits the idea that natural phenomena can signal future events. This is why he undercuts false causation like the phenomenon of "an infinity of enormous ravens and rooks flying out [of] the mouth of a cave" as predicting Don Quixote's eminent demise (636). When these "creatures of the night" fly out of the mouth of the cave, Don Quixote, being "a good Christian and [a wise] Catholic," does not take their presence "as a bad omen," rather he shows people how silly they are to believe that a bunch of bats flapping their wings in flight are underworld harbingers of death and destruction (636). Don Quixote makes this point quite clear when he says that "what the common herd calls omens are not based on any natural process of causation [therefore they] should be viewed by intelligent people as mere happy coincidences [because] wise Christians should not pry into what Heaven intends to do" (636, 876). In support of this idea Sancho Panza says that his "village priest said once that sensible Christian persons shouldn't pay any attention to omens" or prophetic signs, since bunk prophecies cannot portend good or evil (972). Finally, to set himself apart from the crowd Don Quixote emphasizes that he is not "superstitious as some people are" (757). Evidently, Don Quixote disbelieves omens because he rappels into Montesinos's cave despite being knocked off-balance by a bunch of bats; despite Sancho Panza taking the sign of the bats as an omen of his imminent demise; despite their fellow traveler, a young poet, relating bats to hellish creatures that inhabit the accursed underworld. By undercutting phenomena believed to predict future gloom-and-doom, Cervantes highlights the idea that good Christians and devout Muslims should dismiss mystical omens as unsubstantiated coincidences. Similarly, idolatry, to Cervantes, or the worship of false Gods venerated through propitiation ceremonies does not factor into his hero's dream quest at all. This concept is best expressed when Don Quixote says that the reason why a wooden horse that he rides vaporizes into thin air is because objects that assume magical powers

– like the ability to fly – should hold no place in the minds and hearts of good Christians and sincere Muslims. Since Sancho Panza believes that it is impossible for "a [flying] wooden horse [to be] controlled by a peg in its forehead" he thinks that it is only right that "Clavileno the Swift burn" rapidly out of existence (751, 779). Eighth, faith healing, to Cervantes, is a "diabolical [and] foul [pretend] science" that has no place in well-ordered societies (728). Since several of the book's characters systematically refute the idea that spirits can appear as shadowy forms or that ghosts can cause eerie sounds or that spirits can move objects by transubstantiation or that phantoms can predict the future by magical premonition or that spurious miracle potions can mysteriously cause certain natural effects, Cervantes undermines blasphemous beliefs associated with a misversion of Christianity and a misversion of Islam, so that both faiths are free from the absurdity of misbelief.

Cervantes also expresses the idea that a faith-based promise to God, or Allah, is a serious commitment to the truth, whether it is a Christian who swears to tell the truth in the name of God or a Muslim who swears to tell the truth in the name of Allah. This is why when Cide Hamete El Benengeli, the Moorish author of *Don Quixote*, argues that Don Quixote's chronicles are true, he "swears as a Christian and a Catholic, to tell the whole truth in everything he says [because] everything he writes about Don Quixote" reflects how he is recorded in historic journals (671). Here, Cervantes adds "that when Cide Hamete swears as a Christian and as a Catholic [to tell the whole truth and nothing but the truth] he only means to say that just as a Christian and Catholic swears [that] something [is true so] he swears to tell the truth in everything he says" (671). This statement suggests to readers that a solemn promise given in the name of a divine being is a serious way of avowing that something is, or is not, true, no matter who the promise is given to, or what the reason is. In other words, it does not really matter if an oath is given by a Muslim to God or a Christian to Allah because, ultimately, the meaning is the same.

Another commonality between Christianity and Islam that Cervantes identifies in his story is the exercise of one's free-will to reach God consciousness through faith and penitence. By emphasizing an individual's free-choice in matters of the spirit, Cervantes not only believes that human beings can come to know God, and his works, by worshipping Him directly, but also, Cervantes believes, that faith in God must be a product of a person's individual volition, and not a result of a warped form of social conformity that is coerced, or compelled, or forced, upon people by an ascetic religious entity that defines what is, or is not, pious. To emphasize the idea that human beings should not be restricted and regulated against their will by an authoritarian religious power structure, Cervantes expresses freedom of thought and action in his story through charactertorial statements like "freedom should not be sold for all the gold in the world;" or "our free-will is sovereign;" or "it seems excessively harsh to make slaves of those whom God and nature made free;" or by "free-will [a person] chooses a life" fit for him; or "you must do as you please [within reason];" or "freedom, Sancho, is one of the most precious gifts bestowed by heaven on man; no treasures that the earth contains and the sea conceals can compare to it [because] for freedom, as for honour, men can and should risk their lives and, in contrast, captivity is the worst evil that can befall them;" (Prologue, 180, 183, 207, 212, 628, 730, 863). By emphasizing the condition of being free as necessary for social independence, Cervantes shows Christians and Muslims that it is one's own personal choice whether they want to bring God and faith into their lives, or not.

Similarly, since Cervantes believes that the condition of being free is a universal desire of good Christians and pious Muslims he purposely has his characters free one another despite having different belief systems. This is why when Cervantes recounts the tale of "Melisendra being set free from the Moors in Spain" he reiterates the point that sometimes a person must fight for their freedom by force of arms (663). Similarly, Cervantes has Christian soldiers grant Muslims shipmen their freedom like when a Spanish infantry Captain "offers Moorish sailors [their] liberty by telling them that they weren't being taken captive" (363). Since Christians and Muslims made slaves of their defeated foes in medieval times, a Moor is genuinely surprised "that [his Christian captors] are going to hand [him his] liberty [since they] took [great] risks to deprive [him] of it in the first place only to give it back so generously, [especially because they can make] so much money ransoming [his liberty to the highest bidder]" (437). To highlight the fact that it is not just Christians who free Muslims but Muslims who also free Christians, Cervantes has a Moorish woman named Lela Zoraida "break the chains [binding a group of Spanish prisoners together] [to] free [them] from captivity" (451). Together, these examples show readers that since liberty of action, arising from freedom of thought, is a basic tenet of natural law, civil liberties should be an essential feature of all well-ordered Christians communities, and all highly organized Muslims societies.

Moreover, Cervantes contrasts freewill with force, or consent with its opposite, to express to Christians and Muslims that a society that introduces compulsion into social relationships is not only an unjust arrangement of human affairs but also that fighting for one's freedom is sometimes necessary. In effect, Cervantes argues for the absence of antecedent causal determinations that act against the action of a person's free-will, through the events of the story. For example, Don Quixote expresses this precept in action when he compels a group of "men in white to [set] free a lady in black [by telling them that they] must at this very instant set free that beautiful lady, whose tears and sorrowful face are clear proof that [she is being] borne off against her own [free] will" (470). Though the woman Don Quixote thinks is being held prisoner is only a statue of the Virgin Mary in procession, the larger point that Cervantes makes by her example is that "there's no happiness on earth [that can match] regaining one's liberty [since] freedom is a God given right worth fighting for" (369, 383, 386, 387). Another example of a person fighting for the principles of a free society occurs when Sancho Panza, as governor, repulses "enemies that attack by night [and by day] thanks to the [great] might of [his invincible] arm" (863). In addition, when Don Quixote thinks that people are being held against their will he "tells [a group of] millers and fishermen that he will gladly pay for the boat [he destroyed] on the condition that they hand over to him, free and without ransom, the person, or persons, imprisoned in the castle" (686). Since Don Quixote does not condone the use of force against a person who has committed no crime, he fights for justice by using force against those he thinks initiates it. Evidently, since freedom is such a vital part of one's moral life, Cervantes has his characters fight for their liberty throughout the book. Indeed, Don Quixote even argues that:

> there are four reasons for prudent men and well-ordered communities to take-up arms, draw their swords and put their lives and their possessions at risk: first, to defend their own lives in accordance with natural law; second to defend their honour, their families [honor] and their [own] possessions [especially from unlawful search or seizure;] third, in service of their king in a just war; and fourth, to defend their country" in times of grave danger

(183, 176, 675).

In other words, Don Quixote wants people to exert volitional self-control over their lives by deciding what to do, or not do, in a particular situation as opposed to having some arbitrary course of action dictated upon them from without. In this sense, Cervantes argues for the liberation of restraint of the despotic power of another so that people are free to think and act for themselves throughout life. In this sense the author argues for a free Christian church and a liberal Muslim Mosque that is not based on state enforcement of theological dictates at gun point but based on a willing sense of devotion to God, instead. Since Cervantes wants to limit the ability of fanatics to impose their beliefs on others, he shows us that a person can be committed to high ideals without being forced to believe in a warped brand of faith. This is why he presents the idea that religious freedom is a hallmark of a healthy nation-state. In short, since freedom of belief is a large part of any moderate Christian state, or any temperate Islamic society, Cervantes views religious worship not as a mandatory form of compulsion to be imposed by a theological dictator but as an act of freewill to be governed by a person's own moral choice. In some cases, suggests Cervantes, this leads to the acceptance of God in one's life but in other cases it does not and should not because no amount of force can compel someone to truly believe or not believe in a thing, especially if that belief does not take shape in the deepest recesses of a person's mind and heart.

Finally, to foster a spirit of unity and understanding between Christians and Muslims, Cervantes has a Christian man marry a Muslim woman so that through intimate pair-bonding they draw closer together in concept; not further apart in practice. To see just how Cervantes argues for a unification of Christianity and Islam through romance let us analyze the *Captive Captain's Tale*, with particular emphasis on the connection between Ruy Perez de Viedma, a Spaniard, and Lela Zoraida, a Moor. By way of background information, Captain Ruy Perez de Viedma is a Spanish infantry Captain who "enlists [as a Spanish naval officer] in Piedmont [to serve] the Duke Of Alba" on a military expedition against the Ottoman Turks (362). In his capacity as a Christian crusader he campaigns for "Don John of Austria [and sails with] the Venetian fleet [stationed in] Messina to fight against the Turk [for] Pope Pius [the fifth]" (362). Fighting for "Venice and Spain against their common Ottoman enemy" Captain Viedma is taken prisoner at the naval battle of Lepanto on October 7th 1571 in which an alliance of Mediterranean and Christian states defeat the main fleet of the Ottoman Empire off the coast of western Greece (362). Despite this victory, however, when Captain Viedma boards an Ottoman galley to claim his prize, his ship is pushed apart by the sea from the enemy ship so that he is besieged with only a few of his soldiers. Soon thereafter he is overwhelmed, overpowered, and "covered with wounds" by the Sultan's soldiers and taken captive "with [his] hands manacled and [his] feet fettered" (363). A tied-up Captain Viedma is transported to Constantinople by the Turkish fleet where he is brought to "the Grand Turk [Sultan] Selim" who decides his fate (363). Sultan Selim decides that his punishment for fighting the Ottomans is first to row as a galley slave in the Pasha's navy and then to be held captive as a bagnio prisoner in Algiers until his family, friends, and relatives can raise a large enough ransom to secure his timely release. This is when he meets Lela Zoraida, a "beautiful and young" rich Moorish woman, "a heiress [to a grand] estate," who gives him gold coins, gems, and other treasures of great value so that he can escape from Algiers back to Spain (373, 374). Since Lela Zoraida falls in love with captain Viedma, she travels to Spain where she is free to marry him. Evidently, Lela Zoraida likes the captive captain's gentlemanly behavior so much, she proposes that he "become her husband" once they are in "Christian lands" together (373). Stimulated by her generous spirit, great beauty, and lavish wealth, the captive captain agrees that she shall "become [his] wife" (374). So begins an epistolary letter exchange between Captain Viedma and Lela Zoraida where they discuss how they can be together. So they flee from Algiers to Spain to formalize their affection for one another. To achieve a sense of nuptial devotion for one another, Captain Viedma and Lela Zoraida enlist the help of a Catholic priest who unites them as man and woman—irrespective of their religion. By entering into a married state by choice, Cervantes shows his readers that people of two different faiths can establish a permanent romantic liaison if they love one another enough and thus willingly align themselves with each other despite having slight differences of belief. By marrying a Christian man and a Muslim woman in this way, Cervantes makes the point that since choosing a spouse is a defining quality of volitional self-determination, people should be free to marry who they want to. And, what is true of the microcosm of Lela Zoraida and Captain Viedma's marriage is also true of the macrocosm of 17th century Spain because by marrying these two companions, Cervantes sends a signal to other Spaniards that it is fine for a Christian man to marry a Muslim woman (or vice versa) if the fit is right.

Cervantes also brings Christians and Muslims together by moving his Christian translator's opinion of the Moorish author from a pejorative and stereotypical conception to complementary and individualized one. Said differently, through the device of a Muslim author and a Castilian translator, Cervantes unwinds popular Christian prejudices for Muslims by addressing them, voicing them, and dissipating them. This, in turn, cleanses the souls of Cervantes's Christian readers so that they overcome a bigoted conception of Muslims and replace it with an objective evaluation of foreign others. To see just how *Don Quixote's* Christian translator evolves his mental outlook towards Muslims let us analyze his view of the original Moorish author of the story. When translating *Don Quixote* from Arabic to Castilian the Christian translator comments on the original author quite extensively—sometimes in a spirit of negative criticism; sometimes in a favorable light. For example, early in the story the Christian translator says that Cide Hamete El Benengeli is unreliable, at best, or downright duplicitous, at worst, by calling him a "liar [and a] dog of an author" (125). Yet as he translates more and more of the book the translator's mental attitude shifts from total distrust of Cide Hamete El Benengeli to respect for him as a writer. This is why, later in the book, the translator says that Cide Hamete El Benengeli is "a careful and meticulous historian; [a philosophical] sage who chronicles" Don Quixote's life accurately" (268). Why, then, does *Don Quixote's* Christian translator insult Cide Hamete El Benengeli only to complement him later? What do these two conflicting attitudes and accounts of the Muslim author do? Is such a divergent viewpoint paradoxical and inconsistent or is there some sort of methodical transition of attitude here? One answer is that the translator's divergent viewpoint signals his evolving mental attitude towards the Muslim narrator. As the Christian translator reads more and more of Cide Hamete's elegant prose he finds himself reluctantly admiring his great verbal artistry and sensitive intelligence even though he is a Muslim. Said differently, as he translates more and more of his novel, the Castilian interpreter evolves his opinion from the bigoted belief that "all Arabs [are] liars" to the idea that Cide Hamete is "a scrupulous historian" (243). In other words, as the Christian translator translates more of Don Quixote, he comes to harbor a reluctant sort of respect for the Muslim author. Said differently, even though he once viewed Cide Hamete as his traditional enemy—the Christian translator overcomes his negative typecasts of all Muslims to see some Islamist's as individual human beings who have goodness within them.

Perhaps, this shift in mental attitude mirrors the evolution of thought Cervantes is trying to instill in his readers. Like his Morisco translator who starts-off negative about Cide Hamete El Benengeli only to praise him later denigrate Cervantes. Said differently, Cervantes tries to replicate this shift of views in his readers, so that they, like his translator, judge Islamic theologians not merely as religionists of an entirely evil racial group but as individual human beings with a unique set of cultural characteristics. By thwarting negative typecasts of Arabs and Muslims in this way, Cervantes suggests that Muslims should be judged not as a collective force of harm but as individual human beings who should be praised, or scorned, according to their merits, or demerits. In this way, Cervantes brings Christians and Muslims together in a spirit of harmony so that they view each other not with suspicion and distrust and fear but rather with a sense of tolerance and acceptance and friendliness instead. It can be argued, then, that *Don Quixote's* translator only insults Cide Hamete el Benengeli at the beginning of his tale to gain a tow-hold over the minds of prejudiced Christian readers to move them away from a stereotypical way of viewing Muslims to a more open minded stance. Said differently, by moving his readers away from a biased prejudgment of all Muslims to a positive evaluation of some Islamists, Cervantes argues for a more objective approach of evaluating another person—an approach that is fair and reasonable and factual. Inexorably, this leads to the conclusion that since some Muslims are good people one can grow to appreciate a culture other than one's own. This, in turn, proves that instead of judging a person based on the social group to which they belong, each person should be judged by the content of his, or her, individual character, defined by the nature of their overall thoughts and actions.

In conclusion, by presenting Christian and Muslim readers with a new look on each other, Cervantes hopes to direct race relations between the Middle East and the Secular West in a more favorable direction. This is why he suggests a positive interfaith relationship between Christians and Muslims, so that they are not suspicious of or threatened by one another but rather come to understand each other from an enlightened point of view. It is in this way that Cervantes strives to begin a constructive dialogue between these two great religions to generate a moral rapprochement between them. In conclusion, by exploring and refuting stereotypes that Christians have for Muslims and Muslims have for Christians, Cervantes shows his readers that there is more that unites these two religions than divides them.

ESSAY 7

The Role of the Picaresque Conversion Narrative In Don Quixote: *Criminal Reform*.

In *Don Quixote De La Mancha* real-life villains – like Roque de Guinart – or low-born rascals – like Gines de Pasamonte – are shown that lying, cheating, and stealing to extract money or property from society is an unsettled, unsound, indefensible lifestyle that results in either a long-term prison sentence for the offender or a life of perpetual exile for the perpetrator or a state of constant fear for the reprobate concluded with a sudden gruesome death. Unlike Don Quixote the idealistic knight-adventurer whose aim is "to do good to all and harm to none," these picaros wander about from place to place under the cover of darkness preying on people to survive (660). As such they are "casteless, [amoral,] outsiders who feel inwardly unrestrained by [society's prevailing] mores and only appear to conform to them when [they] think it suits their [needs]."[1] "Never soiling their hands with an honest day's work they express a spirit of resistance" that is unhealthy to them because Roque and Pasamonte soon find themselves hunted for their crimes by the usual assortment of crusading lawmen, trigger-happy bounty hunters, resident do-gooders, and other mercenary killers, who all seek to benefit from

---

1   **"Picaresque Novel."** <u>Encyclopedia Britannica</u>. 2007. Encyclopedia Britannica Online. Jan. 2007. http://www.search.eb.com.proxyau.wrlc.org/eb/article-9059900. 1.

their death somehow[2]. By sketching their sudden horrible demise in this way—with all its attendant worries, associated anxieties, and linked detriments—Cervantes shows his readers that if they choose to live by their wits rather than by honest work then ultimately they will pay for their crimes.

The narrative of these two picaros also "portrays a clear vision of the world as seen from below" with "a rich mine of observations" about how people in low walks of life function.[3] By exposing the cons, the swindles and the scams of two wandering and dissolute antiheroes, Cervantes warns his readers against certain categories of obnoxious people who devise secret, cunning, and often complicated schemes to prey on society by dishonest means. As such, he focuses on the clever but dishonest adventures of two unprincipled rogues who assume "all the beatings, suffer all the affronts, and undertake all the dangers so that we as readers can grow in honor and can avoid the hidden dangers that the story of their lives reveal."[4]

Besides warning readers away from a life of crime, Cervantes also encourages fallen-men to regain their moral consciences by breaking free of their "prior psychological maladies" to take on the qualities of a "refined essence".[5] Evidently, Captain Roque's pangs of regret coupled with Senor Pasamonte's contrite speech suggests a modicum of ethical remorse on their parts, which implies, however faintly, that it is still possible for them to overcome their infamous origins by undergoing a "radical process [of] repentant self-analysis".[6]

---

2   **Elliott**, J.H. Imperial Spain 1469-1716. New York: Penguin Books, 1963. (299, 318, 295, 393).

3   **Picaresque Novel.**" Encyclopedia Britannica. 2007. Encyclopedia Britannica Online. Jan. 2007. http://www.search.eb.com.proxyau.wrlc.org/eb/article-9059900. 1.

4   **Bandero**, Casareo. The Humble Story of Don Quixote: Reflections on the Birth of the Modern Novel. Washington D.C., Catholic UP, 2006. (49).

5   **Bandero**, Casareo. The Humble Story of Don Quixote: Reflections on the Birth of the Modern Novel. Washington D.C., Catholic UP, 2006. (49).

6   **Bandero**, Casareo. The Humble Story of Don Quixote: Reflections on the Birth of the Modern Novel. Washington D.C., Catholic UP, 2006. (51).

By giving readers some insight into the mental projections of these two criminals, Cervantes matches the minds and dispositions of his readers to that of his criminal characters so that people are not only warned away from crookery but also so that they act in their long-term intellectual and psychological self-interests.

To set the historical context of *Don Quixote*, "brigandage was [fairly] common in and south of the Sierra Morena" during the 17th century.[7] "It reached its greatest heights in Catalonia, where it began in the strife of the peasants against the feudal extractions of the landlords."[8] "It had its traditional [underground figure,] Roque Guinart," who is named after Perot Rocaguinarda, an infamous Catalan bandit who is regarded as a hero by some and as a villain by others[9]. In written histories he is depicted as a blackheart: a highwayman who preyed on the rich, victimized the nobles, and terrorized society. On this view, he followed sudden irrational impulses characterized by quick changes in mood and plan; he was "anti-intellectual in that he was deaf to any and all principles;" he resented all authority, be it the law of the state, the morality of the church, or the precepts of the culture; he had "acute feelings of his own victimization characterized by a strong sense of other's people's evil towards himself," therefore he rebelled against society, against culture, against justice, and against its representatives, to undermine the legal system[10]. In oral legend, however, he is described as a generous brigand who fought against the injustices of his times in the only way he could. On this view he is seen as a reluctant hero: a freedom fighter, who lived in the woods, was generous to peasants and fought for social justice. Popular reasoning has it that because he could not

---

7   http://en.wikipedia.org/wiki/Brigandage (5).

8   http://en.wikipedia.org/wiki/Brigandage (5).

9   http://en.wikipedia.org/wiki/Brigandage (5).

10   **Peikoff**, Leonard. "What to Do About Crime?" Ford Hall Forum. 1995. and **Bernstein**, Andrew. <u>Heroism in Modern American Literature</u>. The Ayn Rand Institute. California, 1996.

advance within a corrupt society he had to use retaliatory force as a means of changing the culture from within. Spanish folktales reflect the common view that he led an adventurous and extraordinary lifestyle consisting of death defying feats, pulse-quickening close calls, glamorized love-affairs, quick chases, boisterous merry-making and close comradeship amongst good friends. Which version of events is true? Why did Roque become an outlaw? What were his motivations? Did he live a glamorous life fighting for a good cause, or was he a common thief? Did people rally around him because he fought for their rights or were they tired of his depredations? The answers to these, and many other questions, are found in *Don Quixote*.

In the book, Senor Roque enters the popular imagination as "a real-life outlaw who operated in eastern Spain" during Cervantes's time.[11] When introduced he is described as "a man of thirty four [years] of age, of larger than average build, with a stern look in his eye, dark in complexion, riding a powerful [war] horse, wearing a steel coat of mail [with] four little carbines at his sides" (894). Right away his "lethality as a killer [is emphasized] at the observational level"[12]. There appears to be a certain inflexible quality about Captain Roque signaled by his stern looks, hard eyes, intimidating presence, and four machine guns. His explicit image as a gun toting, horse trampling, death-dealer shows readers that Captain Roque is not to be messed with—if you toy with him you die. To him his machine guns, his bodily strength, and his bullying tactics are real while more abstract concepts are worthless because they are divorced from and thus do not bear on his underground way of life. As such, he stresses the practical over the moral, the short-term over the long term, percepts over concepts, the present over the future, the here-and-now as opposed to the there-and-then. This is why he grabs loot, shoots his machine gun, flits across secret paths, consumes food when he can,

11 http://en.wikipedia.org/wiki/Outlaw (2).

12 **Bernstein**, Andrew. Heroism in Modern American Literature. The Ayn Rand Institute. California, 1996.

sleeps when he can and thinks about avoiding jail when he can by focusing on the next minute, the next hour, the next day, perhaps the next week, and that's it. His focus is tactical and short-term not strategic and long term for right-away he must get what he wants, when he wants, and how he wants to get it, and woe betide anyone, or anything, that stands in his way, especially his own men.

To ensure that his underlings have the same tactics, the same motivations, the same action-plan that he does, Captain Roque tolerates no insubordination from his lieutenants, sergeants, corporals, soldiers, or from any of his subordinates, whatever their reason is, whoever they may be. To enforce the idea that he is to be obeyed without question, Captain Roque compels a strict sense of unflinching loyalty for his person. For instance, when one "unruly Gascon" challenges his captain's authority "Roque raises his sword and almost splits [his] squire's head in two, saying: 'that's how [he] punish[es] insolence and effrontery" (898, 902). Captain Roque imparts a sense of fear and trepidation in his minions to deter them from testing his might. This is why he bullies them, intimidates them, and uses force against them. In turn, however, Captain Roque is uneasy because if he goes too far in his iron-handed rule either he will have to fight to destroy his underlings or will be destroyed by them in turn. In short, while Captain Roque's men follow his lead out of a sense of misguided self-interest, what motivates them is not love of Roque but fear of death. This, coupled with their material greed compels them to follow his lead. Unless they want to battle him, they must do exactly what he says, when he says, and how he says it, otherwise they are on their own. Since Captain Roque, it seems, rules his men through brute force, he intimidates them with alpha-male strength. Yet to Don Quixote's great surprise, Captain Roque is not just a burly knuckle-dragger who overwhelms his foes with brute might, rather he disarms his victims ideologically because he is intelligent enough to speak "sound sense" at times (899).

Contrary to Don Quixote's opinion that anyone "involved

in the business of robbery and murder [is incapable of] clear thinking" Captain Roque proves he has advanced mental contents as his introspective effusions, rhetorical flourishes, and high-flown language suggest (899). He can read, he can write, he can orate, and he can think clearly, which he demonstrates twice: Once when he writes his goons transit passes granting "safe conduct" to his prey, and again when he "writes a letter to [his] friend in Barcelona" about when, where, and how Don Quixote is to be received in the city and for what purpose (901, 902). Obviously, Captain Roque is not an unlettered, uneducated, illiterate pig farmer from the Spanish countryside. Rather he is a cultured and sophisticated man who is well-travelled in Spain, maybe the world too. On the one hand he is "too cultured and refined to be a common thief, yet, on the other hand, he is too much the gun-fighter and gangster to be a part of civilization's moral structure"[13]. His broad range of life experiences, coupled with his overall genteelness, makes him look like a good guy when really he is a bad guy. Yet some people think he is benevolent because he is intelligent with good manners and a refined sort of politeness. By masking his inner nature, even to himself, Roque hides his deep inner emptiness to the general populas. But he is shown to have something fundamentally wrong with his character for he says that "by nature [he is] a compassionate and well-intentioned sort of fellow; but the desire to avenge [himself] for an affront that [he] suffered so overturns all [his] better impulses that [he still] persists in this way of life, even though [he] knows [he] shouldn't" (899). This statement suggests that because Senor Roque has "not lost all hope of emerging safely from the labyrinth of [his] own confusion" with great effort, he can overcome himself to become a better man (899).

Roque, it seems, is not resigned to living a decrepit and hassled lifestyle as a middling criminal because with some thought with some effort and with some initiative on his part he can overcome his blood

---

13 **Bernstein**, Andrew. <u>Heroism in Modern American Literature</u>. The Ayn Rand Institute. California, 1996.

lust to improve his moral character. Much like "cack-handed Juan Palomeque" transfigures himself from an "Andalusian picaroon" to a respectable "tavern owner;" Senor Roque can regenerate his moral life, too, if he tries (33). Why else would Cervantes juxtapose the life of a reformed picaroon turned good with the life of a repentant criminal who has some hope of reform? In so doing Cervantes suggests that even though Juan Palomeque may not make as much money as he did as a sneak thief at least as a tavern owner he is not pursued by the authorities for breaking the law and at least he can feel good about who he is, what he does, and what he is all about. In brief, the innkeeper's example shows us that since there is a path for legitimate advancement even within a closed society dominated by the Spanish Inquisition, a life of crime is not the way to go. By juxtaposing the narrative of a reformed picaroon with the story of a repentant criminal, Cervantes shows us that Captain Roque has another option in life if he creates an honest opportunity for himself. In sum, Cervantes writes about Senor Roque in such a way that we get the sense that he is reachable, he is improvable, he is even reformable, if he reasons his way out of the deep gulf of confusion that he has sunken into over the years. Just how Cervantes suggests that Senor Roque may self-rehabilitate his character is explicated later; for now just understand that Cervantes unglamorizes a criminal way of life by showing that it is not pleasant at all.

To refute the alluring notion that a crook is somehow a special person who leads an extraordinary lifestyle, Senor Roque is depicted as a freeloader coldly driving along for himself at the harm of others. His life is shown to be wretched: full of secrecy and suspicion and fear. When Don Quixote stays with Roque for "three days and three nights," he always moves from "dusk till dawn, waking for breakfast in one place, eating lunch in some other place, sometimes hiding in wait for unknown prey, at other times chasing unknown quarry," yet always moving by "unfrequented roads, secret paths, [and hidden] short-cuts" to transit from one location, to another spot, to the next, with stealth and speed and secrecy (903). Forever kept nervous by a thick network of "spies" and "sentries" and "spotters" and "minders" one moment Don Quixote "sleeps on his feet: [the next moment he] breaks [his] sleep to move from one spot to another" (903). All this disruptive action makes Don Quixote realize how "wretched" Senor Roque's life truly is (903). To avoid being captured, or killed, by his enemies, sentries are forever posted and reposted to determine who is travelling through Roque's territory, how they are moving through it, and what should be done about it. Consequently, "muskets [and] carbines" are loaded and reloaded for quick discharge, swords and daggers are sharpened and resharpend for close combat and snares and snaggles are tied and retied to trap their prey, so that a sufficient amount of force is deployed in the right area, not too much force is assigned to the wrong area, and criminal fighters are prepared to deal with any and all hostile threats, whether from rival outlaws, or turncoat allies, or from citizen do-gooders alike (903). Once external threats are neutralized by Roque's criminal gang he cannot rest easy because internal dangers exist as well. Since internecine strife is a real possibility in Roque's world he sleeps "away from his men in places that they [can't] find out about, because all the edicts published by the Viceroy of Catalonia, putting a price on his head, [keeps] him nervous and [weary] and apprehensive. [So much so, indeed, that] he [doesn't] dare trust anyone in fear that his own men might either [try to] kill him [to usurp his position] or hand him over to the authorities [to gain instant wealth]—a truly wearisome, wretched life" (903). Concerned that his subordinates may overthrow him one day, Captain Roque leads a lonely, friendless, disconsolate way of life suspicious of even his closest associates. Roque has nobody to rely on, no real friends, no true allies, just coconspirators who will betray him at the first opportunity they get. This is why he does not trust other people because a criminal cannot afford to have confidence in others. In short, Roque's distrust of humans runs so deep that he is blocked from deep personal fulfillment at a profound intellectual and emotional level.

It seems that "others are the object of [Captain Roque's] rage. To him they are one and all the enemy"[14]. As such, he is lost in a self-made world of loneliness, bleakness, and emptiness, all because he chose to become a criminal. His life is an utter contradiction because while he claims to be independent really he needs people to leech off of, to drain life from—like cancer infecting a healthy organism—otherwise he will perish. For all his supposed independence, projected self-reliance, vaunted self-confidence, and purported bravado, he is a parasite who depends on other men to live. In this sense he is not independent, he is dependent, he is not strong, he is weak, he is not brave, he is a coward, he is not resourceful, he is empty of inventiveness. Real men, like Juan Palomeque, work hard in an honest profession to make money; they do not terrorize innocent people by robbing them. All Roque has is a strong survival instinct, clever street smarts, physical prowess, and a firm will to do what the other guy will not. This, paired with a set of intimidating bully tactics cows most people into submission, especially those who value their lives, like Don Vicente's "servants," for instance, who "cringe with fear" in Roque's presence (896). But when Senor Roque encounters real heroes willing to counter his compulsion with might of their own he takes flight.

(Is Senor Roque's life an exciting, romantic, lifestyle, full of adventure, full of action, fun to be a part of? No. Is mooching off of society healthy for one's psychological well-being, conducive to one's long-term prospects, marked by mental peace and emotional fulfillment? No. Is the life of a dependant parasite who drains the life-energy of healthy organisms to survive sustainable? No. Can a criminal develop long-term meaningful friendships, significant romantic relationships, and trusting associations to enhance his life? No. Should people become criminals? No. The deepest messages that *Don Quixote* shows us is that a life of crime is not glamorous, does

14 **Peikoff**, Leonard. "What to Do About Crime?" Ford Hall Forum. 1995. and **Bernstein**, Andrew. Heroism in Modern American Literature. The Ayn Rand Institute. California, 1996.

not pay, is a form of base dependence, and is characterized by fear, worry, misery, and death.)

In *Don Quixote* Captain Roque robs a small percentage of his victim's goods to not only avoid making determined enemies amongst the rich and powerful but also so that he can re-rob his prey in the future. If, however, survival by repeat money distribution does not satisfy his men permanently he threatens them with devasting force so that they shut-up and follow his lead. The events of the story prove that if Captain Roque robbed all of the Spanish "Captains two or three hundred escudos [or if he robbed all of] Dona Guiomar de Quinones's six hundred escudos" the soldiers and the judge's wife would have brought him to justice (900). Since "the wife of the president of the Naples tribunal," and the infantry captains, could, if utterly provoked, mobilize the judicial and military branches of the Spanish State against Captain Roque, perhaps he would not have robbed them at all. But he feels he has "to [in order to] keep his men happy," (900, 901). Therefore, from a potential score of "nine-hundred escudos and sixty reals" Captain Roque takes only "one hundred and forty escudos" total since he feels he "must comply with the obligations of his wicked calling" (901). In an attempt to persuade his victims not to hate him too much for doing what he thinks he must do, Captain Roque "begs [for] their forgiveness for the wrong he does [them]" (901). After he distributes a small percentage of their money to his gang of "sixty" bandits they all cheer in unison shouting: "'Long live Roque Guinart, in spite of all those thieving murders who want to do for him!'" (901, 900). Here, we see that Captain Roque creates goodwill amongst his band of thieves and cutthroats by giving them money constantly. This, he does, so they not only lack a fiscal incentive to challenge his dominance but also so that they do not turn him into the authorities for a large monetary reward. But when one of Captain Roque's soldiers mutters under his breath that "if he wants to be so generous again he'd better do it with his money not [theirs Captain Roque] raises his sword and almost splits his squire's head in two" (902). This show of brute, intimidating, strength "dumbfounds [Roque's men], and none of them dares utter another word, such [is] their obedience" (902). Here, we see that Captain Roque squashes any hint of insubordination in his ranks so that his martial dominance reigns supreme. Besides maintaining order by force and intimidation in this way, Captain Roque institutes a warped form of criminal justice amongst his men by "telling [them] to form up in a line [to divide] the clothes, jewels, money, and everything else they'd stolen since the last distribution—making rapid calculations and putting cash in the place of whatever can't be divided" (898). In fact he shares his booty "amongst his company so wisely and so fairly that nobody is given one farthing more or less than what distributive [equity] requires" (898). This, in turn, "leaves everyone perfectly happy and satisfied," which prompts captain Roque to say that "If [he wasn't] so meticulous in [his] dealings with [his criminal associates] it would be impossible to live with them" (898). Here, we see that by distributing plunder amongst his robbers equitably, Captain Roque fosters a sense of goodwill, or at least contentment, amongst his underlings. This practice, in turn, causes Sancho Panza to say that "justice is such a fine thing that it's needed even among thieves" (898). All this dramatic action proves that Captain Roque is not a nice, gallant, thief, as some people suppose. Rather he drains a percentage of his victim's income to survive—to keep the golden goose laying golden eggs. Simply put, Roque's fake niceness is only a ploy to get his prey to accept his extortion with a smile instead of being off-put by it and fighting against him as they should. In sum, Captain Roque's feigned geniality is designed to not only not make enemies out of powerful people—who could crush him if they chose—but also to get his victims to accept his monetary extortion as a necessary evil.

Like the Robin Hood principle of financial redistribution, where a generous thief takes money from the rich and corrupt, and gives it to the poor and deserving, Captain Roque "gives ten [escudos] to two pilgrims and another ten to the worthy squire Sancho Panza, so that [he] can speak well of [his] adventures [with Captain Roque] (901). This tactic is meant to gain Captain Roque supporters amongst the poor and downtrodden thereby fostering a degree of good will for him amongst underclassmen. He does this for two reasons: One, to correct a cultural imbalance, as he sees it, where the rich and corrupt take unearned money from the poor and deserving. Two, so that he has a base of support amongst populist elements of society so that his enemies have a harder time finding him and bringing him to justice because poor people like, and protect, him. Hence, after Captain Roque "hands out safe conduct passes to the leaders of his squadrons, [thereby] letting [his victims] go free, [they are all] amazed at his [dignified] nobility, gallant disposition, and unusual behavior, regarding him as more of an Alexander the Great than a notorious [lowborn] robber" (902). Why, it must be asked, besides the pilgrim and Sancho Panza—who, arguably, have legitimate reasons to be happy because they receive free money—are Captain Roque's robbery victims amazed by his nobility and gallantry? Because he only robbed some of their money? Is robbery honorable? Even if done politely? No, it is not. In fact Captain Roque masks his inner evil by being polite about it. In reality he is a no good criminal who deserves to be thrown in jail, so he can think long and hard about the evil of his life, the consequences of his treachery, and how he may reform himself permanently to take on the virtues of a purified soul.

Theoretically speaking, Cervantes portrays Captain Roque as not only being morally mixed—one part extortionate, one part saccrine, one part benevolent, and one part regretful—but also Senor Roque shows readers that his motivations for his crimes are mixed, too. Essentially, Captain Roque steals people's money to survive since he wants to live as a free, rich man in the dogmatic, authoritarian, climate of the Spanish Inquisition. But he does not want to make unnecessary enemies, either. This is why he robs only a portion of his victim's goods, pretends politeness to his prey, does not rob or hurt

Don Quixote and Sancho Panza, and really does regret his crimes. On the one hand, Cervantes depicts Captain Roque as a polite and gentile do-gooder thief who has polished manners, elaborate speech, and a gentile sort of sophistication. On the other hand, Cervantes shows us that Captain Roque lives a very dangerous hook-and-crook lifestyle full of pressure and danger. We must now ask ourselves if Captain Roque is more of a hardened career criminal unrepentful for his crimes; or if he is really a good guy turned bad out of necessity since he is driven to the underground to survive in the only way he can. What are we to make of this mixed account of Senor Roque's life? Does he lead an exciting and eventful life characterized by vigilante justice or does he live a hassled and worried life preying on people for survival. Is he fighting for right honorable justice or is he fighting to fill his wallet? Answers to these, and many other questions, are found in *Don Quixote*.

In the final analysis Senor Roque lives a rather unsettled and restrictive lifestyle where the notoriety, the obedience, and the booty he gains in the short term, is outweighed by the worries, the fears, and the jeopardy he experiences in the long term. Though he makes a fearsome reputation for himself, which compels instant obedience from others, his grand larceny have many people hunting for him: like "the Viceroy of Catalonia" and his agents, for example, or "the Holy Brotherhood" and their cohorts, for instance—not to mention the usual assortment of crack bounty hunters, eagle-eyed mercenaries, rival outlaws, and other hired guns, who force him to either "fight to destroy them" or escape from their deadly clutches (210, 903). Kill or be killed, crush or be crushed, destroy or be destroyed is the life that Captain Roque leads. Yes, his prey fear him, lest they experience the full wrath of his complete might; as do his men, mainly out of dread that he will visit some grievous harm on them in some crushing way. So he gets what he wants in the short-term. Yet, on the flip side, he has to worry about swift retribution from multiple enemies both internal and external. On the one hand Roque's victims know that his threats of force are to be taken seriously because he can, and often does, match his words with his deeds in concrete physical action. On the other hand, Captain Roque has to cover all bases because if he carries his demands too far he will be held liable for his actions by a variety of hard men who seek to profit from his demise. So he has to maintain a delicate balance between pushing people for all he can get from them while not pushing them over the edge. This bifurcated lifestyle creates anxiety in his soul because in exchange for being feared by people he views as suckers or cowards or a bit of both, he subjects himself to the ever-present specter of being destroyed for harming them. Nevertheless Senor Roque chooses a short-term method of criminal extortion that he follows through to the very-end, come what may, and not a long-term method of honest work that could earn him permanent goods. But he is intelligent enough to know that the life of an outlaw usually terminates in sudden death, perpetual enjailment, physical duress, mental torture, or some other bleak end. Yet he does not break away from a life of crime altogether because he does not see a clear alternative to criminal extortion given that he has practiced it for so long. Because he thinks it would be hard to escape the criminal underworld easily—especially since his associates may try to pull him back in—and because he is driven by an insatiable blood-lust for "revenge," he continues a life of crime, come what may (899). One thing is for sure, though, Senor Roque is sick-and-tired of living an apprehensive, worrisome way of life comprised of constant plotting, incessant scheming and the ever-present anxiety of a premature death. Since Senor Roque's biography suggests that a life of crime is unsustainable—and since he has some vestige of goodness left in his soul—he indicates that he may change his ways, in time, with Don Quixote's help, of-course.

When all seems hopeless for Senor Roque, in comes Don Quixote, a path of redemption, who is surprised that someone whose livelihood is "robbery [and assault] and murder" can speak with such good wisdom, elegance even, sometimes with hope and optimism foremost in his mind (899). Happy that Captain Roque at least accepts his psychological malady – as opposed to denying it outright – Don Quixote tries to restore his mental health insofar as Roque is a sick criminal patient in dire need of basic reform. To redeem Roque's interiority Don Quixote says that the first step of treating any illness is to identify the root cause of the disease, exactly what form it takes, and what course of treatment can bring a sick criminal patient back from the depths of his confusion. Full mental recovery, says Don Quixote, depends on a convalescent's will and effort and grit to recuperate for a sick person, who is determined to recover from any illness, is more likely to self-correct than not. Don Quixote also suggests that "intelligent" evil-doers are closer to reversing their maladies than foolish reprobates since smart malefactors are capable of faulting themselves and then repairing themselves (900). In other words, not only are rational criminals free from a perpetual state of constant denial but they can also see, with their own two eyes, what steps they can take to turn their lives around. For this reason, Cervantes suggests that since the minds of rational criminals are at least open to a course of "gradual" self-improvement, they have some hope of lasting redemption (900). As such Don Quixote invites Captain Roque to practice chivalry with him because "righting wrongs; correcting injustices; relieving the needy; defending maidens; protecting widows; succoring orphans; avenging the offended; punishing treachery; assisting the helpless; redressing grievances; succoring the wretched; favoring the oppressed; defending women's honor; upholding promises; protecting wards; punishing insolence; redressing outrages; remedying distress; forgiving the modest; destroying the cruel; and observing the will to do good to people of all kinds" would certainly earn him penitence in the world of human affairs (36, 85, 111, 134, 139, 150, 177, 183, 205, 284, 584, 643, 701, 739, 840, 879, 887). In this sense Don Quixote is a role model of building and construction to counter Senor Roque's bad example of tearing down and destruction. He uplifts the downtrodden with positive action rather than pulling them down with negative punishment. In sum, the essence of the storyline is that Don Quixote is the only one who can save Roque except Roque.

The first step that Roque takes to reverse his sociopathy is to acknowledge, not deny, that his life "must seem strange to Don Quixote [because] strange adventures, strange incidents, and" strange occurrences characterize his existence (899). In fact Senor Roque is "not surprised that" his lifestyle is bizarre to Don Quixote because to an outsider like him it is (699). Besides being peculiar, Senor Roque's lifestyle is extremely unsettled because "there's no way of life more uneasy or troubled" than the days of a bandit (899). Yet he "persists in [his] way of life [anyway] even though [he] knows [he] shouldn't [because] one revenge has linked up with another in such a chain that [he doesn't] only attend to [his] own revenges but to those of other people as well" (899).

Not only does Senor Roque make his enemies pay for opposing him he also hunts the enemies of his friends. For instance, when "the daughter of Simon Forte [his] special friend [shoots the son of his] deadly enemy Claquel Torrellas Claudia Jeronima [not only asks him to defend her body against a reprisal killing but she also asks him] to defend her father against [his] relatives" lest they take revenge on father Torrellas if they can't find daughter Torrellas (898). By way of abetting Claudia Jeronima, captain Roque agrees to help her escape "to France, offer[ing] to defend her father against the whole world" if need be (898). So caught up is Captain Roque in a vicious cycle of constant blood feuds that he not only safeguards the interests of his kinfolk through clan-vendetta but he also protects the vested interests of clanly friends as well—essentially, to protect and enhance his friendly social and intelligence network. This is why he enacts a policy of clannish reprisal, punishing those he sees as his traditional enemies. In this way he is very different from Don Quixote despite having striking similarities.

Though Don Quixote and Senor Roque are different in fundamental ways, there is *almost* a spiritual affinity between these two characters. Both have a "common thirst for dominance that compels then to venture along the roads of Spain each seeking—in his own way—to address the world and its problems".[15] Both are men of physical action who confront life's challenges at a physical level. Both are can-do sort of guys with a certain element of individual prowess. Both are unconventional non-conformists who choose to live as free-men in a socially restrictive culture. Both are concerned with the wrongs perpetrated against social victims and both feel they can help the powerless regain their independence. Both are chivalrous toward ladies and are ready to redress the grievances of damsels. Most importantly, both are eager to aid the poor and give alms to pilgrims. Here is where their similarity ends. Don Quixote is more intellectual than Roque in that he applies his intelligence to understand profound moral issues of high philosophical significance. As such, he thinks out ethical issues in full-dimension. Roque, on the other hand, while wicked smart, lacks Don Quixote's deep understanding of life. Though Captain Roque has tremendous physical development he lacks cerebral cultivation because he does not understand what motivates the Holy Brotherhood to hang people for thieving linen, selling sex, and having incestuous relations with their cousins. Also, he does not understand why legitimate advancement within society is impossible for people like him. Lastly, he does not understand why free-thinkers are stamped out ruthlessly. Though he has a crafty sort of intelligence, especially when physically applied, all of Don Quixote's reading, studying and thinking to date has cultivated his intellect beyond Roque's. Roque is not unintelligent just unintellectual and his body is strong and he is efficacious in physical terms, while Don Quixote, on the other hand, is somewhat klutzy. Though Don Quixote is sometimes agile, he is a physical bumbler too. When he charges a group of silk merchants,

---

15   **Attansio**, Salvator, Giants of World Literature: Cervantes: *His Life, His Times, and His Works*. Ed. Arnoldo Arnoldo Mondalori. New York: American Heritage Press, 1968. (128).

for instance, he stumbles and falls. When he embeds his lance in a "windmill dial" he is picked-up and slammed down by the force of its' turning blades (64). When he stays in the Duke's castle for several days he is unable to prevent a tenacious cat from "clinging [to his] nose". Roque, on the other hand, displays tremendous physical development (795). He thunders around swiftly on his war horse threatening his men with knock-down drag out brawls if they disobey him. He rides his charger at "top-speed" to look for Don Vicente (896). He constantly moves along "unfrequented roads [hidden] short cuts and secret paths" to get Don Quixote to Barcelona (903). Sometimes Roque "runs away from unknown pursuers;" at other times he "lies in wait for unknown prey" (903). At "dawn [Roque] is in one place [at] lunch [he is] somewhere else" (903). Finally he deposits Don Quixote on a "Barcelona beach" in true ninja style—with stealth and secrecy and speed. All of this physical action proves that Roque is limber, lithe, graceful even, otherwise he could not get around as much or as well as he does (902). In sum, in the realm of bodily motion, Senor Roque surpasses Don Quixote greatly. More fundamentally, however, Captain Roque and Don Quixote have different actuating moral codes. Don Quixote does what he does to right wrongs and do good to all. Roque does what he does to get loot, have mindless sex, avenge himself against society, revolt against a wicked culture. He feels that his anger is righteous, his cause is just, his method necessary, his ends laudable. This is how he operates. When he meets Don Quixote, however, who illustrates another way to advance in life, Captain Roque is thrown into a mental quandary. He thinks to himself: Should I join Don Quixote? Should I pacify my inner rage so that I can collaborate with Don Quixote? Should I eradicate my desire to drain material wealth and replace it with a need to be honorable like a chivalric knight? How will I survive if I do? These are among a few of the questions that Captain Roque asks himself. Observing Captain Roque's urge to join him, Don Quixote holds out hope that though it will be difficult, he can reform his basic nature to become a chivalric knight like him.

Given that Don Quixote tries to reach Senor Roque and given that Don Quixote defies the Holy Brotherhood, Senor Roque begins to like him. He even wants to do good for him. The events of the story prove that senor Roque becomes so fond of Don Quixote that he fights his wicked overlord to protect him. For instance when Don Quixote tells Senor Roque that he can take an "easy shortcut to the road of [his own] salvation [by knight errantry] he laughs" (900). When Don Quixote "makes a speech [to his men] trying to persuade them to give up [a] way of life dangerous to the body and soul" he is amused (898). In fact he likes Don Quixote so much that he praises him in "a letter" he writes "to [his] friend in Barcelona" in which he says that "Don Quixote is the funniest and most intelligent man in the world" therefore his friend should treat him well (902). With such a glowing recommendation Don Quixote is received warmly in Barcelona by Roque's friend: "Welcome to our city, O mirror, beacon and lode star of all knight errantry. Welcome I say, O valiant Don Quixote de la Mancha" (904). In fact a rift develops between the forces of evil, with Captain Roque, Don Antonio Moreno, and his criminal gang on one side of the divide, and the prince of darkness and his minions, on the other. This is why when two little rascals "ram a handful of gorse" in Rocinante and Dapple's rumps by order of "the evil one" Roque's friends "punish the boys for their insolence" (903). We see, here, an ideological split between members of evil in that some want, and perhaps can become good men, while others are so thoroughly corrupted that there is no hope for them at all. Since Roque and his gang are amused by Don Quixote they seek to help him while "the evil one; the source of all evil in this world" plays tricks on Don Quixote for his own private enjoyment (903). Basically, since Don Quixote tries to save Captain Roque's soul he does not harm him or Sancho Panza. In fact an odd relationship develops between them, where they agree to leave each other alone with an open invitation to join each other for good or ill at any time. But since Don Quixote will not become a bad guy for whatever reason, he leaves Senor Roque, while, conversely, senor Roque does not have the strength to become a good guy yet—even though there is clear evidence that he not only wants to but also that he commences to purify his soul. Evidently, since Cervantes leaves Captain Roque's biography unfinished, readers can only hope that maybe, in time, he will reform his ways, thereby transforming his ruling purpose in life, from criminal parasitism, to legitimate economic gains.

In sum, Don Quixote and Senor Roque's relationship is temporary in nature, tentative in form, with a specific finite cause to get Don Quixote to Barcelona and to protect him once there. Though they are completely different from one another and do not really trust each other, they have a common opponent—the radical, religious, militant wing of Spanish society who tries to snuff out individuals who do not conform to their tyrannical power. This is why the Spanish monarchy instituted the Holy Inquisition, this is why Don Quixote breaks their laws repeatedly, and this is the point of commonality between him and Senor Roque. On the one hand Don Quixote fights the authorities because they are dogmatic and authoritarian. On the other hand Roque fights the authorities because they threaten to bust-up his criminal enterprise. Both do not want to be suppressed by society and both fight against it. In sum, Don Quixote and Senor Roque become uneasy associates, at first, then temporary allies a bit later. In the end, neither joins the other, but for a short time, in a very specific way, they have a common purpose, to undermine the Holy Brotherhood. After a brief time together, during which time they travel in the same direction, they part ways neutrally. Each never sees the other again.

What makes Roque so interesting as a person is that he is a paradoxical figure marked by strong contrasts of character "oscillating" between "courtesy and gentleness," on the one hand, and "violence and ferocity," on the other[16]. This makes him both a man of peace and a man of violence whose dual purposes in life are

---

16 **Attansio**, Salvator, <u>Giants of World Literature: Cervantes: *His Life, His Times, and His Works*</u>. Ed. Arnoldo Arnoldo Mondalori. New York: American Heritage Press, 1968. (128).

incompatible and inconsistent. Inherently conflicted, Roque believes in justice and generosity yet he vacillates between helping people and harming people between saying one thing and doing another. The deepest message that Roque's character shows us is that a man cannot live out contradictory goals in life so he must choose one way or the other, not both.

Gines De Pasamonte, on the other hand, is a different type of criminal altogether. Rather than a man of violence, like Senor Roque, he is a "gypsy thief," a trickster extraordinaire, who stages elaborate confidence scams to steal people's money and jewels[17]. He has committed so many crimes, indeed, that in a procession of "twelve" outlaws he:

> is shackled in a different way from [all] the others [with] a chain on his ankle so long that it winds all round his body. [Moreover, he wears] two neck-irons, one linking him to the other convicts and one from which descends two bars to his waist, where his wrists are manacled to them with great padlocks, so that he can neither raise his hands to his mouth nor lower his head to his hands

(176, 181).

These extra safety precautions are taken because Gines de Pasamonte has "committed more crimes than all the other [criminals] put together [and] is so reckless and such a villain that [the guards] fear he is going to escape even though he is shackled up like that" (181). Given his ability to extricate himself from even the most difficult of entanglements, the guards "do not feel safe with him" (181). So they try to diminish his will power, drain his strength, unbalance his emotions, and force him to obey their commands all by: beating him with their "staff[s]" so that he fears the pain of noncompliance;

---

17   http://en.wikipedia.org/wiki/Lazarillo_de_Tormes (4).

frog-marching him mercilessly while burdened by a great iron weight; and insulting him relentlessly by calling him a "double-dyed villain," a "great liar," and an "incorrigible miscreant" (182, 181). To make him docile and quiet and compliant, the guards subject him to a variety of harsh measures so that he hates the consequences of his crimes. Though these actions seem a bit harsh, perhaps they are not entirely unwarranted for Gines is: a "famous" escape artist skilled at eluding his captors by any means necessary; an intimidator who threatens the "sergeant" who guards him; and a vengeful man who vouches to "stop [people from] calling him Ginesillo de Parapilla" (181). Since Gines de Pasamonte is used to steamrolling others he tells Don Quixote to "clear-off because [he is] beginning to get on [Gines's] nerves with all [his] prying into other people's lives" (181, 182). Given Gines de Pasamonte's heinous nature, why does Don Quixote free him in the first place? Do not the standards of moral action enforced by the King's soldiers persuade him to obey the law? Does he not fear the Holy Brotherhood's revenge for trampling their rural laws? Above all, if Don Quixote is such a just man why does he flout the criminal justice system altogether? Answer: because he thinks it is right to do so.

To understand why Don Quixote frees twelve convicts, it is important to understand that most of the accused were whipped for their crimes, faced years of rowing as galley slaves, and underwent cruel and unusual punishment, all for minor, or imagined, offenses like "witchcraft, prostitution, incest, linen-theft, horse-thievery," and premarital sex (178-181). Since these lawbreakers do not have adequate legal counsel they are forced to self-incriminate, they are oversentenced for their crimes, and, above all, they are subject to public-shame and ridicule. The question remains, do people guilty of relatively minor crimes deserve to row in the Spanish Navy as galley slaves? What if their ships are sunk or captured? Should minor offenders be punished for their offenses by death or years of slavery? Do petty criminals deserve to row to the point of exhaustion to eat a paltry amount of food to be subject to poor sanitary conditions and to be susceptible to multiple diseases, mostly, for simple misdemeanors. Punishment, yes they deserve, but all this, no they do not: as least not in Cervantes's judgment. This is why he creates a hero-protagonist who challenges the notion that minor offenders should be enjailed without fair trial, subject to years of hard labor, without possible reprieve. By having Don Quixote free these prisoners, Cervantes wonders if King Phillip the III's Spain is just? To answer Cervantes's primary inquiry, let us examine these men's crimes, one-by-one, to find reasons for, or against, their punishment. Let us investigate why they were arrested in the first place to determine if full justice was served by their incarceration. Let us review their jail terms to judge if their penal sentences fit the nature of their crimes. Finally, let us inspect the nature of their charges to discover if what they did constitutes a major crime.

By way of starting this examination, we will begin with the first convict who was "sent to the galleys for being in love with a washing basket chock-a-block with linen" (177). So much so, in fact, that he "hugged it so tight, that if the law hadn't taken it off [him] by force [he] still wouldn't have let go of it of [his] own free-will" (178). After suffering "a hundred" lash stokes to get him to talk he is sentenced to "three [years] in the tubs" for petty thievery (178). The next convict is "a young man of twenty-four" sentenced to the galleys "for six years for being a canary-bird, a singer, [and] a musician" in that he "sung in his throes" or confessed, when whip-lashed, to being "a prigger of prancers, [or] a horse-thief" (178). By obtaining his confession under duress he gets a half decade for grand theft auto. The third convict is sentenced to "the tubs for five years for the lack of ten ducats to grease the clerk's pen and to liven-up his lawyers wits" (179). Evidently, he is a debtor sent to the clink for reneging on a loan. The fourth convict is "a man with a venerable face and a white beard reaching below his chest who [is sentenced] to the galleys for four years, [after being] paraded in state through the streets, dressed up on a fine horse [to] expose [him] to public shame" (179). Not only is he guilty of "prostitution" he is also accused of "having a touch of the sorcerer about him" (179). The fifth convict is:

> sentenced to the galleys for six years [because he]
> fooled around too much with two girl-cousins of his,
> and with two girl-cousins of somebody else's; and, in
> short, [he] fooled around so much with the lot of them
> that as a result the family tree's become so complicated
> that [he doesn't] know who the devil would be able to
> work it out

(180).

Since these charges were "proved against [him], [and since] there weren't any strings for [him] to pull [this] student, a great talker and a first-rate latiner" was sent to the clink for his transgressions (181). The last convict, the infamous Gines de Pasamonte himself, whose long list of crimes is greater in scope then the wrongs of the previous inmates "put together"— is sent to the galleys for "ten years" for a slew of misdemeanors (181). We must now ask ourselves should it be lawful to extract a person's confession by torture? Do the accused have the right to a public defender? Should people be subject to years of hard labor for minor crimes? Do criminals deserve to be banished to the galleys where hard labor, bad sanitation, little food, and pestilence awaits them?

Since Cervantes believes that Gines de Pasamonte, and his cohorts, are treated unjustly, he has Don Quixote intervene on their behalf. This is why when a "Sergeant raises his staff to hit Gines, Don Quixote thrusts himself between them [to] beg the sergeant not to maltreat the fellow, for it was only to be expected that one whose hands were so tightly bound would loosen his tongue a little" (183). Moreover Don Quixote says that:

> from everything the convicts have told [him], [he]
> gathers that although it is for [their] crimes [they]
> have been sentenced, the punishments [they] are to
> suffer are [excessive] for it could be that one man's
> lack of courage under torture, another's lack of money

[for a lawyer], another's lack of strings to pull [with powerful intercessors] and, to be brief, the judge's perverse decisions, were the causes of [their ultimate] downfall

(183).

As such Don Quixote asks the guards "to release [their prisoners] and allow [them] to go in peace [because] it seems excessively harsh to make slaves of those whom nature made free, for it is not right for honourable men to be the executioners of others if they have no concern in the matter" (183). In response to his request, the guards laugh at his "fine joke" asserting that they do not "have the authority [to] hand over the King's prisoners to him [and Don Quixote does not have] the authority to tell [them] to" (184). Then they tell him to "clear-off and make tracks, and straighten that chamber pot on [his] head, and [to not] go around trying to put the cat among the pigeons" (184). This brusque response compels Don Quixote to "match his deeds to his words [by] tumbling the [guard] with the flintlock to the ground before he has a chance to [fire his weapon]" (184). Seeing "their chance to be free [the] convicts break the chain on which they are threaded" and vanish into the black mountains (184). Speaking through Don Quixote, Cervantes wonders: since when is premarital sex, or incest, a crime? Since when do religious authorities have the right to label any deviant behavior as witchcraft? Since when are men forced to self-incriminate through torture? Since when is it right to send people to their death for minor crimes? Clearly, we get Cervantes view here that King Phillip the III's monarchy used a crushing form of tyranny to pervert natural justice in the name of enforcing it. Since Cervantes saw the harsh treatment of jailed convicts in his own life, he depicts a variety of injustices in *Don Quixote* very realistically.

In light of Cervantes's life story it is not surprising that he takes the strong view of crime that he does. In-and-out of jail all of his adult life, Cervantes projects his own experiences onto readers. The events of his life prove this for on "September 20, 1575, [Cervantes's ship], the Sol, was suddenly attacked by three Ottoman galleys, just off the mouth of the Rhône [river]. After a fierce struggle, his ship was captured and the crew was taken prisoner" to be sold as slaves in Algiers[18]. "Miguel spent five years in slavery," from 1575-1580, where he experienced, first-hand, what it is like to be locked up, to be beaten about, to be commanded by wicked jailers, to be denied all hope.[19] Despite trying to escape thrice, never was he successful. But try he did with a "carefully prepared and organized escape plan [where he, along with a group of] fugitives would be picked up on the [Algerian] coast [by a rebel brigantine to be whisked away to Spain post haste]. Captured by the sultan's cutthroats, Cervantes was dragged before the infamous caliph of Algiers, Hassan Pasha. The pasha was notorious for his hatred of Christians [so] he constantly sent slaves to the gallows on the mere suspicion that they planned an escape."[20] But Cervantes was fortunate because the Pasha admired both his bravery in action and his loyalty to his friends. Impressed that Cervantes did not finger the others—despite facing the prospect of having his nose cut off—the Pasha granted him leniency by segregating him in an isolation cell where he was left alone to think. During his imprisonment he wrote several verse epistles and even penned a play, or two. Though Cervantes was ransomed by his Spanish friends he was again enjailed when he was a tax collector for the kingdom of Granada. Since Cervantes deposited royal tax monies in an insolvent Seville bank, he was enjailed for losing state funds. This time he wrote

---

18 **Attansio**, Salvator, <u>Giants of World Literature: Cervantes: *His Life, His Times, and His Works*</u>. Ed. Arnoldo Mondalori. New York: American Heritage Press, 1968. (13).

19 **Attansio**, Salvator, <u>Giants of World Literature: Cervantes: *His Life, His Times, and His Works*</u>. Ed. Arnoldo Mondalori. New York: American Heritage Press, 1968. (14).

20 **Attansio**, Salvator, <u>Giants of World Literature: Cervantes: *His Life, His Times, and His Works*</u>. Ed. Arnoldo Mondalori. New York: American Heritage Press, 1968. (12, 13, 14).

more dramas, penned more letters, and composed the first part of *Don Quixote*. In 1605, just a decade before his death in 1616, he was sent to jail again because a man was mysteriously and fatally stabbed to death in the street outside Cervantes's house in Seville. This is when he conceived the second part of *Don Quixote De La Mancha* with its extensive picaresque conversion narratives. In sum, Cervantes stints in-and-out of jail shaped his view on crime and punishment, as is evidenced by the sorrow, the shrift and the repentance that many of his criminal characters undergo in his stories.

To show readers the mental set necessary to move one's fundamental character away from a bad makeup to a good identity, Cervantes illustrates the regret, the remorse, and the hope that many of his story's picaros have of overcoming their character flaws to become better men. For example, the third convict, a man sent to "the tubs for five years for the lack of ten ducats to grease his lawyer's pen" is not resigned to live a dark life because he thinks that "God is good, and you've just got to be patient" (179). Although he is jambed-up now he still has some hope of improving his moral stature because he thinks that his eternal soul can be redeemed at a later time. Likewise, the fifth convict "accepts his fate [as] punishment for [his] crime" but claims that since he is "still young long live life [because] while there's life there's hope" (180, 181). Moreover, we are told that Gines de Pasamonte—the most notorious and unsavory criminal of the lot—has "written his own life-history himself and a good one it is too [for] he means to redeem it" (182). When pressed on whether he has "finished" his book yet he retorts: "How can [he] have finished [his book] if [his] life hasn't finished yet?" (182). In short, Gines de Pasamonte's autobiography warns the common man that if they descend into a life of crime then ultimately they will suffer. This is why Gines encourages bad man to become good men so that they "live a good life and speak even better words" (183).

Cervantes also gives his audience a clear picture of how fugitives not only disguise themselves in a variety of clever costumes to avoid detection but he also explores how they steal people's money through fraud, so that we, as readers, avoid being victimized by their protean deceptions. Firstly, Cervantes shows us how to avoid people who use different dialects to escape detection, who take-on diverse accents to elude spotters and who put on sundry disguises to manipulate situations in their favor. By way of exposing con-men for what they are – not what they pretend to be – we are told that to "avoid recognition and to sell his ass Gines de Pasamonte dresses himself in gypsy clothes, because he can speak Romany, as he can speak many other languages, like a native" (278). Despite his elaborate disguise, however, Sancho Panza recognizes him and shouts: "Hey, Ginesillo, you thief! Leave my dearest alone, free my heart's content, unload the comfort of my life, leave my donkey be, leave my beauty alone! Clear off you bugger, go away you robber and give up what isn't yours!" (278). As soon as "Gines hears [Sancho's demands] he jumps off his donkey and departs at a lively trot and [is] far away in an instant" (278). By calling attention to Gines de Pasamonte in such strident terms, Sancho Panza makes him tuck tail and skedaddle, because a master of disguise, who eludes capture by blending into the background, cannot, under any circumstances, be identified and apprehended. After Gines de Pasamonte's gypsy disguise is exposed, he becomes an itinerant, "one-eyed, puppeteer" who uses a fortune telling "ape" to trick gullible people into handing over "two reals per question." (278, 658). This time Gines de Pasamonte avoids recognition by wearing "chamois leather leggings, knee breaches, [and] doublet; [and by covering] his left eye and almost half his left cheek with a patch of green taffeta" complete with a "cart" of tricks and a prognosticating "tailless ape, with buttocks like old leather," perched on his shoulder for show (657). In this guise he becomes a wandering puppeteer named "Master Pedro [who] travels around [the] Aragon end of La Mancha" undetected by the Holy Brotherhood, or anyone else for that matter (658). Not only does Cervantes show readers how they may penetrate the deceptive lies of immoral shape shifters who will say and do almost anything to make a quick buck but he also illuminates their donkey stealing scams, as well, so that 16th century Spanish readers learn to protect their chattel. For example, to steal Sancho Panza's donkey, Dapple, without him knowing it, one night, when Sancho Panza sleeps on his:

> Dun [Gines de Pasamonte] props up the pack-saddle, with [him] sitting there and all, on top of four poles one in each corner, and gets the dun out from underneath [him] without [him] noticing a thing. Dawn breaks and as soon as [Sancho Panza] gives himself a good shake the poles cave in and [he] comes down with an almighty thump, and he looks around for [his] donkey and [can't] find it, and the tears fill his eyes and he makes a [great] lament [over his loss]." [We are told that this Donkey stealing scam was] easy enough to do, and no new occurrence, [since] it is what happened to Sacripante when he was at the siege of Albracca and that the famous thief Brunello removed his horse from between his legs using the same trick
>
> (509, 510).

By describing, in realistic detail, this, and other common tricks, Cervantes equips his Spanish contemporaries with the knowledge that they need to avoid being tricked in a similar fashion. In sum, all these examples prove that Gines De Pasamonte shifts his cosmetic appearance to sink into the human background, much like a vampire squid blends into nature by camouflaging its colors, modifying its hues, changing its patterns, and adapting its textures, to escape detection by predators and prey alike. At the same time, however, vampire squids have to eat to live so they mesmerize their victims with an attractive display of pulsating colors to strike an alluring death blow. Much like a vampire squid throws-off its predators, bamboozles its prey, and kills to survive, Gines De Pasamonte draws his victims into his sordid entertainment web so that he can strike at their wallets with ease.

Master Pedro extracts his audience's money by: alluring them with his fortune telling scam; beguiling them with his sham puppet show; and captivating them with his general legerdemain. Then, once he sets his dramatic bait he reels in his suckers – hook, line, and sinker – with a dazzling array of colorful costumes, a panoply of special effects, and a beguiling voice of tranquil hypnotism, all so that his theatre patrons suspect not a thing and willingly surrender their purses to him. To implement his first scam Master Pedro "buys [an] ape, trains it to jump onto his shoulder [so that it] whispers, or seems to whisper, [replies] in his ear" (672). To ensure that his monkey's answers are correct, Cervantes tells us that:

> before going into a village with his ape, [Master Pedro would] find out in a previous village, or from the best source he came across, what notable events had happened there, and to whom, and he'd carefully memorize them. [Then] he'd perform his [conjuring] show [in which] he described the ape's skills, telling [audience members] that it could divine everything in the past and the present, but it couldn't manage the future. For each answer he charged two reals [per person] and whenever he walked by a house where there were people living about whom he'd received information, he makes the sign to the ape, and then says it had told him this and that and the other, all of it tallying exactly with what really happened. This, [in turn], earns him an incredible reputation [for divination]; and from then on he [is] in great demand

> (672).

As described above, part one of Gines's devious infiltration program is to "shape his answers to the mould of the [audience's] questions [to] fill his money bags" (672). Then, once his audience is captivated by his fortune-telling powers he commences the second phase of extracting their money by staging an elaborate puppet show about "how Don Gaiferos frees his wife Melisendra, [from being held] prisoner [by] the Moors in Spain" (663). Then he hustles the crowd with a dazzling light show that renders the puppet theatre a glittering "sight" to behold (662). On cue a boy with a honey-tongued voice, "acts as [the] announcer and interpreter of the mysteries of the show" while Master Pedro "works the puppets" from above, dangling them enticingly (662). With the audience "hanging on the lips of the announcer; [noises] of war-drums and trumpets and artillery ring-out" enthralling the audience further with their magical sounds (663). The crowd is then enticed by: a bejeweled Emperor Charlemagne flashing his "crown and scepter;" a bedecked Don Gaiferos accoutered in a bright violet "Gascon cape;" and a "beautiful" princess named Melisendra who woos play-goers with her "fine red skirt" (663, 664, 665). Moreover, Gines de Pasamonte lures his human prey into the convolutions of his twisted entertainment web, until they just itch to surrender their gold to him. He does this with a talking ape who Master Pedro claims can understand Spanish; with a spectacular puppet show that conjures sights of brave knights fighting lecherous Moors; with a glib storyteller who narrates historical events with a tranquilizing and cunning voice; with a dazzling array of special sound effects like "trumpets blaring, pipes [chiming], shawms playing, [and] kettle drums beating;" and finally, with a hypnotizing assortment of shimmering lights, glowing candles, and burning torches. In fact, by pretending to be a one-eyed puppet master, Gines de Pasamonte "has gotten very rich" (658).

The question remains: what does Cervantes want his readers to take away from reading about Gines de Pasamonte? With what view? With what understanding? What is the message of his characterization? What is its' point?

Essentially, Cervantes warns his readers away from confidence men by not only delineating their specific character types, but also by exposing their clever schemes so that people are alerted to their devious ploys. Said differently, to inform readers about the general essence of a shyster figure, Cervantes outlines a con man's character traits in realistic detail, so that his audience knows what to look for and avoid. Right away, for example, we told that "Master Pedro [is] a gallant man who lives it up like the best of them; [since] he talks more than six men and drinks more than twelve;" and pays for his expenses by a persuasive "tongue," a mystical "ape and [an alluring] puppet show" (658). Since he depends on clever deception to make a living, "at sleight-of-hand he [is truly] an expert" (672). Evidently, by attracting his opponents with distracting flare he confuses them, greatly. For example, when confronted by an irate Don Quixote, Master Pedro stuns him by playing into his excitement for chivalry. This is why he drops to his knees, "hugs [Don Quixote's] legs and says:

> These legs I embrace as if I were embracing the twin pillars of Hercules, O illustrious reviver of the forgotten order of knight-errantry! O never sufficiently praised Don Quixote de la Mancha, encourager of the faint-hearted, support of those about to fall, helping hand to the fallen, staff and comfort of all the unfortunate!

(659).

Since Gines de Pasamonte wants to move the conversation away from who he is, what he does, and what he wants, he changes the topic to chivalry. With fake gratitude, Master Pedro diminishes the prospect of being exposed as a false impersonator. Therefore, when cornered, Master Pedro controls the situation by soothing his victims into net neutrality so that his vested interests are not threatened. After Master Pedro trots out his ape to stage a spectacular puppet show, Cervantes outlines (as noted before) just how Gines de Pasamonte entices people out of their money, so that medieval Spanish readers are aware of the scams of their times, so that they do not fall victim to them. In short, by presenting Gines de Pasamonte (a.k.a. Master Pedro) as a quick-talking, hard-drinking, picture-painting con man, who dupes his victims with a number of devious ploys, Cervantes warns his readers away from toxic personalities. Yet, the coup-de-grace of Gines de Pasamonte's well-laid plans comes when Don Quixote busts-up his entire money-sucking operation.

Don Quixote ends Master Pedro's ability to gain money through dishonest means by drawing his sword and leaping on stage, hewing his puppets to shreds, and almost decapitating him in the process of chasing him out of town for good. This is why he "springs to his feet and shouts:

> Never while there is still breath in my body will I consent to such an insult being offered in my presence to such a famous knight and bold inamorato as Don Gaiferos. Desist you low-born rabble; do not follow him, or you shall battle with me! [Then he] draws his sword and with one leap positions himself in front of the stage, and with speedy and unprecedented fury begins to hack at the hordes of puppet Moors, knocking some over, beheading others, wrecking this one, destroying that; and one down-stroke among many others would have lopped Master Pedro's head off as easily as if it had been made of marzipan, if he hadn't ducked and crouched and made himself into a ball

(666).

By raining down a variety of cuts and thrusts and two-handers and fore-strokes, Don Quixote demolishes Master Pedro's puppet show, chases his monkey out a "roof[top] window" and cripples his ability to gain money through dishonest means (667). Foiled in his ability

253

to drain money from people "Master Pedro rises before the sun, takes his [frazzled] monkey [as well as] the remains of his puppet theatre" and vanishes into the night (670). In this case the forces of right honorable justice triumph over the forces of a con man's clever tricks.

At the level of physical conflict Senor Roque and Gines de Pasamonte show readers that if they initiate physical force "against the person or property of innocent persons;" if they lie, cheat and steal to seize valuables through force or fraud; "if they defy the world, smash its' structures, break its' laws, and kill its' representatives,[21]" then, ultimately, they will live a short, lonely, fear-ridden life characterized by a bad end. Case in point is Senor Roque who eludes punishment for his crimes by constantly moving about the badlands of the Sierra Morena. Never staying in one place long enough to develop deep personal relationships his own immovable and instinctive defiance against civilization has gained him nothing but utter loneliness. At night he even sleeps away from his thugs to explore the dimensions of isolation around him. Afraid of being gobbled-up from within by his underlings, Senor Roque inhabits the world of a "criminal jungle" where immoral men compete on a "vicious level".[22] As such, he lives in a dog-eat-dog environment where every man is out for himself. In this world peers do not trust each other. They are only grouped together insofar as their mutual fear aligns them. Constantly reminded that the wages of his sins is death, Roque waits until it is his turn to be hung from a tree and forgotten. Gines de Pasamonte is not much better. Introduced as a "chronic adult offender," his attitude in life is "whatever will be will be"[23]. For this reason he is "present oriented short-range

21 **Peikoff**, Leonard. "What to Do About Crime?" Ford Hall Forum. 1995. and **Bernstein**, Andrew. Heroism in Modern American Literature. The Ayn Rand Institute. California, 1996.

22 **Bernstein**, Andrew. Heroism in Modern American Literature. The Ayn Rand Institute. California, 1996.

23 **Peikoff**, Leonard. "What to Do About Crime?" Ford Hall Forum. Boston, Massachusetts, 1995.

impulsive and not reason driven long-ranged deliberative."[24] As such he is a drifter who rides from town to town cashing-in on the gullibility of people he meets along the way. The reward for his criminality is that he is nearly beheaded, his puppet show is torn to shreds and he is destined to wander the lawless hinterlands of the Sierra Morena forever dodging the authorities lest they discover his real identity and lock him up for good. In short, since Senor Roque and Gines de Pasamonte lead miserable lives, Cervantes erases a predisposition for an appetite for crime by drawing forward their negative examples.

To "instill in his readers the ideas and emotions that lead away from crime," Cervantes dramatizes the traits that produce it[25]. Take Senor Roque for example. He is a hardened career criminal who defines his choice in life as me versus them. He "wants something, he has to have it, he grabs it: like his victim's wallet [for example] or his [twin] machine guns [for instance]. [As such] he only cares about what is real and immediate. What moves him is the [direct] satisfaction of a desire, an urge, a wish. To him there is no reason to obey the law or to work for a living. Only weaklings follow the systems rules. Only suckers get jobs. [Though he is] at war with society he has a compassionate sense of [his own] moral entitlement justifying his life of crime as getting back what is owed to him."[26] Hostility, bitterness, and resentment define his inner emotions and he is filled with what he sees as a justified even righteous anger. "Emotionally he is aloof from all people, even his [close] associates," because his sudden attacks of frustration, his quick bursts of anger and his unexplained changes of mood block him from deep psychological fulfillment.[27] Lost in a

24 **Peikoff**, Leonard. "What to Do About Crime?" Ford Hall Forum. Boston, Massachusetts, 1995.

25 **Bernstein**, Andrew. Heroism in Modern American Literature. The Ayn Rand Institute. California, 1996.

26 **Peikoff**, Leonard. "What to Do About Crime?" Ford Hall Forum. Boston, Massachusetts, 1995.

27 **Peikoff**, Leonard. "What to Do About Crime?" Ford Hall Forum. Boston, Massachusetts, 1995.

world of self-made loneliness he is empty inside. Gines de Pasamonte, on the other hand, is a repeat habitual offender, who intentionally misrepresents who he is, what he wants, and how he aims to get it. Unrestrained by moral principles of right and wrong he uses short-term practical methods that generate tangible benefits—nevermind what he has to do to fulfill his immediate desires. Oblivious to any kind of ethical reasoning whatsoever he feels little guilt or remorse over his behavior. Lying is easy to him. In fact he lies so often that it becomes a habitual character trait. By telling untruths he defies the world, gets away with anything, does what he pleases, and succeeds. The world, he thinks, is his for the taking. So he pulls scams on unsuspecting people to con away their goods. By showing that criminal fraud can lead to one's downfall, Cervantes seeks to deflate the ideas and values that motivate crime.

Besides teaching readers to be men of productivity and men of peace not men of force or men of violence, Cervantes shows readers that if society is unjust, noncompliance is the only answer. Take, Senor Roque, for example. Formerly, he was a well-intentioned and compassionate sort of man but a desire for revenge "convulsed his placid heart" (899). Some external force has molded him has shaped him has made him into a man who is "violently pitted against the world around him."[28] He is defiant to the end and refuses to give in to society's demands. To further his own values, to meet his own needs, to succeed on his own terms, he stands up to the system to wrest what he can from it. Since the ruling purpose of Roque's life is to inflict punishment on society he ends up as the wounded part of the culture. In fact Roque's very existence impugns the criminal justice system of 17th century Spain. Since Cervantes's moral ideal is to live in a just society where underclassmen have a chance to prosper he encourages people to fight for justice. Thus, he rails against what he sees as injustice.

---

28 **Bernstein**, Andrew. <u>Heroism in Modern American Literature</u>. The Ayn Rand Institute. California, 1996.

His idea of what constitutes justice is antithetical to how the chain gang is treated. They are condemned to row in the galleys not based on "a logical evaluation of the relevant evidence" but based on a conspicuous sort of injustice instead.[29] Cervantes's "assessment of what constitutes justice turns on the question of how people are evaluated and judged and treated."[30] The events of the story show that since the state is no longer an agent of justice assigned to protect the rights of the innocent but rather initiates excessive force against its population, Don Quixote takes action to change society for the better. He creates truths, he judges right from wrong, he brings about principles in an unprincipled world. He is a rare depiction of a hero who saves the victims of social oppression. He fights the oppressors to save the oppressed; he fights the exploiters to save the exploited. Virtue, to Don Quixote, rests in generating justice for the people. This is why he takes on a certain type of respectability. All of this suggests that if a government violates the rights of its citizens by initiating excessive force against them than it is one's moral obligation to be noncompliant, resistant even.

Similarly, if readers analyze Spain when Don Quixote was written, they might see a need for "a powerful, militaristic, coming apart at the seams" because of their trampling of civil liberties[31]. Therefore, in *Don Quixote* Cervantes asks his readers if the "big, powerful," Spanish Inquisition administered by the state is "morally the good guy"?[32] No, reasons Cervantes, because it does not stand for civil liberties and individual freedoms! Rather, the author presents evidence, in a funny way, that Spain is "heading down the tubes

29 **Smith**, Tera. Passing Judgment: Ayn Rand's View of Justice. The Ayn Rand Institute. Irvine, California May, 9th, 1996.

30 **Smith**, Tera. Passing Judgment: Ayn Rand's View of Justice. The Ayn Rand Institute. Irvine, California May, 9th, 1996.

31 **Bernstein**, Andrew. Heroism in Modern American Literature. The Ayn Rand Institute. California, 1996.

32 **Bernstein**, Andrew. Heroism in Modern American Literature. The Ayn Rand Institute. California, 1996.

because there is a certain rejection of liberality," as well as a certain form of systemic tyranny[33]. There is a certain commitment to the idea in *Don Quixote* that "a free intellect that challenges the status quo is somehow dangerous and therefore ought to be shut-down."[34] By depicting Don Quixote as willing, and able, to buck the powers that be in Inquisitional Spain, Cervantes shows readers that an individual can rise above society to fight for freedom. In this way Cervantes takes on the social injustices of his times by "projecting a hero standing-up to and reaching tremendous heights by his own power."[35] Accordingly, Cervantes shows readers that a hero must have intellectual and physical prowess at the level of mental ability and bodily strength if he to vanquish a clever and forceful opponent. In brief, we see that the evil of the Holy Inquisition is not granted destructive power over goodness, because, heroes, like Don Quixote, fight for, and achieve, in large measure, their own individual freedom, and that of others.

All of this talk of freedom versus force, good versus evil, light versus darkness in *Don Quixote* poses the primary questions of moral philosophy: How should I live? What is right for me to do? What is wrong for me to do? Where does goodness reside? What is deep moral goodness at a sense of life level? Does good have the dominate power in man or does evil? Essentially, by fighting, and defeating a greater evil—the Holy Inquisition—thereby freeing and reforming a lesser evil (i.e. repent criminals like Gines de Pasamonte and Captain Roque) Cervantes illustrates that the triumph of freedom, justice, and goodness, is supreme, while evil, in all forms, should be avoided, fought against, or reformed.

More largely, the picaresque conversion narrative in *Don Quixote*

33 **Bernstein**, Andrew. Heroism in Modern American Literature. The Ayn Rand Institute. California, 1996.

34 **Bernstein**, Andrew. Heroism in Modern American Literature. The Ayn Rand Institute. California, 1996.

35 **Bernstein**, Andrew. Heroism in Modern American Literature. The Ayn Rand Institute. California, 1996.

asks readers to ponder what a "just society" is?[36] What "the rules of a society of justice are"?[37] Basically, Cervantes "isolates the essence of justice," by criticizing the Spanish State, under the Holy inquisition thereby encouraging the authorities to "treat people as they deserve"[38]. Law courts, in Cervantes's world, do not "convict the guilty and acquit the innocent," according to an objective code of morality[39]. Judges in Cervantes's Holy Spain do not base their sentences on a "fair evaluation of the facts relevant to the judgement" and then rule accordingly—assigning the appropriate punishment to offenders to disincentivise negative behavior, while, providing positive incentives to reinforce good conduct[40]. This unjust imbalance, in turn, leads to the inexorable conclusion that justice not only demands objective evaluation for fruition but also that justice requires a judge to pass judgement in a proper way passing an appropriate sentence, as well. Simply put, Cervantes not only presents the view that objective justice requires fair evaluation of the facts relevant to the judgement but also that following a policy of justice is beneficial to all people concerned.

In conclusion, since Cervantes is a romantic writer, he is aware of how one's nature effects his actions. He recognizes, at least at some level, that human virtue, human well-being, and human prosperity can be developed by choosing a proper life for oneself. The view of man presented in *Don Quixote* is that he is capable of goodness, he is capable of prowess, he is capable of courage, he is capable of all these

36 **Smith**, Tera. Passing Judgment: Ayn Rand's View of Justice. The Ayn Rand Institute. Irvine, California May, 9th, 1996.

37 **Smith**, Tera. Passing Judgment: Ayn Rand's View of Justice. The Ayn Rand Institute. Irvine, California May, 9th, 1996.

38 **Smith**, Tera. Passing Judgment: Ayn Rand's View of Justice. The Ayn Rand Institute. Irvine, California May, 9th, 1996.

39 **Smith**, Tera. Passing Judgment: Ayn Rand's View of Justice. The Ayn Rand Institute. Irvine, California May, 9th, 1996.

40 **Smith**, Tera. Passing Judgment: Ayn Rand's View of Justice. The Ayn Rand Institute. Irvine, California May, 9th, 1996.

moral values. There is no presentation of the view that the individual is a helpless victim crushed beneath the weight of social forces. Don Quixote applies individual choice to literature to determine how far he goes in life and in what way. This is how Cervantes shows his readers that they are not what society makes them but what they make themselves. That by choosing to actively pursue their values they have control over the make-up and quality of their lives. This is how he explores the nature of an ideal man and what qualities such a man would have. This is why he suggests a conscious choice to give up crime as a lifestyle. Cervantes looks into his characters, gazes into them, and finds that though many of them are wild and tricky and reckless they can become good men if they try hard enough.

Select Bibliography

Attansio, Salvator, <u>Giants of World Literature: Cervantes: *His Life, His Times, and His Works*</u>. Ed. Arnoldo Mondalori. New York: American Heritage Press, 1968.

Bandera, Casareo. <u>The Humble Story of Don Quixote: Reflections on the Birth of the Modern Novel</u>. (Chapter II. The Picaresque Point of Reference I.). Washington D.C: Catholic UP, 2006.

Bernstein, Andrew. <u>Heroism in Modern American Literature</u>. The Ayn Rand Institute. California, 1996.

Chambers, Leland, H. "Structure and the Search for Truth in the Quijote: Notes Toward a Comprehensive View." <u>Hispanic Review</u> 35.4 (1967) 309-326.

Elliott, J.H. Imperial Spain 1469-1716. New York: Penguin Books, 1963.

Peikoff, Leonard. "What to Do About Crime?" Ford Hall Forum. 1995.

"Picaresque Novel." <u>Encyclopedia Britannica</u>. 2007. Encyclopedia Britannica Online. Jan. 2007. <u>http://www.search.eb.com.proxyau.wrlc.org/eb/article- 9059900</u>>.

Smith, Tera. Passing Judgment: Ayn Rand's View of Justice. The Ayn Rand Institute. Irvine, California May, 9th, 1996.

http://en.wikipedia.org/wiki/Picaresque

http://en.wikipedia.org/wiki/Brigandage

http://en.wikipedia.org/wiki/Outlaw

ESSAY 8

The Generation of the Renaissance in the Quijote: *How the Spirit of Classicism, Chivalry, and Christianity Bypassed Medievalism and Led to Modernity.*

Cervantes dramatizes the ideas and practices of the Renaissance in the "Quijote" in a number of ways. One, by reviving classics in the humanities, he generates a sense of excitement about ideas from the past: a vision of classical simplicity that would lead men to study the achievements of classical scholars. Two, he shows readers that the printing press introduced new and unmistakable signs of a new Renaissance spirit in Spain's political, intellectual, and social life. Three, by noting changes in how books were produced and sold during the Renaissance, Cervantes suggests how feudalism gradually transitioned to capitalism during the early modern era. Fourth, by presenting the Renaissance axioms of esthetics (i.e. its sense of proportion, symmetry, beauty, and perfection) Cervantes marks the rough transition from medieval to modern thought. Fifth, by aggrandizing the Renaissance ideal of universal education, Cervantes notes how the Renaissance improved on the culture of the Middle Ages, especially since the wealth produced at the time meant people had more time for study. Sixth, by highlighting the Renaissance ideal of realistic literature, Cervantes emphasizes that reality and human emotion in art gave rise both to modern fiction and to the modern world. Seventh, Cervantes shows readers that during the Renaissance the willingness to question previously held truths and search for new answers resulted in a period of major scientific advancements. Eighth, by weaving together many different literary genres in his book, Cervantes invents the modern practice of novel writing, which was first practiced during the Renaissance. Ninth, by showing readers that Renaissance men focused on worldly not just spiritual matters, Cervantes illustrates how medieval Christian values were adjusted to a more this worldly spirit. Tenth, Cervantes suggests that the spirit of chivalry led to the Renaissance gentlemen of the modern age by teaching him politeness and self-control. Eleventh, Cervantes notes the emergence of the modern Spanish state by referencing many different legal proceedings and legal language in the "Quijote." Twelfth, patronage in Cervantes's view is not only great for the production of art but to him it is a political strategy. One of the keys to understanding the Renaissance. Thirteenth, Cervantes further shows that the Renaissance deferred to the vernacular, not Latin, as a suitable language for works of beauty and weight so people could gain access to knowledge by reading, especially religious information. Fourteenth, by chronicling and praising grand achievements of real life men from our classical past, Cervantes suggests how these great men merit high-honor in the march to civilization. Fifteenth, to address the lazy indolence that led to the decline of the Spanish Republic, Cervantes tried to encourage a new sense of energy and dynamism by noting the problems of his dissipated age. Sixteenth, by popularizing art forms used during the Renaissance, like the pastoral eclogue, for example, Cervantes ministered to society's modern spiritual needs. Seventeenth, Cervantes shows readers that the Renaissance fascination with the individual human being—with the mental viewpoint of one person—is most prominent in the "Quijote," in contrast to the medieval collectivist perspective, which homogenized people regardless of difference. Eighteenth, Cervantes reflects in his book that during the Renaissance new ideals of humanism sparked a religious reformation by changing the way people viewed their relationship with God. Nineteenth, Cervantes reminds readers that during the Renaissance people advanced themselves more by their ability than by their lineage thus giving rise to the modern concept of social mobility. And finally, Cervantes draws in additional readers, like former feudal lords, for example, by showing chivalry yielding to the Renaissance in a funny way. In all these ways, and more, Cervantes's notes, in the "Quijote," the progress made during the Renaissance towards the early modern age.

In the "Quijote," Cervantes emphasizes "a period of spiritual and intellectual renaissance [based on classicism] when a great literary language was being fashioned. "[1] As you know, "the Renaissance Humanists were interested in the classics, in reading the classics in the original, in editing the classics to make them available"[2]. This is because Renaissance intellectuals thought that the classics provided moral instruction and an intensive understanding of human behavior. Thus, classical authors referenced in the "Quijote" include: "Aristotle; Plato; Homer; Virgil; Aenias; Erasmus; Dante; Cicero; Plutarch; Zoroaster; Thomas Moore; Niccolo Machiavelli; Thomas Aquinas; Augustus Caesar; Julius Caesar; El Cid; and Cato the Elder" (Prologue [12], Prologue [12], 504, 504, 504, ?, ?, Prologue [16], Prologue [15], 435, Prologue [16], ?, Prologue [12], 102, 500, 452, 767). By focusing on great thinkers from the classical period, Cervantes not only showed how the Renaissance style emulated and improved on classical forms but he also attempted to restore direct links to the classical past, thus by-passing medievalism altogether.

Cervantes also breaks clean from the Middle Ages by showing his

---

1   Echevarria, Roberto, Gonzalez. "Spanish 300: Cervantes's Don Quixote." Yale University. New Haven, Connecticut. Fall 2009

2   Echevarria, Roberto, Gonzalez. "Spanish 300: Cervantes's Don Quixote." Yale University. New Haven, Connecticut, Fall 2009

readers how the printing press[3] democratized learning and allowed for a faster propagation of ideas. The fact that the "Quijote" was published at the end of the Renaissance, when improvements to the printing press had created a large readership, is shown in the novel. For example, at the end of the story Don Quixote:

> looks up and sees written in large letters over a door the words 'Books Printed Here,' [which] pleases him to no end, because he'd never seen a printing-house and was keen to know what they were like. [So] in he goes, with all his retinue, and all, [to observe] men printing in one place, correcting in another, setting up type over there, revising over here, and, in short, all the different activities of a large printing-house.

(914)

Basically, all of Don Quixote's observations of and questions to publishers, reflects the fascination that great Renaissance thinkers, like Cervantes, had with the newly invented process of mechanized printing, which rapidly distributed their ideas. To show this point our knight says that he:

> understands that more than twelve thousand copies of [his] history are in print at this moment; just ask [around in] Portugal, Barcelona, and Valencia, where they were printed; and there's a report being printed in Antwerp, and all the signs are that there is no language in the world into which it won't be translated.

(503)

---

3   Before the printing press, books were very expensive to create because they were made from animal skins, not paper. Thus, a whole flock of sheep would give their lives for the creation of one book. So writing and publishing books was much slower than it is today: often taking years.

This is partly because with the advent of the printing press printed books were much cheaper than hand copied books. More largely, though, since the "Quijote" was printed, reprinted, circulated, and translated, in a span of months, no set of ideas had ever travelled so far and so fast in so short a time. Not only did the printing press speed the delivery of new ideas to the public during the Renaissance—thus teaching people to gain access to information by reading—but it also enriched writers who produced those ideas.

To highlight the idea that during the Renaissance money and art went hand-in-hand, Cervantes shows readers that at the time a new economic relationship was developing between people based on writing for profit. Thus, he has Don Quixote and a random author discuss publishing thusly:

> **Q:** But please tell me this: are you having this book printed on your own account, or have you sold the rights to the bookseller?
>
> **A:** I'm printing it on my own account and I'm hoping to make a thousand ducats, at least, from this first printing, of two thousand copies, because they'll sell like hotcakes at six reals each.
>
> **Q:** Your accounts are in a fine way, I must say! You do not seem to know anything about printers' credits and debits, or the agreements that they make with each other. I can promise you that when you find yourself loaded down with two thousand copies of your book you'll soon be so exhausted from trying to sell it.
>
> **Q + A:** What do you mean? Do you want me to let a bookseller have it, and give me three marvedis for the copyright, and think he's doing me a great favour? I don't print my books to achieve fame, because my deeds have already made me well-known; profit is what I want, because without it fame isn't worth a farthing. (916).

Such a focus on writing and profit reflects the Renaissance shift in mentality from a feudal social organization, where human relationships were based on tenant farming, to a capitalistic social organization, where people freely wrote, and freely exchanged, their ideas for money. Or, phrased differently, the "Quijote" infers that commercially producing your own ideas, and getting rewarded for your thoughts by the free marketplace of consumers, was beginning to emerge. To explain, prior to the Renaissance there were no private art markets like we have today. Before the Renaissance you did not make art and put it in a shop window and wait for someone to buy it. But during the Renaissance the phenomenon of creating books, selling books, and letting a consumer marketplace decide who the winners and losers where, was starting to form. Thus, during the Renaissance changes in how art was produced and sold were part of a general economic transition from feudalism to capitalism, which not only preceded and financed the Renaissance but which also shifted Spain away from land owning and tenant farming to merchants and commerce.

Cervantes also revives Renaissance aesthetics in the "Quijote," which is "based on the idea of order, symmetry, and perfection obtained by the imitation of classical models. [4]" This is why the Cannon of Toledo talks about classical narrative unities thusly:

> The soul can only take delight in the beauty and *harmony* that it sees or contemplates in what the eyes or the imagination places before it, and nothing that contains ugliness or dis*order* can give us any pleasure. Because what beauty can there be, what *proportion* of *the parts to the whole, or of the whole to the parts* can there be in poorly plotted and worsely structured tales of chivalry. I have never seen a book of chivalry that could be regarded as a body complete with all its

---

4   Echevarria, Roberto, Gonzalez. "Spanish 300: Cervantes's Don Quixote." Yale University. New Haven, Connecticut, Fall 2009.

members, and in which the *middle corresponds to the beginning and the end with the beginning and middle*; on the contrary their authors give them so many members that their intention seems more to produce a chimera then a well-proportioned figure.

(440)

Here, we see the Cannon of Toledo criticize the medieval structure of fiction—particularly chivalry romances, with their series of break-away tales—in his attempt to restore classical literary esthetics popular during the Renaissance. He further defines the rules of classical literature as follows:

Fictional stories should [enhance a] reader's understanding and be written in such a way that they amaze and astonish, gladden and entertain, so that wonder and pleasure go hand in hand; and none of this can be achieved by the writer who forsakes *Verisimilitude* or the imitation of the truth; because the *perfection* of all writing consists in these qualities.

(440, 441).

Here, the Canon of Toledo suggests that the aim of classic literature is reaching perfection; or a mirror-image of the truth, by emulating the harmonious forms of classical art. Besides showing Renaissance readers these Neo-Platonic ideals, the "Quijote" contains other elements of Renaissance literary esthetics: like the idealized beauty and perfections of Marcela and Dorotea in Part I of the novel. This is significant because Renaissance artists tried to achieve a standard of ideal beauty based on a careful examination of the human form. In sum, Cervantes shows readers that as the Renaissance emerged from feudalism so too did its sense of taste concerning beauty and the beautiful.

Another way Cervantes transitions medieval to modern thought is to present the Renaissance ideal of universal education [5], which the humanists believed prepared them for the afterlife with a perfect mind and body. This is why Don Quixote is greatly learned himself; tries to teach Sancho Panza to read and write; teaches the Duchess about Demosthenes and Cicero [6]; and, ultimately, renews, through his speeches and actions, an interest in adapting the relation of the chivalric tradition to an evolving humanistic vision that suited the needs of a new society. The benefits of universal education is further shown by the "Quijote's" hypothetical narrator, one Cide Hamete el Benengeli, who is "a Muslim philosophical sage, [and] a wise and circumspect historian, [who] answers unspoken questions, clears up doubts, brings arguments to their proper conclusion, and, in short, reveals every last atom of information that the most curious reader could ever want to know" (243, 750). Similarly, Grisostomo,[7] an undergraduate student of Salamanca University is a humanist scholar and first rate poet who "writes carols for Christmas Eve and mystery plays for Corpus Christi" (91). Judge Juan Perez de Viedma is also a graduate of Salamanca University; a civil court judge who travels to Mexico City to take-up an important post as a Supreme Court Justice [8]. Likewise, an anonymous student swordsmen MA "studies Cannon Law at Salamanca, [and] takes pride in expressing [himself] in clear, plain, meaningful, language" (613). The list of learned men in the book is long. The main point here is that Cervantes stressed the interconnection of chivalry and learning in the "Quijote" to

---

5   The modern practice of **Civic Humanism** emerged from the belief that education should promote individual virtue and public service.

6   The modern practice of **Civic Humanism** emerged from the belief that education should promote individual virtue and public service.

7   **Demosthenes** was a prominent Greek statesmen and orator of ancient antiquity while **Cicero** was a Roman philosopher, statesmen, lawyer, and political theorist.

8   "**Grisostomo's** profession was humanism his pursuits and studies consisted in writing books for publication, all of great social value, being both instructive and entertaining" (page #)..

emphasize that both the chivalric ideal and the renaissance ideal of self-management centered on a concept of universal education. In sum, since Don Quixote talks about education in admiring terms, teaches Sancho Panza the value of letters, and populates his story with learned people, he highlights how widespread education was at the time.

Literary realism is another hallmark of the Renaissance that Cervantes depicts in the "Quijote," since Renaissance art is typified by the search for realism in fiction. This is why he "links reality," as he experienced it in his own life to the stories in his novel. For example, Cervantes writes about how he was captured during the battle of Lepanto and how "he was the only man to emerge unscathed from slavery" (370). Basically, as Dr. Echevarria writes, Cervantes "transmutes his own experiences into the stuff of literature to elevate his life into fiction" (Introduction XI). This is why he references real life people in his book, like "Don John of Austria,[9]" the Duke of Alba [10], Ali Alouk Fartach [11], Hajj Murad [12], Hassan Aga [13], Avellaneda[14],

---

9   **Don John of Austria** was a great military commander. His most notable naval accomplishments was defeating the Ottoman Turks in the battle of Lepanto in 1571, which gained for Spain, naval control of the Mediterranean seas.

10   **Duke of Alba:** Fernando Alvarez de Toledo, Duke of Alba (1508-83), was a famous soldier and a member of one of Spain's noblest families. He fought with distinction in Germany and Italy and in 1567 was appointed Governor of the Netherlands.

11   **Ali Alouk** was the King of Algiers then the Admiral of the Ottoman fleet under Sultan Selim.

12   **Hajj Murad** was an important Algerian moor who lived in Algiers, at a place called Oran, on the Mediterranean coast, in the year 1527. He was governor of Algiers for a time..

13   **Hassan Aga** originally a Venetian Renegade who rose to be the King of Algiers. He was Cervantes's captor when he was enjailed in an Ottoman Bagnio, or bathhouse, from 1575-1580.

14   **Avellenda** was the spurious author of the "Quijote's" second part who debased Cervantes's great work to get a free knock-off ride from his literary masterpiece. This is why Cervantes pours scorns on Avellenda in Part II of his novel. Thus, he becomes a character in the novel, who Don Quixote and Sancho Panza always make fun of.

Miguel Cervantes[15], Count Alazar[16], King Phillip the III, Hector of Troy, Magellan[17], Methuselah[18], Thomas Aquinas[19], Prester John[20], Lopa de Vega[21], Augustus Caesar[22], Cicero, Zoroaster [23], Julius

---

15 **Miguel de Cervantes de Saavedra** was author of the world's first novel, the "**Quijote,**" a pastoral romance named "**La Galatea,**" a collection of moral tales named "**Exemplary Novels,**" a poetry folio named "**Journey to Parnassus,**" and a set of plays called "**La Numancia.**"

16 **Don Benardino de Velasco**, the **Count of Salazar**, was put in charge of the expulsions of the Moriscos from Castille, La Mancha, Extremadura and Murcia, between 1609 and 1614.

17 **Magellan** was a famous Portuguese naval explorer who lived from 1480-1521: a navigator who was the first man to circumvent the southern tip of South America in his expedition around the world.

18 **Methuselah**: Was a patriarch, the grandfather of Noah, said to have lived for 969 years (Genesis 5.27). Though, on the one hand, he takes on the ora of a messiah and prophet, since some Christians believed he lived for a millennia, scientists, on the other hand, think he just lived a long time.

19 **Thomas Aquinas** was reasonably the greatest Christian Aristotelian Philosopher of all time because he synergized reason and faith in "**Summa Theologica.**"

20 **Prester John**: Was a legendary medieval Christian King of Asia, ruler of one of the four parts into which the Byzantine Empire was divided in the early 13th Century. This is why he is often mentioned in books of Chivalry. He also ruled Trebizond which fell to the Turks in 1461.

21 **Lope de Vega**: Félix Arturo Lope de Vega y Carpio was a Spanish playwright and poet. He was one of the key figures in the Spanish Golden Century of Baroque literature.

22 **Augustus Caesar**: Was the founder of the Roman Empire and its first Emperor, ruling from 27 BC until his death in 14 AD. He was born Gaius Octavius into an old and wealthy equestrian branch of the plebeian Octavii family. He was the Creator of the Roman Republic, one of the greatest men of all time.

23 **Zoroaster was a Persian King** who reformed his country's religion in about 800 b.c., and was regarded as the inventor of magic. He created the philosophy of Zoroastrianism, which, is based on the notion that fire has important qualities because it brings warmth, and sanitizes food.

Caesar[24], and the Duke of Alba[25]". By referencing real life people and events in his chronicle-novel, and by blending fact and fiction, Cervantes makes his story believable because it is historically accurate. Realistic literature is further addressed by Father Pero Perez when he says "as far as [Tirante the White's] style is concerned [it] is the best book in the world. In it knights eat and [expire] in their beds and make wills before they die, and other things that are usually omitted from books of this sort" (56). Evidently, Father Pero Perez's elevation of realistic tales of chivalry over unbelievable stories of knight errantry highlights the drive during the Renaissance to write about life realistically. In sum, by referencing himself throughout the story, chronicling real-life historical facts, and praising realistic tales of knight errantry, Cervantes imbues a degree of literary realism in his book which was new, or novel, during the Renaissance.

Besides publishing a realistic book depicting everyday events, Cervantes founds the Renaissance practice of novel writing by combing prose and verse for the first time. He did this by synergizing pastoral, picaresque, romantic, devotional, poetic, and realistic fiction, into a new literary element called the novel. The Cannon of Toledo even talks about how the modern novel combines literary genres thusly:

> If [writing a new book] is done in an agreeable style
> and with ingenious inventiveness, and comes as close
> as possible to the truth, it will most certainly weave
> a web of beautiful and varied thread which, once
> complete, will display such perfection and loveliness
> that it will attain the highest goal to which writing
> can aspire: giving instruction and pleasure together,

---

24 **Julius Caesar**: Gaius Julius Caesar was a Roman general, statesman, Consul, and notable author of Latin prose. He played a critical role in the events that led to the demise of the Roman Republic and the rise of the Roman Empire.

25 **Duke of Alba**: Duke of Alba is a Spanish title of nobility accompanied with the dignity Grandee of Spain. In 1472 he was elevated to the title Duke of Alba by King Henry IV of Castille.

because the openness of such books allows the author to display his talent for epic, lyric, tragic, and comic, together with the quantities of the sweet and pleasing arts of poetry and oratory; for epic can be written in prose as well as verse.

(441)

Such a fusion of fictional writing forms, as the Cannon of Toledo describes them, was new to creative literature, since, before, literature consisted of devotional poems praising God, heroic epic written to honor the Gods, romantic ditties written for one's lover, or letter writing books featuring an epistolary letter exchange between several different characters. With the advent of the "Quijote," however, this changed. Now stories were being written about everyday people doing everyday things at locations such as inns, taverns, mountains, roads, and more. We are even told that the "Quijote," "which draws from all the prose genres that preceded it (and some poetic ones too) had no beaten paths to follow" (Introduction XIX). In conclusion, because Cervantes blends many different literary genres, and combines prose and verse for the first time, the "Quijote" was novel, or new, for its time, thus, engendering the literary Renaissance.

Cervantes also suggests in the "Quijote" that the Renaissance saw changes in the way the universe was viewed and the methods sought to explain natural phenomena. This is why a character named Grisostomo, who is particularly well-versed in Astronomy, or the science of the stars, explains the movements of the sun and moon in relation to the earth, predicting, with precise accuracy, the cyclical occurrence of solar and lunar eclipses. This is significant because during the Renaissance people began to approach the world empirically and draw rational conclusions based on observation. Thus, based on his knowledge of the movements of cosmic bodies—which he uses to forecast weather patterns—Grisostomo predicts, with precise accuracy, if a year will be fruitful, or not. Due to his agricultural predictions, Grisostomo's father, and many of his friends, sow barley, wheat, chickpeas, or olives, when, and as appropriate, enriching themselves with bumper crops in the process. Such a reliance on the cosmos to predict climate patterns suggests the scientific spirit of the new times that were coming. Other characters use the stars to navigate. For example, Sancho Panza often resorts "to the lore [he] learned as a little shepherd" by plotting the sun's position relative to the stars (155). This is important because it marks how influential Renaissance astronomy was on the everyday man. One further scientific development during the Renaissance was not a specific discovery per se, but rather the further development of the process of discovery, the scientific method. This is why in the "Quijote's" introduction Dr. Echevarria defines the social context of the novel by saying that "during the Renaissance Spanish humanists had kept up with scientific developments and had developed a method to absorb their findings" (Introduction, VIII). Arguably, Cervantes noted the coming a "scientific revolution," in the "Quijote," thus heralding the beginning of the modern age, especially since during the Renaissance, the willingness to question previously held truths and search for new answers resulted in a period of major scientific advancements.

Another signal that the "Quijote" is a Renaissance book is that it marks the transition from medieval knight to Renaissance courtier by establishing a new set of norms of behavior and moral codes that differed from those of the warrior society of knighthood. This is also how Cervantes begins a fictional conversation about the court as a sociological entity during the reign of King Phillip the III. For example, in the transition from part I to part II of the novel we see how the book exchanges knighthood for courtierhood as the ethical focus of its criticism. As Dr. Alemany explains, during the first part of the "Quijote" life at the court goes almost unnoticed and escapes strong criticism. But part II of the Quixote is very different. Here, Cervantes uses the long stay at the ducal palace to examine current court behavior. Thus, alongside brief remarks about the easy life of the palace in part one, we find a well thought out criticism about the court itself as an institution. Evidently, "the arrival of a progressive courtly sublimation of physical force brought with it a different hierarchy of values to be represented by high society:" attributes in which consideration, temperance, cheerfulness, diligence, and generosity is emphasized[26]. In other words, Cervantes replaces the virtues of a warrior society with those of a courtesan life governed by a different set of morals, because, as Dr. Elias suggests, in every civilizing process one of the most decisive transitions is that of warriors to courtiers. Thus, the civilizing process occurs in the "Quijote" step-by-step, "as a warrior nobility is replaced by a tamed court nobility with more muted effects[27]."

In-line with critical Renaissance attitudes characterized by primary focus on oneself and secondary focus on others, Don Quixote is largely concerned with his own self, or, partaking in physical creature comforts and gregarious social pleasures as a psychological reward for his value questing. Hence, "Dances and song are good for him [because] he likes to see a cheerful spirit [since] his guiding philosophy [in life] is to not be cast down [by] the bumps [that he] receives [on the road]; some [of which, he feels] are bound to come [his] way."[28] Said differently, even though Don Quixote thinks that he must discipline his body and keep fit, if libations are offered to him, he feels there is no need to eschew intoxicating beverages provided moderation is exercised. Thus, Don Quixote enjoys golden cups to drink from, casks of wine, piles of baked bread, and whole roasted oxen, at Basilio and Quiteria's wedding, as a justly earned social

---

26 Alemany, Ignacio, Lopez. "Courting Don Quixote: An Aulic Frame of Reference." Fall 2013. Cervantes: Bulletin of the Cervantes Society of America. 33.2. 49-70.

27 Alemany, Ignacio, Lopez. "Courting Don Quixote: An Aulic Frame of Reference." Fall 2013. Cervantes: Bulletin of the Cervantes Society of America. 33.2. 49-70.

28 Keen, Muarice. Chivalry. Yale University Press: London, 1984. (13).

and bodily pleasure for his dream questing. And when he sees a warm bed, like in the Duke and Duchess's country estate, or a pile of hey, like in the innkeeper's barn, he plops down and slumbers. And, occasionally, our knight enjoys fine food, pig roasts, and warm pies, sometimes sleeping in sheltered domiciles, like taverns, castles, and private homes. In brief, Don Quixote fuels his soul by punctuating his adventures with pleasing song, vibrant dance, scrumptious food, fine wine, and jovial merrymaking, as a spiritual reward for all of the hardships he overcomes on the road. In sum, all of Don Quixote's worldly concerns, like eating, drinking, dancing, and socializing, shows readers that the Renaissance focused on the human not just the spiritual world.

Cervantes also shows readers how the spirit of Christianity was a civilizing influence throughout history and during the Renaissance, since the very existence of this standard was a tremendous factor in the slow development of society out of barbarism into modern civilization. To explain, "for the Church medieval warfare was too cruel, medieval religion too irrational, and medieval love too gross for any permanent harmonization. To the clergy, it was necessary for warfare to be humanized, religion to be rationalized, and love purified.[29]" And the one hope of restraining the bestial love of mere violence, was to penetrate the knightly order with the Church's teachings. This is why Cervantes approves of the Church's[30] campaigns against feudal barbarity in the "Quijote," which he shows by having the Duke of Aragon monitor the joust[31] between Don Quixote and Tosilios closely, instituting a whole host of safety precautions like:

---

29   Keen, Muarice. Chivalry. Yale University Press: London, 1984.

30   Historically, as Muarice Keen noted, quarrels and confusion drove men to choose kings, to defend the people against their enemies and against evil judges, they sought out those among them who were the wisest, strongest, and most handsome, and gave them seniority over others in such a way that they should help the King maintain peace, and from these men are descended those who we call gentlemen.

31

removing the "iron tip" from his "lance" so that Tosilios can defeat Don Quixote "without killing or wounding him;" eluding the first clash of arms that would likely result in Don Quixote's death if they met at full tilt; "surveying" the field of battle to make sure there are "no hidden obstacles" that could cause a trip and fall; and, lastly, ensuring nobody has an unfair advantage because the "sun" is in his opponents eyes" (865, 866). Ultimately, since Don Quixote and Tosilios do not joust at all, Cervantes dramatizes the provisions of the Ecumenical Council of Trent[32] in the "Quijote," which outlawed jousting altogether, at least in the houses of the high nobility[33]. In sum, Don Quixote's chivalric enterprise manifested, if sometimes in a crude and rudimentary form, the elements of virtues and graces, which display themselves as the fine flowers of the cultured and Christian society of a latter-and-better Renaissance age.

Chivalry, as Cervantes depicts it in the "Quijote" also lead to the Renaissance by teaching gentlemen of a succeeding age to place honor at the center of his mental and social world. This is why our knight delivers so many speeches on honor, nobility, and merit, to Sancho Panza, and others. For example, he says that a man "should [not only have] virtue, wealth, and generosity [but he] must concern himself with the administration of justice." (524). This shows readers that chivalry instilled a courtesy, a code of fine manners, based on heartfelt consideration of the intercourse of legal proceedings. Ergo, to Cervantes, to get to the truth of matters, a man, or woman, must have "good judgment [coupled with] a keen and incisive mind; [and

---

32 The **Ecumenical Council** opened at **Trent** on December, 13, 1545, and closed there on December, 4th 1563. Its main object was the definitive determination of the doctrines of the Church in answer to the heresies of the Protestants; a further object was the execution of a thorough reform of the inner life of the Church by removing the numerous abuses that had developed in it.

33 The **Ecumenical Council** of **Trent** reflects the evolution from a martially oriented, society, where knights had to keep their skills sharp for war, to a society based, in part, on a Christian view of morality, where the system of values was geared more towards peace and amity between city states.

above all,] the honest determination to do what is right" (459). Thus, he should:

> march on with a firm foot, and honest intentions, [for] his wisest course [is] to control and conquer himself and show a generous heart [since] what gives [a person] greatest happiness is to find himself with a good name on everybody's lips, while he is still alive, [especially among virtuous and eminent men, [both by speech] and in print.

> (669, 344, 503).

Since, at the time, universal courtesy was a relatively new thing in the hard and general world, this new attitude brought about the Renaissance by showing how honor can get men to act as they should. In sum, Cervantes emphasizes that chivalry grew in breadth and nobility to become the code of the gentleman: a code of moral honor, a standard of good form, and a school of courtesy directed by intelligence and virtue, not, solely, base animal violence.

Cervantes also shows readers that during the Renaissance justice was not only used to end crimes not eliminate the criminal but judicial rules were now fixed by individuals and were operated by professionals and procedure. As Dr. Childers suggests, the "Quijote" is not only "saturated with formulas lifted from legal documents, including arrest warrants, letters of payment, Don Quixote's duly notarized will, a certified register of the galley slaves sentences and several affidavits" but mock trials and other scenes patterned on legal proceedings also recur frequently throughout the book[34]. For example, readers learn that the romance between a knight named Don Clavijo and a young heiress named princess Antonomasia is conceived on the basis on "an iron-clad written contract" tantamount

---

34   Childers, William. L. "Legal Discourse in Don Quixote." 2005. Maester 34.1. 1-17.

to a prenuptial agreement (747). In another episode Don Quixote "presents [a] mayor a petition" asking a character named Don Tarfe to swear he is the real Don Quixote (969). In response, "the mayor takes all the appropriate steps: drawing-up a deposition in front of a notary with all the legal requisites as is proper in such cases" (969). Thus, legal discourse in the "Quijote" draws our attention to a major political change at the time: the role of judicial reforms in the process of the emergence of the Spanish state. Additionally, a popular reading of the galley slave episode, where a group of prisoners account to Don Quixote their crimes and the sentences they received, is that it satirizes the harsh and unjust judicial system at the time implicitly arguing in favor of a more modern approach.

Artistic patronage is also shown in the "Quijote" as a Renaissance activity, since many Renaissance patrons believed in, and thus sought out, the genius of man, the unique and extraordinary ability of the human mind, while artists needed financiers to pay for their works and sustain their genius. To explain, in 17th century Spain there was little commercial artistic activity where artists could put their works on display in shop windows and sell them directly to the public. You only made art when someone commissioned it from you and paid for it more or less in advance. Thus, artists depended on the charity of rich men to commission their work before they started to ensure they were paid. Patrons, in turn, not only wanted to spend their money virtuously by patronizing great artists like Cervantes they also "tried to get power by various public and private dealings," ultimately promoting their image to the rest of the world through art, literature, and having people write about them[35]. This, in turn, served patrons ends, which were to "recognize great ideas, reward talented artists, and take advantage of the public relations opportunities contained

---

35 Empire. Dir. Justin Hardy. Narr. Massimo Marinoni. PBS Home Video. 2003. 220 min.

therein."[36] But since direct criticism of powerful yet corrupt people was dangerous for the artist, Don Quixote counsels Don Lorenzo to write poetry that only denounces sins and vices in general by *not* "launch[ing] bitter invectives against those responsible for the disaster," or propounding ad hominem attacks against villains by name (589). Thus, to earn aristocratic patronage for his writings, Cervantes attacks vice in general, not specific people embodying that vice. This is why he gets two patrons: The Count of Lemos[37] and the Archbishop of Toledo, Don Bernardo de Sandoval y Rojas. This is significant because Cervantes's interaction with the historical patrons of his time signals one reason why the Renaissance produced so many great works of art: because a high number of great and rich men were willing to respect artists who knew their minds and their worth. To express his gratitude to these great men for their financial support and protection, Cervantes writes: "Long live the great Count of Lemos, whose well-known Christian virtue and generosity sustains [him] in the face of all the blows of [his] scant fortune. [And] long live the splendid charity of the Archbishop of Toledo, Don Bernardo de Sandoval y Rojas[38]" (485). In sum, the open-handed liberality of Cervantes's two patrons, coupled with the generosity of different patrons sponsoring other artists at the time, created a literary and artistic Renaissance in Spain and Europe.

Cervantes also shows readers that as a cultural movement the Renaissance encompassed the innovative flowering of vernacular literatures beginning with the 14th century learning based on classical sources. Many people at the time, including Cervantes, called for a translation of the Bible into the vernacular, or everyday language of

---

36   Empire. Dir. Justin Hardy. Narr. Massimo Marinoni. PBS Home Video. 2003. 220 min.

37   The **Count of Lemos**: Dinis of Braganza (1481-1516) was the younger son of Fernando II, Duke of Braganza and Issabella of Viseu who was daughter of Infante Fernando, Duke of Visue and Beatrice of Portugal.

38   **Don Bernardo de Sandoval y Rojas** (1546-1618) was a Spanish bishop and Grand Inquisitor of Spain from 1608 to 1618.

ordinary people—words people use with their friends and amongst their generation. This is why Cervantes says that "there isn't any need to go begging counsel from holy scripture [but rather] to write sentences that depicts what is on your mind [to the best of your ability] setting out your ideas without complicating or obscuring them (Part I Prologue, 16). To explain, the reformers insisted that religion had to be popular, which meant it should be presented in the vernacular – itself a Renaissance notion – and that meant all old settings in Latin had to be discarded. This is why Cervantes tells readers to "avoid Latin expressions, [to] not go for needless complications; [and that] those who indulge in random jargon will get a taste of their own medicine (Part I Prologue, 19). This passages suggests that though Latin had evolved greatly from the classical period and was still a living language used in the Church and elsewhere, the Renaissance obsession with classical purity halted its further evolution and saw Latin revert to its classical form.

In the "Quijote" Cervantes also relates the spirit of chivalry to the social and political needs of the Renaissance to revive a belief system defined by "common attitudes, judicial rules, and accepted manners, which defines and gives life to a common culture.[39]" Since many of the "Quijote's" characters have read, at one point, or actively read, in the novel, popular forms of chivalry, readers immediately see that the movement of popularization of chivalric literature affected not only the beliefs, the knowledge, and the religious attitudes of the reading community as a whole, but, most importantly, it lead to the emergence of new ideals of life, tending towards personal freedom, individual rights, and modern ethical values. Said differently, by keeping "a certain sentimental affection for knighthood in bloom," Cervantes not only deliberately tried to seek in a bygone era the satisfaction that could not be found at the time but he also sought to

39 Duby, Georges. The Chivalrous Society. Trans. Cynthia Postan. Los Angeles: University of California Press, 1980 (173).

look back in time to understand the present[40]. But wistful yearning is not all that Cervantes expresses in the "Quijote." Part of the author's remembrance of chivalry's golden age is not simply to look from the present to a golden past, which differed from the present only in that deterioration had not yet set in, but to "reanimate chivalric worth and glory, with the hope that it would bring about a new era" of Spanish enterprise. [41]In other words, Cervantes seemed to preserve the chivalrous forms so popular in previous centuries to diffuse, in Spain, a well-reasoned, and reasonably, coherent social ideology, based on individual heroism, spiritual rationalism, and Renaissance values.

The widespread popularity of chivalry books in the "Quijote" also signals how important a part literature can play in spreading Renaissance ideals. Since: "the 'Quijote' is full of writers and readers— of books, stories, poems and of people young and old effected by literature," many people in the novel are exposed to the ideas of the Renaissance through books. This is significant since the spirit of our knight's chivalry and the spirit of the Renaissance was both individualistic and non-religious[42]. Indeed, several characters in the "Quijote" have read, do read, or plan on reading chivalry books. For example, Don Quixote's housekeeper reads books of chivalry as does: Cardenio; Luscinda; Lotario; Dorotea; Altisidora; Marcela; Maritornes; Grisostomo; Tosilios; the Curate; the Cannon, and, countless others. Some of these fictional characters "love hearing about [chivalric] goings-on" (290). Others think that chivalric literature has "given [them] new life" (290). Some, "enjoy listening [to chivalry books] at harvest time [since tales of bravery] takes all

---

40   Kilgour, Raymond Lincoln. The Decline of Chivalry: As Shown in the French Literature of the Middle Ages. 1937. Cambridge: Harvard University Press, 1966.

41   Kilgour, Raymond Lincoln. The Decline of Chivalry: As Shown in the French Literature of the Middle Ages. 1937. Cambridge: Harvard University Press, 1966 (34).

42   Echevarria, Roberto, Gonzalez. "Spanish 300: Cervantes's Don Quixote." Yale University. New Haven, Connecticut, Fall 2009.

their worries away" (290). Others, like Dorotea, read chivalry books in the comfort of their own homes. Day laborers, like "reapers," or farm hands, gather under the shady boughs of trees during "rest days," to "listen" to instructive stories of chivalry (290). The Cannon of Toledo has even "written [more than] a hundred pages [of his own] chivalry book," which observes the finer points of literary realism, which he gave to "learned and intelligent men" so they can critic it (442). Together, these people signal the special contribution chivalric literature has played in spreading modern Renaissance values throughout the world.

Cervantes also engages and transforms the popular imagination during the early Renaissance by referencing great heroes from our classical past thus providing models of excellence for Spanish youths to follow. Said differently, by chronicling the deeds of many great men throughout history, Cervantes strengthens the literary energy of chivalry itself, so that new seedling attitudes of classicism could take place beneath and around him. This is why Don Quixote chronicles the lives of so many heroes throughout history. For example, he critiques,

> the wiles of a *Ulysses*, the pity of an *Aenias*, the courage of an *Achilles*, the misfortunes of a *Hector*, the treachery of a *Sinon*, the friendship of a *Euryalus*, the generosity of an *Alexander*, the resolve of a *Caesar*, the honesty of a *Trajan*, and the wisdom of a *Cato* (441)

> Each figure of the eleven notables "had something particular to teach and a particular relevance." *Ulysses*, or *Odysseus*, in Greek myth, not only represents a hero's use of stratagems, or concealed intentions, to outwit and outmaneuver a mighty opponent (like Homer's one-eyed giant Cyclops) but he also represents the tenacity and persistence needed to accomplish a worthy goal, since, ultimately, he won home to his wife Penelope after a "mighty ten year struggle against

Gods, Goddesses, human beings, monsters,"[43] and foes of all sorts.

Aeneis, no doubt, represents mercy and clemency for people who suffer mentally, or physically, or both, because of distressed conditions beyond their control, since, ultimately, *Aeneis* saved himself, and the *Aeneids*, from a life of slavery to the Greeks, because when Troy fell to General Agamemnon, he fought-off his soldiers long enough to escape Troy. After an epic five-year exodus from Asia Minor to Italy, *Aeneis* founded the ancient sanctuary-polis of Rome, which provided relief, comfort, and shelter, to the *Aeneids*.

Achilles, Homer's epic hero, represents the mental, physical, and moral strength needed to overcome danger, fear, and difficulty, since he singlehandedly slayed hundreds of soldiers in the *Trojan War*, including *Hector* outside the gates of Troy.

Hector, represents steadfastness in the face of hardship, since, historically, he was "Troy's greatest warrior," who "fought" legendary heroes, like "Ajax, to a stalemate," and even "killed a Greek champion named Protesilaus."

Sinon, represents wily courage, or hidden-bravery, in the form of fake-treachery, since he pretended to desert the Greeks during the Trojan War. After convincing the Trojans that Odysseus left him behind to die because of gross insubordination, *Sinon* tells them that "the giant wooden horse the Greeks left on the beaches of Troy was a gift to the gods to ensure their safe voyage home." Once the Trojans bring the Trojan horse into Troy, "Greek soldiers disembark

---

43 Bernstein, Andrew. "Heroes and Hero Worship." 2010. Ayn Rand Institute: Irvine, California.

from within and open the gates of the city," to capture Troy.

Euryalus, observe, represents deep friendship, even platonic love, between two men, since "*Euryalus* and *Nisus* [are] inseparable in the aftermath of the Trojan War" under the leadership of *Aeneas*.

Alexander, to wit, is famous for his generosity, since he allowed people he ruled, like the Persian's, for example, to practice their own religion, and keep their own customs and dress. He even "introduced Persian officers and soldiers into Macedonian units," when his men objected to his liberal policies.

Caesar, above all, is legendary for his fixity of purpose, since he defeated Gallic tribes poised against him; pursued and captured Pompey, a rebellious Roman naval general; and, most importantly, was steadfast in his "prosecution of former governors notorious for [their] extortion and corruption." Caesar, was also greatly renowned for his crime fighting skills. For example, when "he was kidnapped by pirates and held prisoner he maintained an attitude of superiority throughout his captivity". He had such a high opinion of himself that when the pirates demanded a ransom of twenty talents of silver, he insisted they ask for fifty talents instead. After the ransom was paid, Caesar raised a fleet, pursued and captured the pirates, and imprisoned them. After giving them a fair trial, Caesar "had them crucified on his own authority," as he had promised while in captivity—a promise the pirates had taken as a joke. As a sign of "leniency, [however,] he first had their throats cut, so they did not agonize for days, dying from thirst, starvation, and blood loss: suffering minute-by-minute and hour-by-hour under the sun's direct rays, drying-up internally from the deadly combination of sun-stroke, perspiration, and salt-spray, dazed and confused from lack-of-food and loss-of-blood, bleeding-out from their wrist wounds."

Trajan, notice, represents how a civil-minded, peaceful, Roman Emperor can form an ideal government, since he "presided over an era of peace and prosperity in the Mediterranean world," by "overseeing public building programs and implementing social welfare policies, which earned him the legacy as the second of the five good emperors."

And, finally, *Cato the Elder*, represents civic humanism incarnate since he not only carried out, with great efficiency, his office of Greek Censor, but, more largely, because he read lengthy papyrus scrolls about practical, city-centric, solutions, night-and-day, like constructing an aquifer irrigation system, for example, or constructing a road-grid system, for instance. (Wikipedia).

In sum, in his drive to recreate society along Renaissance lines, Cervantes tries to get Spanish youths to seek honor as they did in the past through heroic deeds. Thus, he details biographies of great leaders of ancient antiquity to encourage youths of his day to find objects of their intense hero-worship.

The *Cannon of Toledo* seconds this initiative by not only echoing and resonating the concepts of great ancient thinkers but by suggesting how the thoughts and actions of these great men marked an advance on the savagery of the dark ages that came before the Renaissance. Thus, he tells readers that "Portugal had its *Viriatus*, Rome its *Caesar*, Carthage its *Hannibal*, Greece its *Alexander*, Castile its *Count Fernan Gonzalez*, Valencia its *Cid*, Andalusia its *Gonzalo Fernandez*, Extremadura its *Diego Garcia de Paredes*, Jerez its *Garci Perez de Vargas*, and Toledo its *Garcilaso*" (452).

Viriatus, we learn, "was the most important leader of the Lustian people since he resisted Roman expansion into the regions of western Hispania [by leading] the confederate tribes of Iberia who resisted Rome." Accordingly he was able to stave-off Roman expansion for many years because "he was a man of great physical strength, probably in the very prime of life, an excellent strategist [who owned] a brilliant mind." Part of his brilliant strategy was his charming and persuasive personality, which won him many friends and allies, since he was described by those who knew him "to be a man who followed the principles of honesty and fair dealing and was acknowledged for being exact and faithful to his word on the treaties and leagues he made." It is agreed by all, in fact, that *Viriatus* "was valiant in dangers, prudent and careful in providing whatever was necessary, and that which was most considerable of all was that whilst he commanded he was more beloved than ever any was before him." In brief, Viriatus's admirable qualities earned him great renown, thus endearing him to his people.

Caesar, as suggested earlier, was an extremely intelligent, brave, and determined man, since he: unified the Roman territories of Europe, Egypt, North Africa, and the Eastern Mediterranean. Later, he vanquished ferocious mercenaries and barbarian hordes, and defeated great Roman admirals, like *Pompeii*, who rose against him.

Hannibal, to wit, was a Carthaginian military general who was "generally considered one of the greatest military commanders in history [since he] won over many allies of Rome during the outbreak of the second Punic wars" and occupied parts of Italy for many years, as well. In fact, he was such a great military commander that Rome, "came to adopt elements of his military tactics in its own strategic arsenal [meriting him the honorific of] the 'father of strategy.'

Alexander, as previously mentioned, united many disparate lands to establish the Greek republic, most notably ruling Egypt, Babylonia, the Persian Empire, parts of India, and the Ancient Greek kingdom of Macedonia.

Count Fernan Gonzalez, was the first autonomous count of Castile, who laid the foundation towards semi-autonomy from Rome.

Cid, Spain's national hero, is most noted for his sagacious rule in Valencia, ruling over a pluralistic state with the popular support of both Christians and Muslims.

Gonzalo Fernandez was the count of Castile and Burgos.

Diego Garcia de Paredes was a Spanish soldier and duelist, who was a notable figure "in the wars of the end of the 15th and beginning of the 16th century," when personal prowess had a considerable share in deciding the result of battles.

Garci Perez de Vargas was a hero of the Spanish Reconquista who, when his "sword broke in a battle against the Moor, broke a branch from an oak tree and crushed many Moors" with it. *(Likewise, Don Quixote imitates this man by replacing his broken sword-blade with a branch from an oak tree, which he uses to fight a group of footmen who he thinks are abducting a princess in a coach).*

Finally, *Garcilaso* was a Spanish soldier and poet who was not only a member of the royal guard and an honorary member of the order of Santiago but was also "the most influential poet to introduce Italian Renaissance verse forms, poetic techniques, and pastoral themes to Spain." (Wikipedia).

In sum, in-line with classical Renaissance values, Cervantes brings men back to the traditional paths of justice and honor by chronicling the lives of many great men.

Cervantes also tried to avert the universal decadence that was seizing Spain after the Renaissance by moralizing on the dangers of ease. He does this to encourage the energetic age of the Renaissance, which was marked by the absence of the spirit of laziness that led to the decline of the Spanish Empire. For instance, in chapter 17, page 869:

> Don Quixote thinks it high time to put an end to his lazy life in the castle, because he imagined that his person was being sorely missed as a result of allowing himself to remain shut up and idle amid the countless luxuries and delights that the Duke and Duchess lavished upon him as a knight errant. This is why he asks this royal duo to "permit [him] to leave [their country estate] because the luxury and abundance that [he had] been enjoying in the castle [comprised of] delectable banquets [and] snow chilled drinks [rendered him eager] to travel far and wide in search of tournaments and glory, to achieve worldly honor.
>
> (869, 873).

Here, we see that Don Quixote did not wish to stay in the Duke's castle without martial diversion in idleness, indefinitely – but chose, instead, to roam the world in search of chivalrous adventures – because, he thinks that exclusive interest in the pleasures of castle and court life rather than in military duties dissolves his sense of discipline and honor. This is why when Don Quixote "finds himself in open country [he not only] thinks that he is in his own element again [but he feels] that his spirits [are] reviving for the fresh pursuit of his chivalresque goals" (873). In brief, Cervantes tries to restore the energetic spirit of the Renissential epoch—the can-do spirit of Spain's renascent golden age—by showing readers that his hero-protagonist is often eager for adventure.

Another way Cervantes prepares readers for the Renaissance is by harkening back to the golden, spiritual age of chivalry as an aspirational and inspirational model for the future. To explain, when Cervantes wrote the "Quijote" Spain had passed from the golden age of mercantile trade—characterized by a robust trading and bartering system with its colonies in the Americas—to a waning, even tyrannical monarchy, characterized by the intolerant climate of fear instituted by the Holy Inquisition. Evidently, with King Phillip the III at its helm, Spain was in decline. This is why Cervantes criticizes, through a whole host of characters, the Holy Inquisition; effete courtesans [44]; lazy spiritual decadence, and, basically, a national life-sensation which reflects Spain's former greatness without maintaining that greatness in the present or projecting that greatness into the future. Thus, Cervantes tries to revive, through a sense of patriotic nostalgia, the former glory of the Spanish golden age. For this reason, he reanimates chivalric worth and glory, with the hope that it will bring about a new era of chivalric splendor—not, literally, in substance, but figuratively, in spirit—by repeatedly talking about the chivalric golden age. Hence, Don Quixote tells Sancho Panza that "though [he] was born in the [iron] age [his real purpose is] to revive in it the age of gold, or golden age, as it is often called" (154). This statement suggests that Cervantes wants to restore a refreshed Renaissance feeling in people's minds-and-hearts. This is also why he creates, in Don Quixote, a hero-protagonist who "was the first man in [the seventeenth century] to devote himself to the toils and exercise of

---

44

knight errantry" (74). In this sense, Cervantes tries to preserve the true spirit of chivalry in Spain by banishing decadent luxuries that had characterized municipal life at the time. But complaining about how lousy the zeitgeist is in 17th century Spain and how great the golden age was is not all Cervantes does. Rather, he creates a hero protagonist who tries to improve the general culture. This is why Don Quixote says that: "Happy will be the age, the country will be happy, which brings to light [his] famous exploits, worthy to be engraved on sheets of bronze, carved on slabs of marble and painted on boards of wood as a monument for all posterity" (31). This striving reflects that there is an "inherent optimism in the Renaissance because it is hoped that the revival of the classical past will reanimate the present and bring back a golden age"[45].

Similarly, the "Quijote's" bucolic episodes suggests that the pastoral eclogue enjoyed a revival during the Renaissance because it depicts life in an idealized manner: how it should be and ought to be. For this reason, Cervantes projects in the "Quijote" the utopian ideal of a pastoral oasis populated by "lovely shepherdesses roaming from dale to dale and from hill to hill, their hair in plaits, or flowing loose, clothed in no more than is necessary to conceal with modesty that which modesty has always required to be concealed" (85). Thus, in his search for the recovery of an ideal past Don Quixote reflects the natural beauty of the Renaissance through pastoral art. In other words, much like Adam and Eve lived alone together in the Garden of Eden, Don Quixote envisions a perfect garden paradise characterized by:

> limpid fountains and running streams, which offer their delectable and transparent water in magnificent abundance; sturdy oaks, liberally inviting [men and women] to taste [of] their sweet and toothsome fruit; rocks and hollows of trees, [where] diligent and prudent bees form their [social] commonwealths;

45 Echevarria, Roberto, Gonzalez. "Spanish 300: Cervantes's Don Quixote." Yale University. New Haven, Connecticut, Fall 2009.

coark oaks that shed their thick, light bark with which
men first covered their houses; [and finally] acorns,
which dangle gently from the limbs of trees, swaying
ever so lightly in the wind.

(85)

This golden age speech reflects the tendency of the Renaissance
to look back at the past while expressing a desire to return to it.
Moreover, since "utopia is one of the Renaissance's [primary] ideas,"
many Renaissance thinkers, like Cervantes, thought that the perfect
society was attainable through the application of idealism. This is
why Cervantes reminisces back to a time before modern warfare
began, where inventions, "like gunpowder and lead [had not yet]
deprived [warrior knights] of the opportunity to make [themselves]
famous all over the world by the might of [their] arms and the
blade of [their] swords" (358). And though Don Quixote revives the
wistful imaginings of olden day knights who preferred cold steal to
mechanical guns, Cervantes, as scholars note, was concerned that
chivalry was losing contact with and confidence in serious values,
especially since under empire the authorities became more concerned
with order and stability than with advantageous changes.

Cervantes also saw in the Renaissance the modern spirit of
individuality since the Renaissance was not only the work of
individuals but because artists were moving away from a collectivist
presentation of human beings that was so characteristic of medieval
art, portraying them as individuals, instead. Thus, by stressing the
honor to be gained from individual adventuring, Cervantes shows
readers that Don Quixote was an ardent champion of individual
virtue. So, by: freeing a young farm laborer from being whipped
for losing sheep; liberating innocent persons accused of witchcraft
and incest; and convincing a man named Tosilios to marry Donna
Rodriguez's daughter without dueling him in a joust, Don Quixote
meets self-imposed tests of personal enterprise and endurance:

honor to be acquired by individual adventuring. In other words, through feat of arms Don Quixote emphasizes the stress laid upon his outstanding individual – and individualistic – achievement, which ultimately paved the way for the take-over of the Renaissance spirit, since Chivalry and the Renaissance are both based on individual achievement. In brief, the "Quijote" shows readers that during the Renaissance a new modern spirit of individualism was displacing the medieval paradigm of Catholic religious and political control.

Cervantes also shows readers that the Renaissance had a profound effect on contemporary theology, particularly the way people perceived their relationship to God. To explain, many people at the time were disturbed by the corruption in the church, including Cervantes. So they called for Church reform to bring about a moral and religious revolution. Thus, to express this critical spirit the first innkeeper tells Don Quixote that "in his castle there isn't any chapel where he could keep the vigil of arms because it had been demolished" (37). This helps explain why Cervantes's picture of Chivalry, deeply Christian as it is, is so remarkably free of priestly overtones, so humane and in many ways so secular in its outlines.

Another chivalric act that Cervantes reanimates in the "Quijote" is the secular practice of the making of a new knight, which was practiced in Florence[46], Italy, during the Renaissance, by the Medici and their followers. This ritual consists of: the girding on of the sword; the blow to the neck; the tap on the shoulder; the vigil of the knight; and the blessing of the sword. Early in the novel, for example, we learn that "what most bothered [Don Quixote] was that he hadn't been knighted, because he knew that he couldn't lawfully embark on any adventure without having been admitted to the order of chivalry" (35). For this reason, he travels to an inn/castle, to find a knight to

---

46 **Florence**: Cervantes emphasizes the spirit of the times of the Renaissance by having the Tale of the Inappropriate Curiosity set in Florence, Italy, which was the birthplace of the Renaissance—a rich and famous Italian city in the province of Tuscany in the San Giovanni Area.

dub him. Mistaking the innkeeper "for the governor of the castle" he falls "upon his knees and says:

> I shall never, o valorous knight, arise from where I kneel, until your courtesy vouchsafes me a boon which I desire to beg of you and which will redound to your own praise and to the benefit of humankind. Tomorrow you shall knight me, in the chapel of your castle.

(33, 36).

But since the making of a knight in the "Quijote" is an entirely worldly ceremony, "symbolic of the Old Germanic custom of delivery of arms, which is in origin secular," there is no need for a priest or for the Church's altar for its accomplishment[47]. But since Don Quixote wants to replicate the vigil of a new knight, complete with a ritual spiritual cleansing, he "gathers his armour together and places it on a water trough next to a well, and, taking up his leather shield and seizing [his] lance, he begins with stately bearing to pace back and forth in front of the trough" (38). As mentioned before, the significance of the water trough is to signify the baptismal cleansing of sin; the significance of Don Quixote's arms and armor is to remind him of his duty to protect the weak and uphold justice; and the significance of the dubbing is to remind the new knight that justice and loyalty must go together. Indeed, the ceremony of knightly dubbing is best signified by the innkeepers laying on of secular hands on Don Quixote. This is why he "raises his hand and cuffs him on the neck and then with Don Quixote's own sword, gives him a thwack on the shoulder" (40). This, "vigorous blow on the nape of the neck, was purposely energetic, for it was intended to fix in the memory of the young knight both the ceremony and the lord who administered

---

47   Kilgour, Raymond Lincoln. <u>The Decline of Chivalry: As Shown in the French Literature of the Middle Ages</u>. 1937. Cambridge: Harvard University Press, 1966 (73).

the blow"[48]. And, though, typically, each candidate for knightly admission had to take an oath to observe his Christian duties as a knight—to defend the Church, uphold justice, protect orphans, and Christ's poor—Don Quixote takes no such overt oath, in line with his emerging spirit of Renaissance secularism.

Characteristic of Renaissance Humanism, part of Cervantes attempt to instill in his readers a thoroughly modern belief system, was to project, in the "Quijote," a moving away from the idea that noble birth alone gives renown to a person to the belief that a man of low estate can occupy a high social station. He does this in one main way. By telling Sancho Panza to: "take pride in being a virtuous man rather than a lofty and sinful one [for] there are innumerable men who, born of low stock, have risen to the highest positions, both pontifical and imperial" (770). Thus, a squire's drive to better his station through honorable acts reflects Cervantes's modern view that deserved rank in society only comes from good character. Don Quixote then tells Sancho Panza that if he "make[s] virtue [his] method, and take[s] pride in doing virtuous deeds, [he] will not have to envy those descended from lords and noblemen; because blood is inherited and virtue is acquired, and virtue has in itself a value that blood lacks" (771,772). This quote suggests that since virtue is one of the qualities of nobility it makes eligible those, like Sancho Panza, who did not come from high birth. In sum, Cervantes highlights the idea that during the Renaissance, individual virtue and achievement are the true keys to nobility, rather than blood and descent, thus advocating for a political system that would allow for more social movement on the basis of personal merits, which, itself, is a very modern notion.

Cervantes also ushers in the Renaissance by bringing cheer to feudal lords no longer engaged in military exploits by providing a fond remembrance of a heroic past. Since many an old knight could

---

48   Kilgour, Raymond Lincoln. <u>The Decline of Chivalry: As Shown in the French Literature of the Middle Ages</u>. 1937. Cambridge: Harvard University Press, 1966. (Introduction XIV).

recall with the fondness of romantic memory his service long ago, Cervantes uses this nostalgia for a heroic age to subtly impart the Renaissance spirit to former feudal lords. He does this in a number of ways. First, Cervantes emphasizes how important horses are for knights. Thus, he has Don Quixote

> spend four days considering a name of [great] eminence for Rocinante a name which in his opinion is lofty and sonorous and expresses what the creature had been when it was a humble hack, before it became what it was now – the first and foremost of all hacks in the world.

(28)

This is important for a lord since a horse is both his primary means of transport and identifies his essential qualities. Second, Cervantes appeals to a feudal lord's sense of a fair-fight by continuously looping back to the idea that knights can only fight other knights and squires can only fight other squires. This is why Don Quixote tells Sancho Panza that he:

> must not seize [his] sword to defend [him], unless [he] sees that those who attack [him] are common people, in which case [he] can most certainly come to [his] aid; but should they be knights or gentlemen, it is on no account licit or permitted by the laws of chivalry for [Sancho Panza] to assist [him], until [he is himself] knighted.

(66)

By creating combat rules for a squire defining who he can and cannot fight; and by devising a ranking ladder whereby a squire can become a knight, Cervantes appeals to a former feudal lord's sense of hierarchy and protocol. Third, by appealing to a feudal lord's Spanish patriotism and loyalty to his King, Cervantes attracts these erstwhile knights to a solemn vision of knight errantry. To explain, treason, to Knight's Errant, to betray one's lord was from the earliest days of chivalry the darkest of all crimes with which a knight or a warrior could be charged with. Cowardice and treason were still more serious affairs, as was to be expected in a society whose ethic was essentially martial. But:

> loyalty was one of the greatest virtues that there can be in any person, and especially in a knight, who ought to keep himself loyal in many ways. The principal ways are two: first to keep loyalty to his lord, and secondly to love truly her in whom he has placed at heart.
>
> (Keen, Maurice. Chivalry. Yale University Press: London, 1984.)

Fourth, the "Quijote" also appeals to a feudal lord's sense of loyalty by showing readers that once given a knight keeps his word. Thus, knights in the "Quijote," like the Duke of Aragon, can never be induced to break their plighted word. This is why the Duchess tells Sancho Panza that "though her husband is not that errant, that does not stop him from being a knight." (716). This harmony of word and deed, this honoring of one's sacred word, appealed to erstwhile feudal lords, since it crystallized around the knightly ideal the morality of a kept promise. Fifth, by appealing to a Lord's sense of wisdom to choose a wise course of action, Cervantes appeals to their sense of learning the truth about the world around them. This is why Don Quixote says that "the lord of an estate must concern himself with the administration of justice in his realm, [determined by] his good judgment and [keen ability], to honestly do what is right" (459). In conclusion, by presenting a realistic but funny picture of chivalry, Cervantes sought to entertain feudal lords of a bygone era, so he could subtly impart Renaissance principles to erstwhile knights who had found that there time had ended.

Evidently, the Renaissance, as seen in the "Quijote," is the period when western thought breaks away from medieval ideas. Thus, the ideas behind the Renaissance, particularly the overwhelming desire, in letters, to get at the truth and, in art, to present the truth as we see it, were a force that pushed writers and artists like Cervantes to the highest levels. But the Renaissance was not determinative. Artists, in particular, were not forced to conform to its aims by its compulsive spirit. Rather, it gave artists much greater opportunities than in medieval times to be themselves and develop their capacities to the full. Hence, it unleashed the geniuses. Indeed, Cervantes expresses the critical spirit of the times that were coming by writing a superb satire directed towards the outworn ideology of the Middle Ages. Through a pathetic but infinitely appealing character, he depicts an outmoded way of life. And in this stirring of new attitudes we may find the beginnings of ideas that ultimately matured into the Spanish Renaissance. Thus, thanks, in part, to Cervantes, eventually, the ideas and attitudes of medieval culture disappear completely and are replaced by those of the Renaissance. And, though, instinctively, Don Quixote adhered to the old order, the old values, insofar as he drew inspiration for the present from the experience of the past, he made way for the Renaissance's new system of values by not only marking the decline and transformation of chivalry in his book but also by noting the shifting intellectual climate of his day.

Select Bibliography

Alemany, Ignacio, Lopez. "Courting Don Quixote: An Aulic Frame of Reference." Fall 2013.

Cervantes: Bulletin of the Cervantes Society of America. 33.2. 49-70

Bartlett, Kenneth. "The Study of the Italian Renaissance." The Teaching Company. Chantilly, VA. 2005.

Bernstein, Andrew. "Heroes and Hero Worship." Ayn Rand Institute: Irvine, California: 2010.

Cervantes, Saavedra Miguel. <u>The Ingenious Hidalgo Don Quixote de la Mancha</u>. New York: Penguin, 2003.

Childers, William. L. "Legal Discourse in Don Quixote." 2005. Maester 34.1. 1-17.

<u>Da Vinci and the Code He Lived By</u>. DVD. Dir. Robert Gardner. The History Channel. 2005. 91 min.

Duby, Georges. <u>The Chivalrous Society</u>. Trans. Cynthia Postan. Los Angeles: University of California Press, 1980.

Elias, Norbert. <u>The Civilizing Process</u>. Trans. Edmund Jephcott. Oxford: Blackwell, 2000.

Echevarria, Roberto, Gonzalez. "Spanish 300: Cervantes's <u>Don Quixote</u>." Yale University. New Haven, Connecticut, Fall 2009.

<u>Empire</u>. Dir. Justin Hardy. Narr. Massimo Marinoni. PBS Home Video. 2003. 220 min.

Ferguson, Arthur. B. <u>The Indian Summer of English Chivalry</u>. Durham: Duke University Press, 1960.

Keen, Muarice. <u>Chivalry</u>. Yale University Press: London, 1984.

Kilgour, Raymond Lincoln. <u>The Decline of Chivalry: As Shown in the French Literature of the Middle Ages</u>. 1937. Cambridge: Harvard University Press, 1966.

Kirsch, Johann Peter. "Council of Trent." The Catholic Encyclopedia. Vol. 15. New York: Robert Appleton Company, 1912. 30 Sept. 2014

<http://www.newadvent.org/cathen/15030c.htm>.

Occonline.occ.cccd.edu/online/Idanzige/DonQuixote[1].doc.

Prestage, Edgar. Chivalry: It's Historical Significance and Civilizing Influence. New York: Routledge, 1996.

Volman, Cole. Don Quixote: The Humanist. English 308W-3 Final Paper. April 4, 2012.

https://www.google.com/search?q=Wiki+Ulysses&gws_rd=ssl

https://www.google.com/search?q=Wiki+Aenas&gws_rd=ssl

https://www.google.com/search?q=Wikipedia+The+Renaissance&gws_rd=ssl

https://www.google.com/search?q=Wiki+Achilles&gws_rd=ssl

https://www.google.com/search?q=wiki+Hector&gws_rd=ssl

https://www.google.com/search?q=Wiki+Sinon&gws_rd=ssl

http://en.wikipedia.org/wiki/Alexander_the_Great

https://www.google.com/search?q=Wiki+Trajan&gws_rd=ssl

https://www.google.com/search?q=Wiki+Cato&gws_rd=ssl

https://www.google.com/search?q=Wiki+Ulysees&gws_rd=ssl

https://www.google.com/search?q=Wiki+Odysseus&gws_rd=ssl

https://www.google.com/search?q=Wiki+Aeneids&gws_rd=ssl

https://www.google.com/search?q=Wiki+Euralus&gws_rd=ssl

https://www.google.com/search?q=Wiki+Nisus&gws_rd=ssl

https://www.google.com/search?q=Wiki+Trajan&gws_rd=ssl

https://www.google.com/search?q=Wiki+Cato+the+Elder&gws_rd=ssl

https://www.google.com/search?q=Wiki+Viriatus&gws_rd=ssl

https://www.google.com/search?q=wiki+Hannibal&gws_rd=ssl

https://www.google.com/search?q=Wiki+Count+Fernan+Gonzalez&gws_rd=ssl

https://www.google.com/search?q=Wiki+Diego+de+Parades&gws_rd=ssl

https://www.google.com/search?q=Wiki+Garci+Perez+de+Vargas&gws_rd=ssl

https://www.google.com/search?q=Wiki+Garcilaso&gws_rd=ssl

https://www.google.com/search?q=Wiki+Pompeii&gws_rd=ssl

https://www.google.com/search?q=wiki+Hannibal&gws_rd=ssl

https://www.google.com/search?q=Wiki+El+Cid&gws_rd=ssl

https://www.rtsd.org/.../Chapter_10_Notes--Renaissance_and_Discovery.docx

https://www.google.com/search?q=Wiki+Gonzalez+Fernandez&gws_rd=ssl

Reference Guide

Explanation

For individuals who enjoyed reading **Don Quixote Explained: ** *The Story of an Unconventional Hero,* there is also a **Don Quixote Explained Reference Guide** available through amazon books, and, elsewhere.

This comprehensive reference guide analyzes almost all of the novel's 111 characters—both from the main story itself and from the two interpolated tales. Moreover, readers who want to understand the meaning and significance of certain scenes and objects from the book, like Montesinos's cave, for example, or Mambrino's helmet, for instance, can refer to my reference guide for clarifying analyses. Likewise, students who wish to understand certain *Don Quixote* themes—like how the book is Metafictional, or how the book juxtaposes letters versus arms, or why women are always going to convents—can find extensive discussion of these topics in my reference guide. Lastly, since my reference guide defines and explores the book's many literary genres—like Chivalry, Pastoral, Epistolary, Romance, Epic, History, Drama, and Poetry—it facilitates a clear understanding of how these genres relate to and are woven into *Don Quixote.* In short, my **Don Quixote Explained Study Guide**, at 558 pages, is the most extensive, and perhaps, most insightful, reference guide on the market.

Sample

Characters

Don Quixote

<u>Appearance</u>- Don Quixote is a tall man with a wrinkled face, long skinny arms, and an eagle like nose that is somewhat hooked and graying. Typically, he has a dried-up face, a knotted and grizzled beard, a brown, stretched neck, and a big black droopy mustache to disguise his bony underbite. On his backbone is a mole with long stiff hairs growing out of it.

<u>Age</u>- Don Quixote is 49 years old, which, for the 17th century is old, since the typical life-span during the early renaissance was 50 years of age.

<u>Occupation</u>- Since Don Quixote is a nobleman of the lowest rank he derives a small income from his acres of arable land. Besides having a bit of ready money passed down from his forebears Don Quixote makes a small profit on his vineyards. When he is not managing his property, which is most of the year, either he hunts boar, to while away the time, or reads chivalry books, as a leisure activity.

<u>Sanity/Insanity</u>- When Don Quixote is in his right mind he talks with good sense and a clear and balanced judgment, which makes people think he is clever, studious, and to the point. But when he focuses his mind on chivalry he interlards sense and nonsense, reason and unreason, reality and unreality because what he says is coherent, elegant, and well-expressed, yet what he does is absurd, foolhardy, and stupid. Since he performs mad actions in the world—but speaks words that dissipate the effects of his deeds—most people think that he is mad, in streaks, complete with lucid intervals. Unable to decide whether he is more sane than mad or more mad than sane,

his examiners conclude that he is a sane man with madness in him, and a mad man with sane tendencies.

Injuries- Don Quixote's first injury comes when his ribs are bruised and battered by a muleteer who pounds him with a piece of his broken lance pummeling him until he is well-threshed like the finest chaff. Then his shoulder is half-dislocated when a windmill's sails yank him off his horse with enough force to send him rolling over the Montiel plain in a very sore predicament indeed. Later, half his ear is lopped off by a Basque who sends a large part of his helmet, along with a bloody chunk of his ear, to the ground in hideous ruin. Next a group of Yanguasian mule carriers pound him with their walking-staffs until he is knocked senseless. Then a muleteer at a tavern delivers such a terrible punch to Don Quixote's lantern jaws that his mouth is bathed in blood. Not content with his opening blow, the muleteer climbs on top of Don Quixote's ribs and trots up and down from one end to the other until he lays unconscious atop a ruined bed. To top off his loss of blood, a peace-officer smashes an oil lantern on Don Quixote's head leaving a good size dent there and raising two sizable lumps as well. Later, a group of goatherds break two of Don Quixote's ribs, smash three or four of his teeth, and crush two of his fingers in retaliation for their dead sheep. Next, a group of convicts fire a hailstorm of rocks at Don Quixote hitting him with enough force to knock him to the ground. Once Don Quixote is down, a student outlaw snatches a barber's basin from off his head and smashes it three or four times on Don Quixote's back leaving him in a sorry state indeed. Afterwards, when Don Quixote hurls a loaf of bread at a goatherd's face, the goatherd climbs on top of Don Quixote and flails away at his face until blood pours from the poor knight's face. Later, a penitent delivers such a blow to Don Quixote's sword arm that he smashes his shoulder to smithereens. Next, a snarling cat latches onto Don Quixote's nose leaving his face riddled with holes. Then Don Quixote is scorched and singed and hurled to the ground by an exploding wooden horse. Finally, Don Quixote is stampeded into the mud by a herd of pigs. Though Don Quixote's injuries heal over a number of years—sometimes in his own bed and sometimes in the battle field—it is a wonder that he musters the strength to continue after such numerous and extensive beatings.

<u>Chivalric Delusions</u>- Don Quixote mistakes: inns for castles; windmills for giants; sheeps for armies; wine-filled pigskins for headless giants; black-clad mourners for shadowy enchanters; copper basins for golden helmets; country barbers for warrior knights; simple farm girls for noble damsels; sweat smelling peasants for perfume smelling princesses; wooden horses for flying steeds; air pumping bellows for the earth's natural wind; water mills for castle fortresses; dinghies for ships; and blanket tossers for enchanted ghosts, to name just a few of his chivalric delusions.

<u>Family</u>- Besides having a twenty two year old niece, Don Quixote has no blood relations to speak of.

Sancho Panza

<u>Appearance</u>- Sancho Panza has a short body, a plump paunch, long shanks, and a thick, unkept, beard.

<u>Age</u>- Sancho Panza is in his mid-thirties.

<u>Occupation</u>- Sancho Panza is a poor country farmer who was a swineherd then a geese keeper later a steward and finally a country beadle. During his later years, before he squires for Don Quixote, Sancho Panza is a farm laborer.

<u>Family</u>- Sancho Panza comes from a medium sized family consisting of an older brother who is a priest, a wife who runs his house, his two children (Sanchico 15, Sanchita 14) his maternal grandmother, who he often quotes, as well as two wine-connoisseur forebears on his father's side. Thus, his nuclear family consists of four people, and his extended family consists of 3 people.

Practicality- Sancho Panza has a practical sense of what it takes to live in hard-reality. This is why he: eats out of his saddle-bags to avoid starvation; treats his injuries by mixing poultices; heals his wounds by fastening bandages; avoids jail by paying at inns; and earns money to take care of himself and his family. What's more, since Sancho Panza not only solicits a fixed salary from Don Quixote, but also sells a hunting outfit he acquires, he is always looking for ways to make money. This, in turn, signals his practicality, since earning money is required to maintain his house, provide food and clothing for his family, and pay for his children's education, too. In short, Sancho Panza's desire to earn money is definitely a sign of his practicality.

Glutton- Sancho Panza is prone to excessive eating and drinking binges. From devouring pies by flowing rivers to stuffing himself with geese and hens at Basilio's wedding, Sancho Panza eats like there is no tomorrow. Sancho Panza also likes to drink a lot, since he takes swigs of wine from his leather bottle, sometimes drinking before breakfast. Though he likes to eat and drink to excess, the Duchess puts Sancho Panza on a restraint enhancing diet, during his governorship of Barataria, by assigning him a good doctor to limit his food and liquid consumption. Indeed, before taking office, Sancho Panza says that he has never drunk wine to get drunk, but rather drinks intoxicating beverages to not seem choosy, or rude, because, asks Sancho Panza, what can be more hard hearted, if a friend drinks to your health and one does not drink to his back?

(more characters in the study guide)

Themes

Meta-fiction

Don Quixote is a unique novel because it discusses itself within the pages of itself. For example, when an old notebook of the history of Don Quixote is found at a bazaar in Toledo, a Catholic Cannon reminds us that chivalry books do not follow the rules of Aristotelian writing. Also when Cide Hamete El Benengeli, the book's narrator, analyzes *Don Quixote's* artistic genres he shows a concern for literature and language that signals *Don Quixote's* Metafictionality. Given *Don Quixote's* self-reflexive nature the book's author becomes a character in the story who steps in-and-out of the tale to comment on the art of storytelling. Also, during the Captive Captain's tale, we are told that Miguel Cervantes was the only man who emerged unscathed from his slavery. By referring to the author throughout the story, *Don Quixote* does not let the reader forget that he is reading a fictional work. Another feature which defines Don Quixote as a work of Metafiction is that it mentions several works of fiction. For example, during the inquisition of Don Quixote's library, Cervantes's *Galatea* is retained for its original style. Later, when the innkeeper produces *Rinconete and Cortadillo*, another story by Cervantes, a local priest decides to read *The Tale of Inappropriate Curiosity* instead. Finally, since *Don Quixote* tends to call attention to itself as a literary artifact characters within the story are acutely aware that they are in a work of fiction. In brief, since Don Quixote self-consciously evaluates itself throughout its' story-telling it is fiction about fiction, or Metafictional in nature.

(more themes in the study guide)

FULL-BIBLIOGRAPHY

Alemany, Ignacio, Lopez. "Courting Don Quixote: An Aulic Frame of Reference." Fall 2013. Cervantes: Bulletin of the Cervantes Society of America. 33.2. 49-70

Allen, John Jay. Don Quixote: Hero or Fool. Gainesville: University of Florida Press, 1971 (Part I) 1979 (Part II). Reprinted in Newark: Juan de la Cuesta Hispanic Monographs, 2008.

Auerbach, Eric. Mimesis: The Representation of Reality in Western Literature. 1953. Trans. Willard R. Trask. New Jersey: Princeton University Press, 2003.

---. "The Enchanted Dulcinea." Mimesis: The Representation of Reality in Western Literature. Contributors: Edward W. Said,

Bandera, Casareo. The Humble Story of Don Quixote: Reflections on the Birth of the Modern Novel. Washington D.C.: Catholic UP, 2006.

Barber, Richard. The Knight and Chivalry. London: Longman, 1970.

Bartlett, Kenneth. "The Study of the Italian Renaissance." The Teaching Company. Chantilly, VA. 2005.

Bell, Aubrey, F.G. Cervantes. 1947. Republished by Permission of University of Oklahoma Press. New York: Collier Books, 1961.

Bergin, Thomas, G. Edition. Giants of World Literature Cervantes: His Life His Times and His Works. Eds. Of Arnoldo Mondadori Editore Milano (Attanasio, Bergin). Trans. Salvator Attanasio. New York: American Heritage Press, 1968.

Bernstein, Andrew. "Heroism in Modern American Literature." The Ayn Rand Institute. Irvine, California: 1996.

Bernstein, Andrew. "Heroes and Hero Worship." Ayn Rand Institute: Irvine, California: 2010.

Bjornson, Richard (Editor). <u>Approaches to Teaching Cervantes</u>: Don Quixote. New York: The Modern Language Association of America, 1984.

Bloom, Harold (Editor). <u>Miguel de Cervantes</u>. Bloom's Modern Critical Views. Philadelphia: Chelsea House Publishers, 2005.

---. <u>Cervantes's Don Quixote</u>. Modern Critical Interpretations. Philadelphia: Chelsea House Publishers, 2001.

Byron, William. <u>Cervantes</u>: A Biography. 1978. New York: Paragon House Publishers, 1988.

Cascardi, Anthony, J. <u>The Cambridge Companion to Cervantes</u>. Cambridge U.K.: New York, N.Y. USA: Cambridge University Press, 2002.

Cameron, Ann. <u>Sidekicks in American Literature</u>. Studies in American Literature Volume 55. Ontario: The Edwin Mellon Press, 2002.

Campbell, Joseph. <u>The Hero With a Thousand Faces</u>. 3rd edition. Novato, California: New World Library, 2008.

Cervantes, Saavedra Miguel. <u>The Ingenious Hidalgo Don Quixote de la Mancha</u>. New York: Penguin, 2003.

Childers, William. L. "Legal Discourse in Don Quixote." 2005. Maester 34.1. 1-17.

Chesterton, G.K. <u>A Handful of Authors</u>: Essays on Books and Writers. New York: Sheed and Ward, 1953.

Clausen, Christopher. "Literature and Society." The Pennsylvania State University. State College, Pennsylvania: 2002.

Close, Anthony, J.. <u>Cervantes Don Quixote</u>. Landmarks of World Literature. Cambridge University Press: Cambridge, 1990.

---. <u>The Romantic Approach to Don Quixote</u>: A Critical History of the Romantic Tradition in Quixote Criticism. London: Cambridge University Press, 1977.

---. "Sancho Panza: Wise Fool." <u>Modern Humanities Research Association</u> 68.2 (1973) 344-357.

<u>Da Vinci and the Code He Lived By</u>. DVD. Dir. Robert Gardner. The History Channel. 2005. 91 min.

Davis, Nina. "Ways of Remembering Cervantes and the Historians: Don Quixote, Part I." Don Quixote Across the Centuries. (2005). 153-160.

Duby, Georges. <u>The Chivalrous Society</u>. Trans. Cynthia Postan. Los Angeles: University of California Press, 1980.

Duran, Manuel. Eds. Gerald E. Wade and Janet Winecoff Diaz. <u>Cervantes</u>. Twayne's World Author Series: *A Survey of the World's Literature*. Boston: Twayne Publishers, 1974.

Duran, Manuel and Fay R. Rogg. <u>Fighting Windmills</u>: Encounters With Don Quixote. New Haven: Yale University Press, 2006.

Duby, Georges. <u>The Chivalrous Society</u>. Trans. Cynthia Postan. 1980. University of California Press: Berkley, Los Angeles, London (Print on Demand).

Echevarria, Roberto, Gonzalez. "Spanish 300: Cervantes's <u>Don Quixote</u>." Yale University. New Haven, Connecticut, Fall 2009.

Efron, Arthur. <u>Don Quixote and the Dulcineated World</u>. Austin: University of Texas Press, 1971.

Elias, Norbert. <u>The Civilizing Process</u>. Trans. Edmund Jephcott. Oxford: Blackwell, 2000.

Elliott, J.H.. Imperial Spain: 1469-1716. 1963. Pelican Books, Louisiana, 1970.

El Saffar, Ruth. "The Function of the Fictional Narrator in Don Quijote." MLN: The Hispanic Issue. 83.2. (1968) 164-177.

Empire. Dir. Justin Hardy. Narr. Massimo Marinoni. PBS Home Video. 2003. 220 min.

"epistolary novel." Encyclopedia Britannica. 2007. Encyclopedia Britannica Online. 29 Aug. 2007. <http://www.search.eb.com. proxyau.wrlc.org/eb/article-9032818>.

Eschevarria, Roberto Gonzalez. Cervantes' Don Quixote: a Casebook. Oxford England-New York: Oxford University Press, 2005.

Fajardo, Salvador, J. "Don Quixote Wins by a Nose." Hispanic Review. 70.2. (2002). 191-205.

Ferguson, Arthur, B. The Indian Summer of English Chivalry. Studies in the Decline and Transformation of Chivalric Idealism. Durham: Duke University Press, 1960.

Ferguson, Arthur. B. The Indian Summer of English Chivalry. Durham: Duke University Press, 1960.

Finello, Dominick. Pastoral Themes and Forms in Cervantes's Fiction. New Jersey: Associated University Presses, 1994.

Forcione, Alban, K. Cervantes, Aristotle, and the Persiles. Princeton, N.J.: Princeton University Press, 1970.

---. Cervantes and the Humanist Vision: A Study of Four Exemplary Novels. Princeton, N.J.: Princeton University Press, 1982.

Ghate, Onkar. "Seminar on the Philosophy of Objectivism." The Ayn Rand Institute. Irvine, California. October 2008-March 2009.

Gilman, Stephen. The Novel According to Cervantes. Berkley: University of California Press, 1989.

Glover, Douglas. The Enamored Knight. 2nd Edition. Illinois: Dalkey Archive Press, 2004.

Graf, E.C.. Cervantes and Modernity: Four Essays on Don Quixote. Lewisburg: Bucknell University Press, 2007.

Grierson, Herbert. Don Quixote: Some War Time Reflections On Its Character and Influence. Ithica: Cornell, January 1921.

Haley, George. "The Narrator of Maese Pedro's Puppet Show." MLN: Spanish Issue. 80.2. (1965). 145-165.

Herzman, Ronald, B. "Great Authors of the Western Literary Tradition." Part IV: Literature of the Renaissance. Lecture 46: Miguel de Cervantes. The Teaching Company. Virginia. 2004.

Higuera, Henry. Eros and Empire: Politics and Christianity in Don Quixote. Lanham: Rowman & Littlefield Publishers, 1995.

"historical novel." Encyclopedia Britannica. 2007. Encyclopedia Britannica Online. 29 Aug. 2007. <http://www,search.eb.com. proxyau.wrlc.org/eb/article-9040597>.

Hunt, Morton. The Natural History of Love: A Brilliant Panorama of the Ways Men and Women Have Loved and Felt about Love—from the Early Greeks to the Present Day. New York: Knopf, 1959.

Immerwahr, Raymond. "Structural Symmetry in the Episode Narratives of Don Quijote, Part One. Comparative Literature. 10.2. (1958). 121-135.

Iventosch, Herman. "Cervantes and Courtly Love: The Grisostomo-Marcela Episode of "Don Quixote." PMLA. 89.1. (1974). 64-76.

Jacobson, Karen. Shakespeare's Romeo and Juliet. Cliff's Complete. Ed. Sydney Lamb. New York: Hungry Minds, 2000.

Johnson, Caesar. The Great Quixote Hoax; or, Why Wasn't Cervantes Burned at the Stake? New York: Exposition Press, 1972.

Johnson, Carol, B.. Don Quixote: The Quest for Modern Fiction. Boston: Twayne Publishers, 1990.

---. "A Second Look at Dulcinea's Ass: Don Quijote, II.10." Hispanic Review. 43.2. (1975). 191-198.

---. Cervantes and the Material World. Urbana: University of Illinois Press, 2000.

Johnson, Robert, A.. <u>Transformation</u>: Understanding the Three Level of Masculine Consciousness. San Francisco: Harper San Francisco, 1991.

Keen, Maurice. <u>Chivalry</u>. New Haven: Yale University Press, 1984.

Kilgour, Raymond. <u>The Decline of Chivalry</u>: As Shown in the French Literature of the Late Middle Ages. 1937. Gloucester: 1966.

Kilgour, Raymond Lincoln. <u>The Decline of Chivalry: As Shown in the French Literature of the Middle Ages</u>. 1937. Cambridge: Harvard University Press, 1966.

Kamen, Henry. <u>Empire</u>: How Spain Became A World Power 1492-1763.

Kenner, Ellen. "The Rational Basis of Romance (part 2): Courting Success in Romance." 2003.

Kirsch, Johann Peter. "Council of Trent." The Catholic Encyclopedia. Vol. 15. New York: Robert Appleton Company, 1912. 30 Sept. 2014 <http://www.newadvent.org/cathen/15030c.htm>. Occonline.occ. cccd.edu/online/Idanzige/DonQuixote[1].doc.

Locke, Edwin and Ellen Kenner. <u>The Selfish Path to Romance</u>: How to Love with Passion and Reason.

Mackey, Mary. "Rhetoric and Characterization in Don Quijote." Hispanic Review. 42.1. (1974). 51-66.

Madariaga, Salvador. <u>Don Quixote</u>; an Introductory Essay on Psychology. Translators Salvador de Madariaga and Constance H.M. de Madariga. Newton, Whales: Gregynog Press, 1934.

Mancing, Howard. <u>The Chivalric World of Don Quijote</u>: Style, Structure, and Narrative Technique. Columbia: University of Missouri Press, 1982.

March, James G. and Thierry Weil. On Leadership: Imagination, Commitment, and Joy in Don Quixote. Malden: MA: Blackwell Publishing, 2005.

Martin, Adrienne. Cervantes and the Burlesque Sonnet. Los Angeles: University of California Press, 1991.

Martinez-Bonati, Felix. Don Quixote and the Poetics of the Novel. Trans. Diane Fox. New York: Cornell University Press, 1992.

Mandel, Oscar. "The Function of the Norm in Don Quixote." Modern Philology. 55.3. (1958). 154-163.

Mauer, Kate. The Taming of the Shrew. Cliff's Notes. New York: Wiley Publishing, 2001.

McCrory, Donald. No Ordinary Man: The Life and Times of Miguel de Cervantes. 2002. Mineola: Dover, 2006.

Milton, Joyce. Miguel De Cervantes's Don Quixote. Barron's Book Notes. Hauppauge: Barron's Educational Series, 1985.

Northup. G.T. "Cervantes's Attitude Towards Honor." Modern Philology. 21.4. (1924). 397- 421.

"novel." Encyclopedia Britannica. 2007. Encyclopedia Britannica Online. 31 Jan. 2007. <http://www.search.eb.com.proxyau.wrlc.org/eb/article - 50974>.

"novella." Encyclopedia Britannica. 2007. Encyclopedia Britannica Online. 29 Aug. 2007. <http://www.search.eb.com.proxyau.wrlc.org/ eb/article-9056382>.

Ortega y Gasset, Jose. Meditations on Quixote. Translators Evelyn Rugg and Diego Marin. Notes by Julian Marias. New York: Norton, 1961.

Parr, James. "Don Quixote; On the Preeminence of Formal Feature." Ingeniosa Invencion: Essays on Golden Age Spanish Literature for Geoffrey L. Stagg in Honor of his Eighty Fifth Birthday. 1.1. (1999). 167-182.

"pastoral literature." <u>Encyclopedia Britannica</u>. 2007. Encyclopedia Britannica Online. 29 Aug. 2007. <http://www.search.eb.com. proxyau.wrlc.org/eb/article-9058684>.

Peikoff, Leonard and John Ridpath Vs. Jim Chaplin and Jill Vickers. "Capitalism vs. Democratic Socialism" (Debate). Moderator Jack Clark.

Peikoff, Leonard. "What to Do About Crime." Ford Hall Forum, 1995.

"picaresque novel." <u>Encyclopedia Britannica.</u> 2007. Encyclopedia Britannica Online. 31 Jan. 2007. < http://www.search.eb.com. proxyau.wrlc.org/eb/article-9059900>.

Pike, David. <u>Readings in Genre: Novel</u>. American University, Washington, DC. Spring, 2007.

Predmore, Richard L. <u>The World of Don Quixote</u>. Cambridge, Harvard University Press, 1967.

Prestage, Edgar. <u>Chivalry</u>: Its Historical Significance and Civilizing Influence. 1928. The History of Civilization. New York: Routledge, 1996.

Prestage, Edgar. <u>Chivalry: It's Historical Significance and Civilizing Influence</u>. New York: Routledge,

Quint, David. <u>Cervantes's Novel of Modern Times</u>: A New Reading of Don Quixote. New Jersey, Princeton University Press, 2003.

Riley, E.C.. "Three Versions of Don Quixote." The Modern Language Review. 68.4. (1973). 807-819.

---. "Who's Who in Don Quixote? Or an Approach to the Problem of Identity." MLN Spanish Issue. 81.2. (Mar. 1966). 113-130.

Russell, Peter-Edward.. <u>Cervantes</u>. New York and Oxfordshire (Oxford): Oxford University Press, 1985.

Riley, E.C. Cervantes's Theory of the Novel. Oxford, Clarendon Press, 1962.

Roy, Gregor. <u>Cervantes's Don Quixote</u>. Monarch Notes and Study Guides. New York: Simon and Shuster, 1965.

Russell, P.E. "Don Quixote as a Funny Book." The Modern Language Review. 64.2. (1969), 312-326.

Selig, Karl-Ludwig. <u>Studies on Cervantes</u>. Kassel [Germany]: Edition Reichenberger, 1993.

---. <u>Essays on Art and Literature in Honor of William Sebastian Heckscher</u>. "Don Quichote and Sancho Panza Visit the Duke and the Duchess." The Hague: Van der Heijeden, 1993.

Smith, Tera. "Passing Judgement: Ayn Rand's View of Justice." Recorded May 9th, 2006.

Sobre, J.M. "Don Quixote, the Hero Upside-Down." Hispanic Review. 44.2. (Spring: 1976).

Soons, C.A. "Cide Hamete Benengeli: His Significance for Don Quixote." The Modern Language Review. 54.3. (Jul. 1959). 351-357.

Spadaccini, Nicholas. "Cervantes and the Question of Metafiction." Vanderbilt E-Journal of Latino-Hispanic Studies.

Spark Notes Editors. <u>Don Quixote</u>: Miguel de Cervantes. Spark Notes. 2003. 2nd Edition. New York: Stark Publishing, 2007.

Sturman, Marianne. <u>Cervantes's Don Quixote</u>. Cliff Notes. New York: Wiley Publishing, 1964.

Suarez, Manuel. <u>The Revelations of Don Quixote</u>. 1947. New York: Harbinger House, 2007.

Taplin, Sam. <u>The Official Knight's Handbook</u>. 1456. Ed. Lesley Simms. London: Usborne Publishing, 2006.

Unamuno, Miguel. <u>The Life of Don Quixote and Sancho According to Miguel de Cervantes Saavedra</u>. Trans. Homer P. Earle. New York & London: A.A. Knopf, 1927.

Van Doren, Mark. <u>Don Quixote's Profession</u>. New York: Columbia University Press, 1958.

Volman, Cole. <u>Don Quixote: The Humanist</u>. English 308W-3 Final Paper. April 4, 2012.

Wardropper, Bruce W.. "Don Quixote Story or History." Modern Philology. 63.1. (August 1954). 1-11.

---. "Cervantes's Theory of the Drama." Modern Philology. 55.4. (May: 1955). 217-221.

Weiger, John. <u>The Individuated Self</u>: Cervantes and the Emergence of the Individual. Athens: Ohio, 1979.

http://en.wikipedia.org/wiki/Alexander_the_Great

http://en.wikipedia.org/wiki/Battle_of_Lepanto

http://en.wikipedia.org/wiki/Brigandage

http://en.wikipedia.org/wiki/Catalan_people

http://en.wikipedia.org/wiki/Christanity

http://en.wikipedia.org/wiki/Don_Quixote

http://en.wikipedia.org/wiki/Holy_Brotherhood

http://en.wikipedia.org/wiki/Islam

http://en.wikipedia.org/wiki/Lazarillo_de_Tormes

http://en.wikipedia.org/wiki/Listof_DonQuixoteCharacters

http://en.wikipedia.org/wiki/Matafiction

http://en.wikipedia.org/wiki/Moriscos

http://en.wikipedia.org/wiki/Outlaw

http://en.wikipedia.org/wiki/Picaresque

http://en.wikipedia.org/wiki/Ricote

http://en.wikipedia.org/wiki/self-flagellation

http://en.wikipedia.org/wiki/Spanish_Inquisition

http://www.bookrags.com/notes/dq/TOP5.html

http://www.donquichote.org/cervantes.php

http://www.neh.gov/news/humanities/2008-2009/OneMaster.html

https://www.google.com/search?q=Wiki+Achilles&gws_rd=ssl

https://www.google.com/search?q=Wiki+Aenas&gws_rd=ssl

https://www.google.com/search?q=Wiki+Aeneids&gws_rd=ssl

https://www.google.com/search?q=Wiki+Cato&gws_rd=ssl

https://www.google.com/search?q=Wiki+Cato+the+Elder&gws_rd=ssl

https://www.google.com/search?q=Wiki+Count+Fernan+Gonzalez&
gws_rd=ssl

https://www.google.com/search?q=Wiki+Diego+de+Parades&gws_rd=ssl

https://www.google.com/search?q=Wiki+El+Cid&gws_rd=ssl

https://www.google.com/search?q=Wiki+Euralus&gws_rd=ssl

https://www.google.com/search?q=Wiki+Garci+Perez+de+Vargas&
gws_rd=ssl

https://www.google.com/search?q=Wiki+Garcilaso&gws_rd=ssl

https://www.google.com/search?q=Wiki+Gonzalez+Fernandez&
gws_rd=ssl

https://www.google.com/search?q=wiki+Hannibal&gws_rd=ssl

https://www.google.com/search?q=wiki+Hannibal&gws_rd=ssl

https://www.google.com/search?q=wiki+Hector&gws_rd=ssl

https://www.google.com/search?q=Wiki+Nisus&gws_rd=ssl

https://www.google.com/search?q=Wiki+Odysseus&gws_rd=ssl

https://www.google.com/search?q=Wiki+Pompeii&gws_rd=ssl

https://www.google.com/search?q=Wiki+Sinon&gws_rd=ssl

https://www.google.com/search?q=Wiki+Trajan&gws_rd=ssl

https://www.google.com/search?q=Wiki+Trajan&gws_rd=ssl

https://www.google.com/search?q=Wiki+Ulysees&gws_rd=ssl

https://www.google.com/search?q=Wiki+Ulysses&gws_rd=ssl

https://www.google.com/search?q=Wiki+Viriatus&gws_rd=ssl

https://www.google.com/search?q=Wikipedia+The+Renaissance&gws_rd=ssl

https://www.rtsd.org/.../Chapter_10_Notes--Renaissance_and_Discovery.docx

Williamson, Edwin. The Half Way House of Fiction: Don Quixote and Arthurian Romance. Oxford: Clarendon Press, 1984.

Ziolkowski, Eric. The Sanctification of Don Quixote: From Hidalgo to Priest. University Park, Pennsylvania 1991.

INDEX

310, 311, 312, 313, 314, 315, 316, 317, 318, 320

Don Quixote's 116

Don Vicente 229, 238

Dorotea 26, 39, 41, 42, 43, 85, 98, 269, 283, 284

Dorotea 39, 43

Dr. Aguero 160, 161, 163

Drama 303, 318

Dramatic 14, 195, 231, 250

Dramatists 111

Drinking 159, 253, 277, 307

Ducal 275

Duchess 14, 15, 35, 36, 72, 74, 75, 77, 101, 111, 125, 126, 127, 129, 153, 154, 155, 171, 270, 277, 290, 298, 307, 317

Duchess 74, 127, 154

Duchess of Aragon 74, 126

Duke 19, 72, 73, 74, 75, 77, 101, 109, 113, 120, 125, 126, 127, 128, 129, 138, 139, 143, 153, 154, 155, 157, 158, 163, 164, 165, 169, 171, 214, 238, 271, 273, 277, 281, 290, 298, 300, 312, 317

Duke of Alba 113, 214, 271, 273

Duke of Aragon 19, 77, 101, 277, 298

Dulcinea 38, 57, 58, 61, 63, 64, 76, 95, 96, 100, 105, 106, 111, 113, 175, 176, 177, 178, 179, 180, 181, 182, 183, 184, 185, 186, 187, 188, 189, 190, 191, 192, 193, 194, 195, 196, 197, 200, 309, 314

Dulcinea 182, 183, 184, 187, 188, 189, 190, 193

Dunce 75

E

Earl 10, 17, 19

Earthly Pleasures 87

Eat 161

Eat 160

Ebro 93

Ecclesiastical 56

Economic 2

Educate 87

Egocentric 76

El Cid 113, 265

El Toboso 106, 189

Emercia 180

Emperor Charlemagne 251

Enchanters 61, 94, 95, 105, 306

Enchantment 205

Epistolary 303

Erasmus 265

Escudos 136, 230

Esplandian 110

Ethical 9, 60, 70, 145, 152, 172, 190, 194, 201, 222, 237, 256, 275, 282

Euryalus 284, 286

Excommunicating 177

Executioner 148, 245

Extortion 71, 86, 231, 234, 286

F

Faith 34, 56, 58, 60, 65, 76, 77, 79, 86, 190, 200, 201, 210, 211, 214, 272

Faithfulness 42

Faith Healing 210

Family 2, 6, 11, 20, 29, 30, 32, 65, 66, 71, 144, 166, 194, 201, 215, 244, 272, 306, 307

Farm 18, 120, 121, 178, 191, 195, 202, 284, 293, 306

Farmer 120, 130, 139

Fat 14, 153, 154, 162, 163

Father Pero Perez 26, 273

Female Social Agency 175

Feud 165, 185

165, 171, 175, 176, 192, 197, 200, 202, 211, 217, 218, 237, 240, 257, 258, 260, 264, 270, 279, 282, 283, 293, 294, 296, 303, 318

Infidelity 2

Innocent 22, 68, 69, 95, 126, 127, 132, 138, 143, 151, 229, 254, 257, 259, 293

Inns 92, 96, 108, 117, 274, 306, 307

Inquisition 65, 67, 70, 71, 75, 79, 85, 86, 87, 89, 176, 227, 232, 240, 257, 258, 291, 319

Insults 73, 74, 83, 96, 98, 109, 218

Integrity 7, 86, 123, 134, 142, 144, 145, 166, 167, 172

Irrational Mysticism 77

Islam 65, 106, 201, 202, 204, 205, 208, 209, 210, 211, 214, 318

Islamic 204, 214

Island 11, 16, 17, 19, 21, 123, 126, 141, 145, 147, 148, 157, 158, 163, 164, 204

Italian 117, 290, 294, 300, 309

J

Jailer 127, 137, 246

Jarifa 200

Jealousy 2, 131

Jesters 125, 129

Joke 75, 87, 97, 99, 118, 123, 124, 125, 129, 160, 162, 179, 191, 245, 286

Jokery 127

Joshua 113

Jousting 188, 278

Juan Haldudo 118

Juan Palomeque 227, 229

Judas 113

Judge 82, 123, 127, 133, 134, 135, 136, 138, 140, 144, 152, 171, 230, 243, 245, 259, 270

Judgment 61, 134, 136, 139, 162, 169, 171, 172, 201, 243, 257, 259, 261, 278, 298, 304

Judicial 133, 135, 138, 230, 279, 280, 282

Julius Caesar 78, 113, 265, 272, 273

Juno 113

Jupiter 77

Justice 82, 83, 120, 124, 133, 134, 136, 137, 141, 142, 190, 200, 201, 213, 223, 230, 231, 232, 233, 241, 242, 243, 245, 254, 256, 257, 258, 259, 261, 270, 278, 279, 290, 295, 296, 298, 317

K

King 65, 67, 70, 80, 82, 83, 111, 113, 166, 176, 195, 203, 213, 242, 243, 245, 271, 272, 273, 275, 277, 291, 298

Kingdom 100, 136, 149, 246, 289

Kinship Relations 165

knight errant 108, 111, 182, 187, 290

Knight of The Cross 110

Knight of the Forest 77, 78, 95

Knight of the White Moon 95, 188

Knight Plantir 110

Knotted-Rope 59

Knowledge 73, 87, 91, 110, 111, 113, 114, 116, 128, 151, 170, 192, 201, 249, 264, 274, 282

L

Lace Making 35

Lady Oriana 179

Ladyship 10, 22, 153, 154, 189

Landlords 118, 223

T

Printed in the United States
By Bookmasters